DISCIPLINES
for the
INNER LIFE

BOB BENSON, SR.
&
MICHAEL W. BENSON

DISCIPLINES
for the
INNER LIFE

BOB BENSON, SR.
&
MICHAEL W. BENSON

Deeper Life
PRESS

Second Revised Edition

ISBN 0-9677725-0-8

Cover photo: Captiva Beach, January 1977, John T. Benson, III

Revised Edition, Copyright © 1989 by Bob Benson and Michael W. Benson

Printed in the United States of America.

Library of Congress Cataloging-in-Publication Data

Benson, Bob.
    Disciplines for the inner life / by Bob Benson and Michael W. Benson.
        p.   cm.
    Originally published: Waco, Tex.: Word Books, © 1985.

    1. Devotional calendars.   2. Spiritual life.

BV4811.B46   1989

Deeper Life Press
612 Cumberland Hills Drive
Hendersonville, TN 37075
615/830-9000
email: deeperlife@juno.com

If you wish to live richly, deeply and spiritually you must cultivate the "world within." It is a thrilling world . . . with the Heavenly Father as our companion . . . .

The Nashville Tennessean (Mid-1940s)

To
JOHN T. BENSON, JR.

father and grandfather
who long ago,
by example and by precept,
as expressed in the words he wrote above,
led his family in the quest
to know God.

contents

preface

"To acknowledge and take up the double obligation to the seen and the unseen, in however homely and practical a way, is to enter consciously upon the spiritual life," writes Evelyn Underhill.

Too much of modern day Christianity concentrates on the outward obligation of what is seen and is visible rather than on the inward obligation of what is unseen and is hidden. This book grew out of a concern that we Christians give time and attention to the hidden, inner life with God. If we are going to enter more deeply into the invisible arena, into the realm of the spiritual, we will have to make a conscientious effort to move past the superficial in order to enter into a deeper knowledge of God.

The beginning of such an effort must be the construction of a pattern in our lives in which the voice of God has access to us. We need to develop a personal ascetic. As we are generally creatures of habit, we need a routine, a discipline, to cultivate the inner life. It is the purpose of this book to help you establish such a pattern or routine, hence the use of the word *discipline* in the title.

In our respective spiritual journeys, we have come to see that deeply committed Christians of many traditions have handed down tools to help us as we take steps toward such a discipline. Throughout Christian history we have received from them various spiritual principles, rules, disciplines, and practices that have aided the believer in the quest for a deeper knowledge of God. There were liturgies, lectionaries, prayer books, and guides for the hours and days of one's spiritual journey. The Spiritual Rules, the Spiritual Director, the Liturgy of the Hours, Spiritual Journals, Confessionals, the early Methodist Class Meetings, and many other requirements and customs arose from the need to develop a disciplined, ongoing relationship with God.

One of the common threads of these tools of spirituality was the recognition of the need for constancy in the establishing and deepening of a person's spiritual relationship with God. And underlying the writings of all those whose works have stood the test of time is the theme of faithfulness and regularity in spiritual practice.

Unfortunately for most of us, we are often ignorant of the wide use of such offices or disciplines in days gone by. And even though it seems at times that there is a dearth of materials to be used, it is also very true that we have not exposed ourselves to the ones that are available to us.

Despite the variety of excuses for our lack of contact with such disciplines and materials, our ignorance of them seems to have some roots in at least two philosophical underpinnings.

One of them is that as Christians in our twentieth-century western culture, we have grown up being so pragmatic in our philosophy of living that the developing and nurturing of our spiritual life often begins to revolve around the same pragmatic values that govern other parts of our lives: "What will get this done efficiently? What is the most cost productive? Is this a resourceful use of my time in light of my agenda for today?"

As a result, many of us feel quite sure, both from the hunger in our hearts and from the meager Christian fruits in our lives, that we are far from a life rooted in the deep resources of God. Times of trial and other adverse circumstances may sometimes cause us to renew our intentions and resolves in this regard for a season. Usually though, with the return of better times, or simply under the myriad pressures of life itself, we gradually relax our grip on our resolutions and return to our more pragmatic, "real-world" concerns.

Regretfully, the second of those powerful underpinnings is our prejudice against other traditions. Our unwillingness to cross the boundaries of tradition quite often leaves us to make our forays into the depths without availing ourselves of the counsel and wisdom of those across the centuries who have made similar journeys fruitfully and victoriously. Indeed, we often find ourselves attempting to make our spiritual pilgrimage entirely on our own.

For example, we do not even have a common term that we all understand that can be used to describe the process. For many of us, *devotions* is the term most often used. Terms like *inner life, spiritual formation, spiritual life, interior life,* and others simply do not have the same common meaning to us, if they have any meaning to us at all.

A remarkable similarity and continuity to both the hindrances and aids to piety across the centuries exists. Journals and treatises of early and present-day saints and saintly people record the struggles and the victories in virtually all the matters pertaining to the implementation of our inner intentions. Those writings have something to say to all who would take up the journey into the inner life.

We have collected in this book a sampling of hymns, scriptures, and readings that will provide insight and guidance for the formation and nourishment of the inner life. Our hope is that the daily services will provide a foundation upon which you can begin to build strong disciplines into your life.

While some of the material has been gathered during the study and research for this book, most of the readings have come from books long ago underlined and from writers who, through the years, provided health and hope to our spirits. Likewise, much of the scripture is taken from those verses and passages that came to our minds in thinking of the weekly subject we had chosen.

One more word needs to be spoken to those who would take up a discipline for the inner life. To maintain a discipline of contemplation and prayer one must commit his or her self to the way of faith. The injunction to live "by faith" the life you are now living is applicable in the disciplined life also.

To begin in prayer today may have no visible fruits tomorrow. But that is no reason for stopping. One who begins on Monday to train for a marathon surely wouldn't stop training because his muscles still ached on Friday. More than likely, you will start out enthusiastically in the life of prayer, only to find that you enter some dry, desertlike time after a few days along the way. *Keep going.* Remember that these are disciplines that you have undertaken in response to a call to move deeper into your life with God.

The call to walk with God is a call to a life of prayer and

devotion. The cost of answering, the cost of following, must be counted as best we can. But because we don't know where it will lead us, when we make an attempt to arrive at a sum, we must be prepared to add a great deal more to what we already know to be the cost. The cost will always be greater than our ability to measure it.

The words of Jesus to those who would join him on the journey are, "Come, and you will see" (John 1:39). And that is the order of things in answering the call to follow God on the journey into the inner life. We are not given the privilege of "seeing first" and then deciding if we are willing to make the journey. However, the process of following God can be trusted.

The prayer of the psalmist must become our prayer:

I rise before dawn and cry for help;
I wait for Thy words.
My eyes anticipate the night watches,
That I may meditate on Thy word.
Psalm 119:147–148

May this book be a faithful companion to you on your journey.

Bob Benson
Michael W. Benson

making this book work for you

This book is divided into a series of fifty-two patterns or services for personal worship. They are arranged to be used a week at a time—but if your heart and spirit seem to need to dwell longer with a particular theme or emphasis you should move at your own pace.

Since it is deeply true that we all are beginners in prayer the topics are arranged in a natural progression. We hope this will lead you along the pathway to a deeper life in God. The first weeks deal with awakening spiritual awareness and exercising that awareness in prayer and study. Next there is a section concerning hindrances to living the spiritual life followed by studies of patterns for making this true in our lives. The final weeks are given to considering both the inner graces and outer fruits which come to us as the result of a life centered in God. If there is some area of your inner life that surfaces at a given time you may wish to spend a week or so in the scripture and readings under that heading—even though it may not be the next in order. This is the journey of your soul and you alone can best determine your present location and need.

The journey each day will follow this pathway:

INVOCATION

We have chosen and written prayers to guide you in coming to God and opening your time with him. To make it a very personal time all of the prayers have been changed to first person, singular. Also we have changed the "Thees" and "Thous" to "you," hoping to make your praying a very real conversation with the Father. Obviously, if it is your habit to use the more formal language then pray the prayers in the way that is most helpful to you.

PSALM

The best-known sourcebook of Christian prayers is the Psalms. To many they are rich sources of strength in the varying conditions and circumstances of life.

Some people have difficulty, however, in reading the Psalms devotionally. Part of their reluctance stems from the apparent "bloodthirstiness" of many of these "prayer poems." It is to be remembered that the Psalms were written when the enemies were real and would pour across the countryside as conquering armies. Death literally stalked the writers. And while it is true that we are not engaged in battles with marching armies—and with lions and tigers—we do well to remember that we are also beset by enemies even though they be inward. And if we are going to be victorious in our spiritual warfare it will be as God helps us to defeat a host of enemies such as pride, lust, worry, divided loyalty, depression, lack of willpower, anger, greed and countless other contestants for our souls.

When we read and pray as embattled strugglers on our spiritual pathways the Psalms become deep sources of comfort and help to us.

DAILY SCRIPTURE READINGS

For each day there are portions of scripture listed that relate to the theme for the week. It should help you by example, admonition or insight to gain strength in the area of spiritual development being considered.

As a final aid to scripture reading there is a listing or Lectionary of scripture in the back of the book from which you may find additional chapters to include in your daily readings. The sixty-six chapters listed in the Lectionary, from both the Old and New Testaments, were compiled by members of The Church of the Saviour in Washington, D.C., for reading to keep the "body" intact as they pursued various ministries in scattered locations in the area.

Here again, one must establish his or her own pace in reading. It may be that you will want to spend your Bible reading time in slowly reading and praying the shorter passages related to the theme. If it seems as if you are not reading enough of the Bible each day, you may wish to augment your scripture reading from the Lectionary.

Whether your choice may be for the entire year or for

some particular period of time, it is recommended that you adopt a program and faithfully adhere to it. If you decide to read the selected passages in the morning and the chapter or chapters at night, for instance, try not to let the day go by until you have honored your commitment to the Word.

It will probably also be helpful to you in maintaining your diligence to indicate the passages you have read with a dot or a checkmark both in your Bible and in the Discipline as well. You will probably also want to use a marking pencil to underline in your Bible words or verses that speak especially to you in your reading.

A word of caution: the schedule, the checkmarks and the markings are only to aid you in being faithful to the Word as a means of grace. At best they can help you form some good habits in your devotional life. The Bible must be read with an open heart and mind so that its truth and grace begin to flow into you. You will learn to come to the Bible believing that God is speaking through his living Word to you. The function of the Disciplines is to help you reach the place where the call of the Word is strong enough to bring you to the reading.

SELECTIONS FOR MEDITATION

Even though it is true that one's inner journey is a very personal matter it is also evident that the experience of others can be a most needed help to us. In the instance of every theme in this book, whether it be an important step in learning to pray or some obstacle that seems to be blocking the way, there is ample counsel and guidance from those who have reached the same places in their pilgrimages.

In the readings selected for meditation we have tried to provide help in two ways. Some of the readings will challenge you; they will create a desire in you to reach in some new direction to cultivate your inner life. The richness and conviction with which some people write is readily apparent and their words describe trust, rest, worship and knowing God in ways that arouse deep hunger within the heart of the reader.

Other readings around each theme were selected for their down-to-earth practicality in outlining steps that we may take to begin to possess these new areas. There are specific ways to overcome distractions and obstructions and patterns of devotion. These will enlarge our hearts as we learn to practice them.

You may choose to read all the selections for each week every day—or it may be the better part of wisdom for you to consider one or two selections a day. If you read all of them each day it may be helpful to you to wait until the third or fourth day to begin marking them. Give the words and ideas some time to begin to build up strength as they speak to you.

Some of the readings will come to you at a particular moment in your life and they will be life-changing words for you. In your heart you will become a fellow pilgrim with the writer whether it is Brother Lawrence, a seventeenth-century French monk, or Emilie Griffin, a marketing consultant living in New Orleans.

PERSONAL MEDITATION

If you have allowed the various steps of your worship—the invocation, the Psalm, the scripture readings and the readings—to do their work, your heart and mind should have slowed their pace and freed themselves of the events and responsibilities of your ongoing life. Now perhaps you are ready to meditate and reflect upon how the scripture and the readings have spoken to you.

Your meditations should be silent as new insights, areas for growth, praise, admonition, words, thoughts and feelings come to you in quietness.

The surest way to capture and make the most of the times of meditation is to use a journal. Write down these deep inner words and messages in a notebook. There will be times when there is praise and grace—and there will be other times when you will be discouraged and downhearted. In the faithful recording of these stages of your spiritual development you will come to know both the shape of your own inner space and the gentle workings of the Spirit of God in meeting the ebb and flow of your heart's needs and aspirations.

If your journal is to be a "safe" depository—a place where you are willing to honestly assess your weaknesses and failures—you will have to determine that it remain a private record between you and God. If there is the slightest chance that it will be read by others it will be almost impossible to keep your words from presenting matters and yourself in the best light. The true forgiveness and healing that you need come only as you are entirely honest. The journal will give you a place to express yourself unreservedly to God in a way that welcomes his coming to you.

You may wish to have a place in your journal to list the names of people for whom you are praying. Many times these people will come to you in your meditation. Sometimes, circumstances or tasks to be done will come to mind while you are being silent. Adding them to a list of people and things to be prayed for will move them along in your consciousness and keep your heart and mind open.

Read your journal periodically (at monthly or quarterly intervals) to give you some overview of your journey. You will be heartened by progress you have made, by some answers that have come in prayer. You will probably also see that some of the worries which loomed large to you were not so fearsome after all. And there will be areas of your lifestyle to which you need to devote additional diligence and prayer.

The times of meditation (including the use of the journal) will become times of reflection in which life will begin to be seen in its proper perspective.

PRAYER

"Prayer is the movement of God to humanity and humanity to God, the act of meeting." In a sense, all you have been doing in the daily prayer time is praying. The invocation, the reading of both scripture and the selections, the meditation in silence and in writing have been "acts of meeting."

There is time now given for you to converse with God in the way most meaningful to you. As you read through the book, you will discover many forms of prayer. These move from petition and intercession to adoration and contemplation. There are prayers gathered up in words, whether they be ours or those of another, and there is a kind of praying that is beyond words. There are prayers that have no intention except to be in touch with God and to hear whatever he wishes to say. There are prayers that seek specific answers such as those for a child's well-being or the recovery of an elderly father.

It is not that one of these ways of praying is better than another. More likely, each of the forms should become some part of your praying. At the outset the important thing is to pray the way you know how to pray. As someone has said, "Pray as you can, don't pray as you can't." Believe that God will lead you along the pathway of prayer and will teach you to pray as you should.

A short paragraph of direction is given each week to be used for guidance in learning to use the different forms of prayer. Try praying for a part of the prayer time in the direction that is indicated.

As it was noted with the reading of the scripture, nothing is more important than being consistent. A specific time and a particular place, as discussed further on, will prove invaluable aids to the sense that "the act of meeting" truly takes place for you.

HYMN

Each section of readings includes the text of an old and familiar hymn. These may be sung or prayed.

BENEDICTION

A prayer is included to help you acknowledge that you are a citizen of two worlds and that you have to move back and forth between them. So you need his presence with you as you move outward to live your daily life.

CONCLUSION

The regular use of this book will offer you some structure and, we hope, some insight into seeking to establish or strengthen the process by which you give attention to the inner life. This spirituality is not a part or a piece of you; rather it underlies the fabric of all that you are. You will find that diligence in this part of your life can and will bring healing and well-being to all the rest of life. It will be a significant step on your way to wholeness.

It is often said that "prayer changes things." Probably the first and most obvious changes are wrought in the heart of the one who prays. If you are willing to commit to this journey in the light of real change; if under the bonds of faithfulness you will submit yourself to the disciplines that the inner life requires for this year, you will come to a new knowledge of God and his transforming power at work in you.

SECTION ONE
disciplines for the inner journey

The first section of this book is devoted to some areas which must be given attention in providing the foundation for our continuing spiritual formation.

The topics for the beginning weeks were selected to aid readers in an awakening awareness of their own spirituality—the inwardness of the issues that control and give life meaning. We have all had times when there was nothing particularly different happening in the outward circumstances of our daily living but during which, nevertheless, we possessed a marked calm and happiness. And we can also remember such occasions as vacations when we should have been at peace but were actually in turmoil. The recognition that one's life is meant to be lived from the inside out is a milepost on our spiritual journey. In a society which lays such great stress on outward appearances, labels and symbols of success it will take an earnest concentration on our part to free ourselves from this highly touted living on the circumference.

The middle weeks of this section deal with the different kinds of prayer as ways of living in the awareness of the presence of God in the center of life. Adoration, confession, petition, intercession and meditation are all facets or forms of prayer to be learned. Gradually we will come to explore and make each of them a part of our effective, personal prayer life. And they in turn will aid us in making the prayer experience carry over into all of our daily round of activities.

The concluding weeks of the section are considerations of some practical, concrete aids to the building of this inner sanctuary. Study, Bible reading, journaling, developing a spiritual partnership and fasting are some of the tested and true ways of giving attention to spiritual formation that we will practice.

Take time to read and pray through this section. There are nineteen weekly divisions but every reader must travel at his or her own pace. If it seems that one should tarry at some point until he or she feels at home there, certainly do so. It is not easy to break the patterns of our past manner of living. Persist, for it is a rewarding journey.

1. Authentic Experiences

Eternal God, you have been the hope and joy of many generations, and who in all ages has given men the power to seek you and in seeking to find you, grant me, I pray you, a clearer vision of your truth, a greater faith in your power, and a more confident assurance of your love. Amen.

John Baillie in *A Diary of Private Prayer*

PSALM 46

DAILY SCRIPTURE

Monday	2 Corinthians 12:7–10
Tuesday	Genesis 32:22–31
Wednesday	Philippians 3:7–12
Thursday	John 4:1–26
Friday	1 Corinthians 2:6–16
Saturday	Jeremiah 17:5–10
Sunday	Job 42:1–6

SELECTIONS FOR MEDITATION

PERSONAL MEDITATION

PRAYER

Let your praying this week be for a true sense of being heard. Do not particularly pray for feeling or for specific answers. Rather pray for the quiet confidence that you are in conversation with your Heavenly Father.

HYMN   "I Know Whom I Have Believed"

I know not why God's wondrous grace
To me He hath made known;
Nor why, unworthy, Christ in love
Redeemed me for His own.

I know not how this saving faith
To me He did impart,
Nor how believing in His Word
Wrought peace within my heart. . . .

I know not when my Lord may come,
At night or noonday fair,
Nor if I'll walk the vale with Him,
Or meet Him in the air.

But I know whom I have believed,
and am persuaded that He is able
To keep that which I've committed
Unto Him against that day.

D. W. Whittle

BENEDICTION

Heavenly Father: Let me see your glory, if it must be from the shelter of the cleft rock and from beneath the protection of your covering hand, whatever the cost to me in loss of friends or goods or length of days let me know you as you are, that I may adore you as I should. Through Jesus Christ our Lord. Amen.

A. W. Tozer in *The Knowledge of the Holy*

SELECTIONS FOR MEDITATION

✦ He is the one who can tell us the reason for our existence, our place in the scheme of things, our real identity. It is an identity we can't discover for ourselves, that others can't discover in us—the mystery of who we really are. How we have chased around the world for answers to that riddle, looked in the eyes of others for some hint, some clue, hunted in the multiple worlds of pleasure and experience and self-fulfillment for some glimpse, some revelation, some wisdom, some authority to tell us our right name and our true destination.

But there was, and is, only One who can tell us this: the Lord himself. And he wants to tell us, he has made us to know our reason for being and to be led by it. But it is a secret he will entrust to us only when we ask, and then in his own way and his own time. He will whisper it to us not in the mad rush and fever of our striving and our fierce determination to be someone, but rather when we are content to rest in him, to put ourselves into his keeping, into his hands. Most delightfully of all, it is a secret he will tell us slowly and sweetly, when we are willing to spend time with him: time with him who is beyond all time.

—From *Clinging—The Experience of Prayer*
by Emilie Griffin

◆ By reducing everything we do to some kind of means to an end, we impose upon ourselves a strait jacket of rigidity and conventionality. Oddly enough, we are not aware of this until at some point or another we break out of the strait jacket. At that very moment I rubbed my eyes in astonishment and realized that I had been dead, that the way I had acted toward other people was empty, devoid of all genuineness, depth, and authenticity. I had been wearing masks, playing out roles, going through the motions. I had thought I could handle this television interview in the same way I was accustomed to doing other things—like ticking off a list. Indeed, I had thought that I could avoid any risk of talking about myself. But it had not occurred to me that not to talk about myself would have made me do something worse—say nothing that was of substance. I had thought that I could talk about religion and theology. But one of the strange things about the language of religion and theology is that it does not permit itself to be used. The reason for this is fairly clear. It is not something neutral, a mere instrumentality. When we use such language simply for the sake of using it, the result is sheer nonsense, garbled communication. The language of religion is the vehicle of collective experience and it is meaningful only when it speaks of experience and addresses itself to experience.

—From *Death by Bread Alone* by Dorothee Soelle

◆ Our situation, say the Greek Fathers, is like that of the Israelite people in the desert of Sinai: we live in tents, not houses, for spiritually we are always on the move. We are on a journey through the inward space of the heart, a journey not measured by the hours of our watch or the days of the calendar, for it is a journey out of time into eternity.

. . . Christianity is more than a theory about the universe, more than teachings written down on paper; it is a path along which we journey—in the deepest and richest sense, the way of life.

There is only one means of discovering the true nature of Christianity. We must step out upon this path, commit ourselves to this way of life, and then we shall begin to see for ourselves. So long as we remain outside, we cannot properly understand. Certainly we need to be given directions before we start; we need to be told what signposts to look out for, and we need to have companions. Indeed, without guidance from others it is scarcely possible to begin the journey. But directions given by others can never convey to us what the way is actually like; they cannot be a substitute for direct, personal experience. Each is called to verify for himself what he has been taught, each is required to re-live the Tradition he has received. "The Creed," said Metropolitan Philaret of Moscow, "does not belong to you unless you have lived it." No one can be an armchair traveller on this all-important journey. No one can be a Christian at second hand. God has children, but he has no grandchildren.

—From *The Orthodox Way* by Kallistos Ware

✦ But there is a wider voluntary entrance to prayer than sorrow and despair—the opening of our thoughts to God. We cannot make Him visible to us, but we can make ourselves visible to Him. So we open our thoughts to Him—feeble our tongues, but sensitive our hearts. We see more than we can say. The trees stand like guards of the Everlasting; the flowers like signposts of His goodness—only "we" have failed to be testimonies to His presence, tokens of His trust. How could we have lived in the shadow of greatness and defied it?

Mindfulness of God arises slowly, a thought at a time. Suddenly we are there. Or is He here, at the margin of our soul? When we begin to feel a qualm of diffidence lest we hurt what is holy, lest we break what is whole, then we discover that He is not austere. He answers with love our trembling awe. Repentant of forgetting Him even for a while, we become sharers of gentle joy; we would like to dedicate ourselves forever to the unfoldment of His final order.

—From *Man's Quest for God* by Abraham Joshua Heschel

✦ I said I was searching for the roots of Christian mysticism. Now I say unhesitatingly that there are three sources of Christian mystical experience: (1) the Word of God in sacred scripture, (2) the sacraments, particularly the Eucharist, and (3) the Word of God in the community called church.

If, then, you ask for practical advice on how to enter the Christian mystical life, I do not advise you to take the plane to Tel Aviv and the bus to the Judean desert. I do not tell you to travel to Cairo and then to Sinai or to the desert south of Alexandria. I do not tell you to sit in the lotus and breathe from your abdomen. All this is good, very good, but in the end peripheral. Instead I say:

Listen to the word! Read the Scriptures! Read them again and again with faith and love until the word comes to life within you, penetrating the deepest layers of your unconscious.

Again, celebrate the Eucharist! Break bread with the community! Be present to the mystery of faith and partake of the bread of life. This will lead you into that rich inner desert of silence and joy where your life lies hidden with Christ in God. This will lead you to say with Paul: "It is no longer I who live, but Christ lives in me" (Galatians 2:20). This will lead you to cry out with Jesus: "Abba, Father!"

Again, listen to the community. Be part of the community. Get guidance from some representative of the community; read the mystical literature the community has produced. Never get isolated. Never go out on a limb. Community!

—From *Christian Mysticism Today* by William Johnston

✦ I entered Union Theological Seminary in the fall of 1954. If anyone had told me as little as a year or so earlier that I was going to do such a thing, I would have been no less surprised than if I had been told I was going to enter the Indianapolis 500. The preceding year I had become in some sense a Christian, though the chances are I would have hesitated to put it like that, and I find something in that way of expressing it which even now makes me feel uncomfortable. "To become a Christian" sounds like an achievement, like becoming a millionaire. I thought of it rather, and think of it still, as a lucky break, a step in the right direction. Though I was brought up in a family where church played virtually no role at all, through a series of events from childhood on I was moved, for the most part without any inkling of it, closer and closer to a feeling for that Mystery out of which the church arose in the first place until, finally, the Mystery itself came to have a face for me, and the face it came to have for me was the face of Christ. It was a slow, obscure process and the result of it was that I ended up being so moved by what I felt that I found it inadequate simply to keep it inside myself like a secret but had to do something about it.

—From *Now and Then* by Frederick Buechner

✦ There must be always remaining in every man's life some place for the singing of angels, some place for that which in itself is breathlessly beautiful and, by an inherent prerogative, throws all the rest of life into a new and creative relatedness, something that gathers up in itself all the freshets of experience from drab and commonplace areas of living and glows in one bright white light of penetrating beauty and meaning— then passes. The commonplace is shot through with new glory; old burdens become lighter; deep and ancient wounds lose much of their old, old hurting. A crown is placed over our heads that for the rest of our lives we are trying to grow tall enough to wear. Despite all the crassness of life, despite all the hardness of life, despite all the harsh discords of life, life is saved by the singing of angels.

—From *Deep Is the Hunger* by Howard Thurman

✦ I once thought, "I would like to feel the contours of these times with my fingertips." I was sitting at my desk with no idea what to make of life. That was because I had not yet arrived at the life in myself, was still sitting at this desk. And then I was suddenly flung into one of many flashpoints of human suffering. And there, in the faces of people, in a thousand gestures, small changes of expression, life stories, I was suddenly able to read our age—and much more than our age alone. And then it suddenly happened: I was able to feel the contours of these times with my fingertips. How is it that this stretch of heathland surrounded by barbed wire, through which so much human misery has flooded, nevertheless remains inscribed in my memory as something almost lovely? How is it that my spirit, far from being oppressed, seemed to grow lighter and brighter there? It is because I read the signs of the times and they did not seem meaningless to me. Surrounded by my writers and poets and the flowers on my desk I loved life. And there among the barracks, full of hunted and persecuted people, I found confirmation of my love of life. Life in those draughty barracks was no other than life in this protected peaceful room. Not for one moment was I cut off from the life I was said to have left behind. There was simply one great, meaningful whole. Will I be able to describe all that one day? So that others can feel too how lovely and worth living and just—yes, just—life really is?

—From *An Interrupted Life* by Etty Hillesum

2. Going Inward

O God, in all ages you have imparted yourself to man and set alight the fire of faith in his heart, grant to me the faith which comes from search. Cleanse my life from all that negates and crushes out faith, and fill it with the purity and honesty which foster it. Cleanse me from the evil which makes unbelief its friend, and drive it far from me, so that, being willing in all things to do your will, I may know the truth which shall set me free. Through Jesus Christ, our Lord. Amen.

Samuel M. Shoemaker in *Daily Prayer Companion*

PSALM 139

DAILY SCRIPTURE

Monday	Isaiah 55
Tuesday	John 3:1–8
Wednesday	2 Corinthians 4:7–18
Thursday	Matthew 15:1–20
Friday	John 15:1–17
Saturday	Ephesians 3:1–21
Sunday	Matthew 11:25–30

SELECTIONS FOR MEDITATION

PERSONAL MEDITATION

PRAYER

Your prayers this week should be to recognize the reality and depth of your inner being and to ask God to meet you there. For him to come to abide in this realm of your hopes, values, joys, hurts, and loneliness.

HYMN   "It Is Well with My Soul"

When peace, like a river, attendeth my way,
When sorrows like sea billows roll;

Whatever my lot, Thou hast taught me to say,
"It is well, it is well with my soul."

Though Satan should buffet, tho' trials should come,
Let this blest assurance control,
That Christ hath regarded my helpless estate,
And hath shed His own blood for my soul.

My sin—oh, the bliss of this glorious tho't—
My sin—not in part, but the whole—
Is nailed to His cross and I bear it no more,
Praise the Lord, praise the Lord, o my soul!

And, Lord, haste the day when the faith shall be sight,
The clouds be rolled back as a scroll,
The trump shall resound and the Lord shall descend.
"Even so"—it is well with my soul.

It is well—with my soul.
It is well,
It is well with my soul.

H. G. Spafford

BENEDICTION

Now to Him who is able to do immeasurably more than all I
ask or imagine, according to His power that is at work within
me, to Him be glory in the church and in Christ Jesus,
throughout all generations, forever and ever. Amen.

Paul in Ephesians Three

SELECTIONS FOR MEDITATION

✦ "When thou prayest, enter into thy closet, and when thou
hast shut thy door, pray to thy Father which is in secret"
(Matt. 6:6).

The closet also is twofold, outer and inner, material and
spiritual: the material place is of wood or stone, the spiritual
closet is the heart or mind: St. Theophylact interprets this as
meaning secret thought or inner vision. Therefore the material closet remains always fixed in the same place, but the
spiritual one you carry about within you wherever you go.
Wherever man is, his heart is always with him, and so, having
collected his thoughts inside his heart, he can shut himself in
and pray to God in secret, whether he be talking or listening,

whether among few people or many. Inner prayer, if it comes to a man's spirit when he is with other people, demands no use of lips or of books, no movement of the tongue or sound of the voice: and the same is true even when you are alone. All that is necessary is to raise your mind to God, and descend deep into yourself, and this can be done everywhere.

—From *The Art of Prayer* by Igumen Chariton of Valamo

✦ Theories about religious experience, such as Laing's journey or Jung's descent into depth-consciousness, are merely tools, aids by which to test one's own experience. Each step of one's own is worth more than all the knowledge and insight of others.

But how does one arrive at such steps? Certainly not by waiting for the experiences. The inward journey is an exercise, something that is cultivated; it requires concentration and attentiveness. Above all, the inward journey requires the greatest sincerity of which we are capable. It entails a risk—the risk of shame if nothing is there, the risk of emptiness if one does not change as a result, the risk of one's own person—and this risk is no less than that encountered on the way to another person. For us moderns, perhaps, fear of being ridiculous in our own eyes is the greatest shame.

—From *Death by Bread Alone* by Dorothee Soelle

✦ As we start learning to pray, I would like to make it clear that what I mean by "learning to pray" is not an attempt to justify or explain this in a speculative way. Rather, I would like to point out what one should be aware of, and what one can do if one wishes to pray. As I am a beginner myself, I will assume that you are also beginners, and we will try to begin together. I am not speaking to anyone who aims at mystical prayer or higher states of perfection, because these things will teach themselves. When God breaks through to us or when we break through to God, in certain exceptional circumstances, either because things suddenly disclose themselves with a depth we have never before perceived or when we suddenly discover in ourselves a depth where prayer abides and out of which it can gush forth, there is no problem of prayer. When we are aware of God, we stand before Him, worship Him, speak to Him.

—From *Beginning to Pray* by Anthony Bloom

✦ People who pray, really pray, don't talk about it much. After you have looked into the matter carefully, you may be able to puzzle out who is really praying. In general, though, prayer is something of an underground. Is it because people who pray are too possessive about their experiences to share them? On the contrary, people who pray usually share their experiences generously. But on the whole they don't advertise their prayer lives. Perhaps the energy that might be used in talk goes to prayer instead.

In order to find a person who prays, you have to look for clues: charitableness, good temper, patience, a fair ability to handle stress, resonance, openness to others. What happens to people who pray is that their inward life gradually takes over from their outward life. That is not to say that they are any less active. They may be competent lawyers, doctors, businessmen. But their hearts lie in the inner life and they are moved by that.

—From *Clinging—The Experience of Prayer* by Emilie Griffin

✦ When St. Paul described our mysterious human nature as a "Temple of the Holy Spirit"—a created dwellingplace or sanctuary of the uncreated and invisible Divine Life—he was stating in the strongest possible terms a view of our status, our relation to God, which has always been present in Christianity; and is indeed implicit in the Christian view of Reality. But that statement as it stands seems far too strong for most of us. We do not feel in the very least like the temples of Creative Love. We are more at ease with St. Teresa, when she describes the soul as an "interior castle"—a roomy mansion, with various floors and apartments from the basement upwards; not all devoted to exalted uses, not always in a satisfactory state. And when, in a more homely mood, she speaks of her own spiritual life as "becoming solid like a house," we at last get something we can grasp.

The soul's house, that interior dwellingplace which we all possess, for the upkeep of which we are responsible—a place in which we can meet God, or from which in a sense we can exclude God—that is not too big an idea for us. Though no imagery drawn from the life of sense can ever be adequate to the strange and delicate contacts, tensions, demands and benedictions of the life that lies beyond sense: though the important part of every parable is that which it fails to express: still, here is a conception which can be made to cover many of the truths that govern the interior life of prayer.

—From *The House of the Soul and Concerning the Inner Life*
by Evelyn Underhill

◆ Yet it is difficult to write or speak of the Holy Spirit. We are rather hesitant to claim the Spirit as "ours" in spite of our ease in praying "our" Father, "our" Lord, "my" Jesus. There is a reserve, a humbleness, a muteness before the Spirit. Perhaps it is the adjective "Holy" prefixed to the Spirit that makes us reluctant to say "our" Holy Spirit, "my" Holy Spirit. To say "Father" or "Son" is to speak in terms of definite, clear, human images and correlatives having some tangible reference. The Spirit does not lend Himself to such tangible human categories, descriptions or definitions. Our vocabulary, our language, even our theology clouds the Spirit and conceals more than reveals. Light cannot be put into a bushel or the ocean into a bucket. It is the Spirit which gives life to the word; the word itself is often deadly.

The Spirit is elusive, unobtrusive, as imperceptible as time and season, growth and age. Yet man has a deep sense of Spirit from the breath of his life, the pulse of his heart, the stirring of his conscience, the restlessness of his soul. In this, modern man is not far removed from primitive man. Aloneness, silence, darkness, sleep and death touch us too deeply to allow us to forget the mystery of the absolute. How intuitive ancient man was in sensing that the Spirit was in all things.

—From *Surprised by the Spirit* by Edward J. Farrell

◆ Each of us is the artist of his own life. The materials we are given to work with, the conditions we work under and what happens to us, are part of the drama of what we shall do with our lives. But materials and conditions and events are not, in themselves, the determining factors. Whether a man arrives or does not arrive at his own destiny—the place that is peculiarly his—depends on whether or not he finds the Kingdom within and hears the call to wholeness—or holiness, as another might say. The man who hears that call is chosen. He does not have to scramble for a place in the scheme of things. He knows that there is a place which is his and that he can live close to the One who will show it to him. Life becomes his vocation.

—From *Journey Inward, Journey Outward* by Elizabeth O'Connor

◆ Meister Eckhart wrote, "As thou art in church or cell, that same frame of mind carry out into the world; into its turmoil and its fitfulness." Deep within us all there is an amazing inner sanctuary of the soul, a holy place, a Divine Center, a speaking Voice, to which we may continuously return. Eternity is at our hearts, pressing upon our time-torn lives, warming us with intimations of an astounding destiny, calling us home unto Itself.

—From *A Testament of Devotion* by Thomas R. Kelly

◆ There are no "mere" men. Moral splendor comes with the gift of life. Each person has within him a vast potentiality for identification, dedication, sacrifice, and mutuality. Each person has unlimited strength to feel human oneness and act upon it. The tragedy of life is not in the fact of death but in what dies inside us while we live.

—From *Human Options* by Norman Cousins

◆ It is late evening. We are alone, perhaps for the first time since we woke. Bits and pieces from the day dart in and out of our consciousness. Little desires and fears for tomorrow scatter us further. The more that rushes through our minds, the more complicated and anxious life seems. Maybe TV will help settle us down—or the newspaper—or some work—or sex—or a big snack. Less seems to gnaw at us then. Life stays put for a moment. We feel in control again—we're "doing" something—anything.

The aftereffect of the doing leaves us less anxious, but more drugged. We've exchanged a gnawing anxiety for a dulled sensibility. Maybe, at least, we can sleep now. We do, on the surface. But not below. Our dreams are troubled. Fragments of life whir round and round without a center. We wake tired, and struggle out for another round.

You and I share such an "underlife." It usually is bearable; it even seems "normal," out of sheer habit. Sometimes it is even fun. But it is not fulfilling. We are grown for more than that. When this becomes most clear, when the whole daily round feels most wearisome, we hear ourselves crying out in the Psalmist's lament:

> How long, O Lord? Will you forget me forever?
> How long will you hide your face from me? (Ps. 13:1)

How long will, must I tromp through this dense jungle half crazed and blind before the clearing appears?

—From *Living Simply Through the Day*
by Tilden H. Edwards

✦ To know oneself is a vital element in prayer. For all prayer begins with questioning, with quest for meaning and identity, with hunger. St. Bernard calls self-knowledge "the highest knowledge, the best, the one that brings us nearer to God, the knowledge of ourselves." Or in the words of Johann Tauler (1300–61):

> I will tell you the shortest way, the most direct: enter your own depths, find out what it is that most hinders your own progress, and keeps you back. Retire within yourselves, for the Kingdom of God is within you . . . Go back into yourself, enter into yourself, with the knowledge of what you are.

—From *True Prayer* by Kenneth Leech

3. Addressing God

INVOCATION

O Lord of Hosts, you are Lord alone. You have made the heavens and the earth and all living things that dwell there. Your hand is the soul of every living thing. I would come before you with worship and honor this day. In the name of Christ I pray. Amen.

PSALM 84

DAILY SCRIPTURE

Monday	Luke 10:25–28
Tuesday	Matthew 6:1–4
Wednesday	Exodus 20:1–17
Thursday	John 1:1–18
Friday	Proverbs 8:22–36
Saturday	Romans 5:1–11
Sunday	Luke 18:9–14

SELECTIONS FOR MEDITATION

PERSONAL MEDITATION

PRAYER

Let at least the beginning of your prayer time this week be spent in remembering the wonder of God into whose presence you are coming.

HYMN   "O God, Our Help in Ages Past"

O God, our help in ages past,
Our hope for years to come,
Our shelter from the stormy blast,
And our eternal home.

Under the shadow of thy throne,
Still may we dwell secure;
Sufficient is thine arm alone,
And our defense is sure.

Before the hills in order stood,
Or earth received her frame,
From everlasting thou art God,
To endless years the same.

O God, our help in ages past,
Our hope for years to come,
Be thou our guide while life shall last,
And our eternal home.

Isaac Watts

BENEDICTION

Father, you clothe the sky with light and the depths of the
ocean with darkness. You work wonders among the sons of
men. Give me eyes to see your handiwork this day. Amen.

SELECTIONS FOR MEDITATION

✦ Let us think of our prayers, yours and mine; think of the
warmth, the depth and intensity of your prayer when it concerns someone you love or something which matters to your
life. Then your heart is open, all your inner self is recollected
in the prayer. Does it mean that God matters to you? No, it
does not. It simply means that the subject matter of your
prayer matters to you. For when you have made your passionate, deep, intense prayer concerning the person you love or
the situation that worries you, and you turn to the next item,
which does not matter so much—if you suddenly grow cold,
what has changed? Has God grown cold? Has He gone? No, it
means that all the elation, all the intensity in your prayer was
not born of God's presence, of your faith in Him, of your longing for Him, of your awareness of Him; it was born of nothing
but your concern for him or her or it, not for God.

—From *Beginning to Pray* by Anthony Bloom

✦ What is decisive is not the mystic experience of our being close to Him; decisive is not our "feeling" but our "certainty" of His being close to us—although even His presence is veiled and beyond the scope of our emotion. Decisive is not our emotion but our "conviction." If such conviction is lacking, if the presence of God is a myth, then prayer to God is a delusion. If God is unable to listen to us, then we are insane in talking to Him.

The true source of prayer, we said above, is not an emotion but an insight. It is the insight into the mystery of reality, "the sense of the ineffable," that enables us to pray. As long as we refuse to take notice of what is beyond our sight, beyond our reason; as long as we are blind to the mystery of being, the way to prayer is closed to us. If the rise of the sun is but a daily routine of nature, there is no reason to say, "In mercy Thou givest light to the earth and to those who dwell on it . . . every day constantly." If bread is nothing but flour moistened, kneaded, baked and then brought forth from the oven, it is meaningless to say, "Blessed art Thou . . . who bringest forth bread from the earth."

The way to prayer leads through "acts of wonder" and "radical amazement." The illusion of total intelligibility, the indifference to the mystery that is everywhere, the foolishness of ultimate self-reliance are serious obstacles on the way. It is in moments of our being faced with the mystery of living and dying, of knowing and not knowing, of love and the inability of love—that we pray, that "we address ourselves to Him who is beyond the mystery."

—From *Man's Quest for God* by Abraham Joshua Heschel

◆ A high school play is more polished than this service we have been rehearsing since the year one. In two thousand years, we have not worked out the kinks. We positively glorify them. Week after week we witness the same miracle; that God is so mighty he can stifle his own laughter. Week after week, we witness the same miracle; that God, for reasons unfathomable, refrains from blowing our dancing bear act to smithereens. Week after week Christ washes the disciples' dirty feet, handles their very toes, and repeats, It is all right—

believe it or not—to be people.

Who can believe it?

—From *Teaching a Stone to Talk* by Annie Dillard

◆ Now this general principle has its special application to prayer. Nothing could be more intensely individual than the prayers of the Bible. Nobody tries to commune with God in any one else's way. Some pray kneeling, like Paul (Acts 20:36); some standing, like Jeremiah (Jer. 18:20); some sitting, like David (2 Sam. 7:18); some prostrate, like Jesus (Matt. 26:39). Some pray silently, like Hannah (1 Sam. 1:13); some aloud, like Ezekiel (Ezek. 11:13). Some pray in the temple (2 Kings 19:14); some in bed (Ps. 63:6); in the fields (Gen. 24:11, 12); on the hillside (Gen. 28:18–20); on the battlefield (1 Sam. 7:5); by a riverside (Acts 16:13); on the seashore (Acts 21:5); in the privacy of the chamber (Matt. 6:6). Moreover all sorts of temperaments are found at prayer; practical leaders like Nehemiah, who in silent ejaculation of the spirit seeks God's help before he speaks to the king (Neh. 1:3, 5); poets like the writer of the twenty-seventh Psalm, who love communion with God; men of melancholy mind like Jeremiah, "Hast thou utterly rejected Judah? hath thy soul loathed Zion?" (Jer. 14:19); and men of radiant spirit like Isaiah, "Jehovah, even Jehovah, is my strength and song; and he is become my salvation" (Isa. 12:2). There are as many different ways of praying as there are different individuals. Consider the prayer of St. Augustine: "Let my soul take refuge from the crowding turmoil of worldly thoughts beneath the shadow of thy wings; let my heart, this sea of restless waves, find peace in thee, O God." And then in contrast consider the prayer of Lord Ashley, before he charged at the battle of Edge Hill: "O Lord, thou knowest how busy I must be this day. If I forget thee, do not thou forget me."

We need always to remember, therefore, that there is no one mould of prayer into which our communion with God must be run. Let each man pray as best he can.

—From *The Meaning of Prayer* by Harry Emerson Fosdick

◆ When I was through, he spoke hesitatingly, then, carried away by the importance of his subject, ever more passionately. "How can you bring yourself to say 'God' time after time? How can you expect that your readers will take the word in the sense in which you wish it to be taken?"

. . . The kindly eyes flamed. The voice itself flared. Then we sat silent for awhile facing each other. The room lay in the flowing brightness of early morning. It seemed to me as if a power from the light entered into me. What I now answered, I cannot today reproduce but only indicate.

"Yes," I said, "it is the most heavy-laden of all human words. None has become so soiled, so mutilated. Just for this reason I may not abandon it. Generations of men have laid the burden of their anxious lives upon this word and weighed it to the ground; it lies in the dust and bears their whole burden. The races of man with their religious factions have torn the word to pieces; they have killed for it and died for it, and it bears their fingermarks and their blood. Where might I find a word like it to describe the Highest! If I took the purest, most sparkling concept from the inner treasure chamber of the philosophers, I could only capture thereby an unbinding product of thought. I could not capture the presence of Him whom the generations of men have honored and degraded with their awesome living and dying. I do indeed mean Him whom the hell-tormented and heaven-storming generations of men mean. Certainly, they draw caricatures and write 'God' underneath; they murder one another and say 'in God's name.' But when all madness and delusion fall to dust, when they stand over against Him in the loneliest darkness and no longer say 'He, He' but rather sigh 'Thou,' shout 'Thou,' all of them one word, and when they then add 'God,' is it not the real God whom they all implore, the One Living God, the God of the children of man? Is it not He who hears them? And just for this reason is not the word 'God' the word of appeal, the word which has become a name, consecrated in all human tongues for all times? We must esteem those who interdict it because they rebel against the injustice and wrong which are so readily referred to 'God' for authorization. But we may not give it up. How understandable it is that some suggest we should remain silent about the 'last things' for a time in order that the misused words may be redeemed! But they are not to be redeemed thus. We cannot cleanse the word 'God' and we cannot make it whole; but, defiled and mutilated as it is, we can raise it from the ground and set it over an hour of great care."

—From *Meetings* by Martin Buber

✦ Jesus teaches us to approach God as "Father." In the Old Testament God is not often spoken of as "Father": in fact, there are only fourteen places where it occurs. They refer to God as the Creator with unique relationship to Israel his first-born (Deut. 14:1). In the prophets, there is a sharp contrast made between God's fatherhood and human faithlessness. But it is the whole community which addresses God in this way. There is no evidence that anyone in Judaism addressed God as "My Father." Yet this is precisely what Jesus did in all his prayers—some twenty-one times. Altogether we find the word Father used for God in the mouth of Jesus one hundred and seventy times in the Gospels. There is only one prayer of Jesus, the cry of dereliction from the cross, in which "My Father" is missing. Also Jesus used the Aramaic word "Abba." Thus in Gethsemane he prays: "Abba, Father, all things are possible to thee; remove this cup from me; yet not what I will but what thou wilt" (Mark 14:36). "Abba" was a very familiar form of address, rather like "Daddy," a childlike form. In the Gospels then "Father" is the description of God. Jesus is clearly encouraging a relationship with God which is marked by childlikeness.

—From *True Prayer* by Kenneth Leech

✦ Unless we can find the right name for God, we have no free, real, joyful, open access to Him. As long as we have to call God by general terms like "The Almighty," "The Lord God," as long as we have to put "the" before the word to make it anonymous, to make it a generic term, we cannot use it as a personal name. But there are moments when the sacred writers, for instance, burst out with something which has the quality of a nickname, something which no one else could possibly say, which is at the limit of the possible and impossible, which is made possible only because there is a relationship. Remember the Psalm in which, after more restrained forms of expression, suddenly David bursts out, "You, my Joy!" That is the moment when the whole psalm comes to life. Saying "O Thou our Lord," "O You are the Almighty" and the like, was stating to God facts about Him, but bursting out and saying "O You my Joy!" was quite a different thing. And when we can say to God, "O You my Joy!" or when you can say "O You the pain of my life, O You who are standing in the midst of it as torment, as a problem, as a stumbling block!" or when we can address Him with violence, then we have established a relationship of prayer.

—From *Beginning to Pray* by Anthony Bloom

4. Discipline

O eternal God, sanctify my body and soul, my thoughts and my intentions, my words and actions, that whatsoever I shall think, or speak, or do, may be by me designed for the glory of your name, and by your blessing may it be effective in your work. Through Jesus Christ our Lord. Amen.

Jeremy Taylor

PSALM 26

DAILY SCRIPTURE

Monday	John 3:25–36
Tuesday	Luke 12:35–48
Wednesday	Matthew 25:14–30
Thursday	Romans 12:1–2
Friday	Luke 2:41–49
Saturday	Deuteronomy 27:1–8
Sunday	1 Thessalonians 4:1–12

SELECTIONS FOR MEDITATION

PERSONAL MEDITATION

PRAYER

May your prayer this week lead you past bent knees and reverent spirit into the determining choices of your daily living. Let it bring your will to bear on all the things that lead you away from serving God.

HYMN   "Sweet Will of God"

My stubborn will at last has yielded;
I would be Thine and Thine alone;

And this the prayer my lips are bringing,
"Lord, let in me Thy will be done."

I'm tired of sin, footsore and weary;
The darksome path hath dreary grown,
But now a light has ris'n to cheer me;
I find in Thee my star, my sun.

Thy precious will, O conqu'ring Saviour,
Doth now embrace and compass me;
All discords hushed, my peace a river,
My soul a prisoned bird set free.

Shut in with Thee, O Lord forever,
My wayward feet no more to roam;
What pow'r from Thee my soul can sever?
The center of God's will my home.

Sweet will of God, still fold me closer,
Till I am wholly lost in Thee.
Sweet will of God, still fold me closer,
Till I am wholly lost in Thee.

Mrs. C. M. Morris

BENEDICTION

Lord, let my life be orderly, regular, temperate; let no pride or self-seeking, no covetousness or revenge, no little ends and low imaginations pollute my spirit and unhallow my words and actions. Let my body be a servant of my spirit and both my body and spirit be servants of Jesus, doing all things for your glory here. Amen.

Jeremy Taylor

SELECTIONS FOR MEDITATION

✦ "Watch, therefore." For life in time is not a stumbling from one ecstatic epiphany to another. The enormous task is to keep your eyes open, your wick trimmed, your lamp filled, your powder dry. Even when the bridegroom tarries. Even when the sky falls into the pond and the pond itself is sucked down some sewer of time that comes to nothing. Even when it all flattens out to triviality. Or the midnight cry, "Behold, the bridegroom cometh!" will catch you sleeping, your lamp overturned, the oil spilled out.

And then it is better if you had never been born. The moment you've been waiting for, the end for which you were made—your time—flies without you. Instead of going out to meet the bridegroom, glorious and infinitely desirable, you're in town haggling with the oil dealers. Life himself passes you by. The light dies out. The pond turns its back, closes the door. Depart. It doesn't know you anymore.

There are no two ways about it. You've got your eyes open or you don't. You're watching at midnight or you're not. You must be ready when it comes flying at you, skimming swiftly over the surface of time.

The cares of this world are no excuse. Not father, mother, wife, nor children. Not burials or births or weddings. Not fixing formula, scrubbing the toilet, peddling pills or prose. Whatever the great human enterprise currently in hand, the point is to watch. All the rest is addenda. Seeking the kingdom is the essential integer.

Keep your eyes open or you might as well be dead. You already are.

—From *And the Trees Clap Their Hands*
by Virginia Stem Owens

◆ So we need delay no longer. It is time to begin. However stumbling or uncertain the beginning it is worthwhile. And the beginning is more than the first stab or the first several stabs. Prayer is a matter of keeping at it. The rewards will come no other way. Thunderclaps and lightning flashes are very unlikely. It is well to start small and quietly. No need to tell one's friends and acquaintances. No need to plan heroic fasts or all-night vigils. You should have it firm in your mind that prayer is neither to impress other people nor to impress God. It's not to be taken with a mentality of success. The goal, in prayer, is to give oneself away. The Lord loves us—perhaps most of all—when we fail and try again.

—From *Clinging—The Experience of Prayer*
by Emilie Griffin

◆ Prayer tomorrow begins today or there will be no prayer

tomorrow. The penalty of not praying is the loss of one's capacity to pray! The promise of tomorrow is the hunger of today. As man reaches out to the stars and touches ever-expanding space, he is drawn to the discovery and value of his inner space. Prayer no longer lies on the edge of life. It moves into the core of the person's life and meaning. Without prayer, there is no way, no truth, no life.

. . . Prayer is a journey, a path that is created only by walking it. It creates and reveals oneself in the process. There are many ways of prayer, some new, some to be rediscovered. Writing is a way of discovering one's own gift of prayer. Scripture, Penance and Eucharist are Christ's way of praying in us. Discovering His gifts is to discover Him and those closest to Him. Eventually one is led out to the desert where one discovers the new creation and becomes a new creature.

—From *Prayer Is a Hunger* by Edward J. Farrell

✦ The denying ourselves, and the taking up our cross, in the full extent of the expression, is not a thing of small concern: It is not expedient only, as are some of the circumstantials of religion: but it is absolutely, indispensably necessary, either to our becoming or continuing His disciples. . . . If we do not continually deny ourselves, we do not learn of Him, but of other masters. If we do not take up our cross daily, we do not come after Him, but after the world, or the prince of the world, or our own fleshly mind. If we are not walking in the way of the cross, we are not following Him: we are not treading in His steps; but going back from, or at least wide of, Him.

—From *The Works of John Wesley, Sermon XLVIII, On Self-Denial* by Albert C. Outler

✦ The whole authentic history of spiritual discipline in the Church and in all deep religious traditions is to aid human digestion of the Holy, so that we do not 1) reject his nourishment 2) throw it up by not allowing room inside for it 3) mistake "artificial flavors" for the real thing 4) use its strength for building an ego empire.

—From *Spiritual Friend* by Tilden H. Edwards

✦ My hour in Carmelite chapel is more important than I can fully know myself. It is not an hour of deep prayer, nor a time in which I experience a special closeness to God; it is not a period of serious attentiveness to the divine mysteries. I wish it were! On the contrary, it is full of distractions, inner restlessness, sleepiness, confusion, and boredom. It seldom, if ever, pleases my senses. But the simple fact of being for one hour in the presence of the Lord and of showing him all that I think, feel, sense, and experience, without trying to hide anything, must please him. Somehow, somewhere, I know that he loves me, even though I do not feel that love as I can feel a human embrace, even though I do not hear a voice as I hear human words of consolation, even though I do not see a smile as I can see a human face. Still the Lord speaks to me, looks at me, and embraces me there, where I am still unable to notice it. The only way I become aware of his presence is in that remarkable desire to return to that quiet chapel and be there without any real satisfaction. Yes, I notice, maybe only retrospectively, that my days and weeks are different days and weeks when they are held together by these regular "useless" times. God is greater than my senses, greater than my thoughts, greater than my heart. I do believe that he touches me in places that are unknown even to myself. I seldom can point directly to these places; but when I feel this inner pull to return again to that hidden hour of prayer, I realize that something is happening that is so deep that it becomes like the riverbed through which the waters can safely flow and find their way to the open sea.

—From *Gracias!* by Henri J. Nouwen

✦ It is imperative that those who are to teach religion and guide souls should steadily enlarge their conception of and capacity for God; yet how many adult Christian workers go on, as they should do, steadily expanding toward eternity? The one thing, I suppose, which more than any other testifies to our spiritual vitality? If we do not grow thus, the origin of that defect is and can only be in the poverty of our own inner lives of prayer and mortification, keeping that spiritual vitality at low ebb. Prayer and mortification are hard words; but after all, that which they involve is simply communion with God and discipline of self. They are the names of those two fundamental and inseparable activities which temper the natural resources of man to his supernatural work; and every Christian worker must have in his life the bracing and humbling influences of such continuous self-surrender and self-conquest. They involve a ceaseless gentle discipline; but being a disciple means living a disciplined life, and it is not very likely that you will get other disciples, unless you are one first.

—From *The House of the Soul and Concerning the Inner Life*
by Evelyn Underhill

◆ God does not demand that we give up our personal dignity, that we throw in our lot with random people, that we lose ourselves and turn from all that is not him. God needs nothing, asks nothing, and demands nothing, like the stars. It is a life with God which demands these things.

Experience has taught the race that if knowledge of God is the end, then these habits of life are not the means but the condition in which the means operates. You do not have to do these things; not at all. God does not, I regret to report, give a hoot. You do not have to do these things—unless you want to know God. They work on you, not on him.

You do not have to sit outside in the dark. If, however, you want to look at the stars, you will find that darkness is necessary. But the stars neither require nor demand it.

—From *Teaching a Stone to Talk* by Annie Dillard

◆ One way to recollect the mind easily in the time of prayer, and preserve it more in tranquillity, is not to let it wander too far at other times. You should keep it strictly in the presence of God; and being accustomed to think of Him often, you will find it easy to keep your mind calm in the time of prayer, or at least to recall it from its wanderings.

—From *The Practice of the Presence of God*
by Brother Lawrence

✦ Some of us are more naturally night people or morning people. Our situations further influence what time is best to set aside. The advantage of early morning is the way it sets our attentiveness for the day. The advantage of evening is the way it reintegrates and settles us down for the night. It is ideal to set aside ten minutes to an hour both morning and night, giving more or less time as our situation allows.

Most important though is not the number of times or duration, but our deciding on some time and duration and sticking to it, at least for a trial period of a few weeks. This means that once we've decided to do it, we treat it like brushing our teeth: it is just something we "do," without agonizing over it each time. Brushing our teeth, once it's a habit, is very simple. So is prayer time. If we leave open a crack for "redeciding" every day, then it becomes complicated. We've undercut the very simplicity that prayer time can reveal.

When you feel resistance to prayer time, just lightly "see" the resistance, and get on with it. Don't judge your resistance. Don't even judge yourself if your resistance is so great that you give up your discipline one day. Judgment complicates our resistance and turns what is simple into a heavy struggle. Just gently notice what has happened, smile, and go back to your discipline the next day.

—From *Living Simply Through the Day*
by Tilden H. Edwards

5. Desire

INVOCATION

Lord, I do not know what to ask of you; only you know what I need. I simply present myself to you; I open my heart to you. I have no other desire than to accomplish your will. Teach me to pray. Amen.

Francois Fenelon in *Little Book of Prayers*

PSALM 1

DAILY SCRIPTURE

Monday	Philippians 3:7–11
Tuesday	Psalm 63:1–8
Wednesday	Luke 9:46–50
Thursday	John 12:1–8
Friday	1 Peter 2:1–10
Saturday	Romans 8:18–25
Sunday	John 7:37–44

SELECTIONS FOR MEDITATION

PERSONAL MEDITATION

PRAYER

Use your prayer this week to affirm that your deepest desire is to know him and to serve him. Seek him first and believe that all the other things that you need will be added to you.

HYMN   "Oh! To Be Like Thee"

> Oh! to be like Thee, blessed Redeemer
> This is my constant longing and prayer.
> Gladly I'll forfeit all of earth's treasures,
> Jesus, Thy perfect likeness to wear.
>
> Oh! to be like Thee, full of compassion,

Loving, forgiving, tender and kind,
Helping the helpless, cheering the fainting,
Seeking the wand'ring sinner to find.

Oh! to be like Thee, while I am pleading,
Pour out Thy Spirit, fill with Thy love;
Make me a temple meet for Thy dwelling,
Fit me for life and heaven above.

Oh! to be like Thee, Oh! to be like Thee,
Blessed Redeemer, pure as Thou art!
Come in Thy sweetness, come in Thy fullness;
Stamp Thine own image deep on my heart.

T. O. Chisholm

BENEDICTION

God be in my head, and in my understanding; God be in my
eyes, and in my looking; God be in my mouth, and in my
speaking; God be in my heart, and in my thinking; God be at
my end, and at my departing. Amen.

Old Sarum Primer

SELECTIONS FOR MEDITATION

✦ But it is vitally important at the outset to emphasize that
there is no need for a log cabin, cottages, huts, in order to
lead a life of prayer. Prayer is interior. The hut, the log cabin,
the chapel, is the human heart in which we must learn how to
pray. Solitude sometimes helps prayer, and for special voca-
tions is the cradle of prayer, and powerful prayer at that. But
for the average Christian, prayer doesn't need a geographic
spot. Prayer is a contact of love between God and man.

Married people don't need a bedroom to make love. One
can make love anyplace and "making love" does not necessarily mean immediately what people think it means! Making
love can mean looking into each other's eyes. It can mean
holding hands tightly. It means being aware of each other in
the midst of a crowd. So it is with prayer. In the intense stillness of a loving heart all of a person strains toward the be-

loved, and words—simple, gentle, tender—come forth, audible or inaudible as the case may be.

—From *Poustinia—Christian Spirituality of the East for Western Man* by Catherine de Hueck Doherty

♦ I find myself asking what I am getting out of this retreat, but I realized today that that is the wrong question. This retreat is not for me, but for him. It is to give him, at least for this little while, the fullest attention and love that I can, freed as I am from many other cares and concerns that ordinarily clutter my life—a chance to live out a bit Mary's part in this house that looks to her as a special patron. Lord, help me to let go and rest quietly at your Feet in complete attention to you. And then my life will be refreshed and renewed.

—From *O Holy Mountain!* by M. Basil Pennington

♦ But there is a deeper, an internal simplification of the whole of one's personality, stilled, tranquil, in childlike trust listening ever to Eternity's whisper, walking with a smile into the dark.

This amazing simplification comes when we "center down," when life is lived with singleness of eye, from a holy Center where the breath and stillness of Eternity are heavy upon us and we are wholly yielded to Him. Some of you know this holy, recreating Center of eternal peace and joy and live in it day and night. Some of you may see it over the margin and wistfully long to slip into that amazing Center where the soul is at home with God. Be very faithful to that wistful longing.

—From *A Testament of Devotion* by Thomas R. Kelly

♦ When we come to the lectio the most important thing is our desire. The Lord will reveal himself and enter into our lives to the extent we believe this is really possible and want it. "Ask and you shall receive, seek and you shall find." No one respects our freedom as completely as he does. "Behold I stand at the door and knock and IF one opens it I will come in." He never pushes the door open. He waits for us to open.

This is what we do in our lectio—we open the door of our mind and heart for him to enter. And he will.

—From *A Place Apart* by M. Basil Pennington

✦ In Abraham Heschel's *A Passion for Truth* I read today the words of the Kotzker (Rabbi Menahem Mendl of Kotzk): "He who thinks that he has finished is finished." How true. Those who think that they have arrived, have lost their way. Those who think they have reached their goal, have missed it. Those who think they are saints, are demons. An important part of the spiritual life is to keep longing, waiting, hoping, expecting. In the long run, some voluntary penance becomes necessary to help us remember that we are not yet fulfilled. A good criticism, a frustrating day, an empty stomach, or tired eyes might help to reawaken our expectation and deepen our prayer: Come, Lord Jesus, come.

—From *The Genesee Diary* by Henri J. Nouwen

✦ Desire is not merely a simple wish; it is a deep seated craving; an intense longing for attainment. In the realm of spiritual affairs, it is an important adjunct to prayer. So important is it, that one might say, almost, that desire is an absolute essential of prayer. Desire precedes prayer, accompanies it, is followed by it. Desire goes before prayer, and by it, is created and intensified. Prayer is the oral expression of desire. If prayer is asking God for something, then prayer must be expressed. Prayer comes out into the open. Desire is silent. Prayer is heard; desire, unheard. The deeper the desire, the stronger the prayer. Without desire, prayer is a meaningless mumble of words. Such perfunctory, formal praying, with no heart, no feeling, no real desire accompanying it, is to be shunned like a pestilence. Its exercise is a waste of precious time, and from it, no real blessing accrues.

And yet even if it be discovered that desire is honestly absent, we should pray, anyway. We ought to pray. The "ought" comes in, in order that both desire and expression be cultivated. God's Word commands it. Our judgment tells us we ought to pray—to pray whether we feel like it or not—and not allow our feelings to determine our habits of prayer. In such circumstance, we ought to pray for desire to pray; for such a desire is God-given and heaven-born. We should pray for desire; then, when desire has been given, we should pray according to its dictates. Lack of spiritual desire should grieve us, and lead us to lament its absence, to seek earnestly for its bestowal, so that our praying, henceforth, should be an expression of "the soul's sincere desire."

—From *The Necessity of Prayer* by E. M. Bounds

✦ To have found God and still to pursue Him is the soul's paradox of love, scorned indeed by the too-easily-satisfied religionist, but justified in happy experience by the children of the burning heart. St. Bernard stated this holy paradox in a musical quatrain that will be instantly understood by every worshipping soul:

We Taste Thee, O Thou Living Bread,
And long to feast upon Thee still:
We drink of Thee, the Fountainhead
And thirst our souls from Thee to fill.

Come near to the holy men and women of the past and you will soon feel the heat of their desire after God. They mourned for Him, they prayed and wrestled and sought for Him day and night, in season and out, and when they had found Him the finding was all the sweeter for the long seeking. Moses used the fact that he knew God as an argument for knowing Him better. "Now therefore, I pray thee, if I have found grace in thy sight, show me now thy way, that I may know thee, that I may find grace in thy sight"; and from there he rose to make the daring request, "I beseech thee, show me thy glory." God was frankly pleased by this display of ardor, and the next day called Moses into the mount, and there in solemn procession made all His glory pass before him.

—From *The Pursuit of God* by A. W. Tozer

✦ All of us are willing to admit pangs of hunger and feelings of emptiness inside us. We experience half-formed dreams and vague drives for something more than human resources can promise or produce. There is in each of us a dynamic, a mystique or drive that, unless detoured by human selfishness, leads to search for God, whether we know it or not. It is this desire that carries us beyond what we can see into the darkness and obscurity of faith. It is a hunger that can be satisfied in God alone. Obviously, God does not intend to satisfy this desire completely in this world; its function is to draw us closer and closer to God who alone can give us complete satisfaction. This is the truth which St. Augustine discovered, after the discouragement of so many blind alleys: "our hearts were made for you, O God, and they shall not rest until they rest in you."

The experience of God touching and involving the human will in search may come to different men in different ways. There are many avenues of attraction to God. Some are drawn to him through his beauty, others to his peace, and still others are attracted by his power. Most men find themselves drawn to God as the source and wellspring of the very meaning of life, the ultimate ground of human existence. But it may be that the first motion of God within the believer-to-be is one of disturbance. Sometimes we forget that God comes to us, not only to give us peace but also to disturb us. He comforts the afflicted and he afflicts the comfortable. For some men life becomes a hopeless mess, and they find themselves aware of a demand to know what it is all about. This inner restlessness and disquiet can well be God sowing the first seeds of faith in the human heart.

—From *A Reason to Live! A Reason to Die!* by John Powell

◆ Here, then, Jesus is confronting his disciples with a promise which is also a challenge and a demand. What he meant by righteousness we shall later have to investigate, but he is saying here: "Do you desire righteousness with that intensity of desire with which a starving man desires food, and a man parched with thirst desires water?" This is a challenge and demand with which Jesus continually confronted men. It was

with this challenge that he confronted the Rich Young Ruler (Matt. 19:16–22; Mark 10:17–22; Luke 18:18–23). The young man came to Jesus pleading to be enabled to find eternal life, real life. He was an attractive character for, when Jesus looked at him, he loved him. In answer to Jesus' questions he claimed that he had kept all the commandments from his youth upwards. Jesus then confronted him with the demand that he should go and sell all that he had and give the proceeds to the poor. In effect Jesus was saying to him: "Do you want eternal life as much as that? Are you prepared to sacrifice the luxuries of this life to gain eternal life?" And, when the matter was put that way, the young man went sorrowfully away. It was with this challenge that Jesus confronted one of the men who wished to follow him. The man said that he would follow Jesus anywhere. Jesus answered: "Foxes have holes, and birds of the air have nests; but the Son of Man hath no where to lay his head" (Luke 9:57–8). In effect Jesus said to that man: "Do you want to follow me enough to face a life like that?" It was this challenge that Jesus confronted his disciples with when he told them that they must love him more than father or mother or any other of their kith and kin (Matt. 10:37; Luke 14:26). In effect he said to them: "Do you want to become my disciple enough to give me the unconditional first place in your life?"
—From *The Beatitudes and The Lord's Prayer for Everyman*
by William Barclay

6. Solitude

INVOCATION

I pause, Father, to commune with you. Help me to be still and know that you are God. Ease awhile any tense muscles or strained nerves or wrought-up emotions. Let me be relaxed in body and calm in spirit so that I may be more responsive to your presence. I pause, Father, to commune with you . . . Amen.

Roy E. Dickerson in *Daily Prayer Companion*

PSALM 91

DAILY SCRIPTURE

Monday	Luke 5:12–16
Tuesday	Matthew 4:1–11
Wednesday	Ecclesiastes 3:1–13
Thursday	Luke 22:39–46
Friday	Galatians 1:11–24
Saturday	Luke 17:20–21
Sunday	Psalm 37:1–7

SELECTIONS FOR MEDITATION

PERSONAL MEDITATION

PRAYER

This week ask God to help you see the value of withdrawing unto him. Aloneness can be blessed when he is in it. It was the pattern of the Master to withdraw for rest. And we need to enter into his rest.

HYMN "I Need Thee Every Hour"

I need Thee every hour,

Most gracious Lord;
No tender voice like Thine
Can peace afford.

I need Thee every hour;
Stay Thou nearby.
Temptations lose their pow'r
When Thou art nigh.

I need Thee every hour,
In joy or pain;
Come quickly and abide,
Or life is vain.

I need Thee every hour,
Most Holy One.
Oh, make me Thine indeed,
Thou blessed Son!

I need Thee; oh, I need Thee!
Every hour I need Thee!
Oh, bless me now, my Saviour;
I come to Thee!

A. S. Hawks

BENEDICTION

O my God, when will silence, retirement, and prayer become
the occupations of my soul as they are now frequently the
objects of my desires? How am I wearied with saying so much
and yet doing so little for You! Come, Jesus, come, You the
only object of my love, the center and supreme happiness of
my soul! Come, and impress my mind with such a lively conviction of Thy presence that all within me may yield to its
influence. Amen.

Thomas à Kempis

SELECTIONS FOR MEDITATION

✦ In solitude we can slowly unmask the illusion of our possessiveness and discover in the center of our own self that we
are not what we can conquer, but what is given to us. In solitude we can listen to the voice of him who spoke to us before
we could speak a word, who healed us before we could make

any gesture to help, who set us free long before we could free others, and who loved us long before we could give love to anyone. It is in this solitude that we discover that being is more important than having, and that we are worth more than the result of our efforts. In solitude we discover that our life is not a possession to be defended, but a gift to be shared. It's there we recognize that the healing words we speak are not just our own, but are given to us; that the love we can express is part of a greater love, and that the new life we bring forth is not a property to cling to, but a gift to be received.
—From *Out of Solitude* by Henri J. Nouwen

✦ Deserts, silence, solitudes are "not necessarily places but states of mind and heart." These deserts can be found in the midst of the city, and in the every day of our lives. We need only to look for them and realize our tremendous need for them. They will be small solitudes, little deserts, tiny pools of silence, but the experience they will bring, if we are disposed to enter them, may be as exultant and as holy as all the deserts of the world, even the one God himself entered. For it is God who makes solitude, deserts and silences holy.

Consider the solitude of walking from the subway train or bus to your home in the evening, when the streets are quieter and there are few passersby. Consider the solitude that greets you when you enter your room to change your office or working clothes to more comfortable, homey ones. Consider the solitude of a housewife, alone in her kitchen, sitting down for a cup of coffee before beginning the work of the day. Think of the solitudes afforded by such humble tasks as housecleaning, ironing, sewing.

One of the first steps toward solitude is a departure. Were you to depart to a real desert, you might take a plane, train or car to get there. But we're blind to the "little departures" that fill our days. These "little solitudes" are often right behind a door which we can open, or in a little corner where we can stop to look at a tree that somehow survived the snow and dust of a city street. There is the solitude of a car in which we return from work, riding bumper to bumper on a crowded highway. This too can be a "point of departure" to a desert, silence, solitude.

But our hearts, minds and souls must be attuned, desirous, aware of these moments of solitude that God gives us.

—From *Poustinia—Christian Spirituality of the East for Western Man* by Catherine de Hueck Doherty

✦ Thus we see an outline of the content and method of Jesus' guidance. There was a rhythm of dealing with individuals, groups and crowds, saying and doing whatever would best reconcile them to their larger life with one another and in the Holy One.

There was one other dimension of this rhythm: solitude. Jesus' culminating preparation for this ministry was alone, in the wilderness, going through the dark, diverting, corrupting forces of evil, until they were faced down and their power shriveled. He emerged empowered, emboldened, with an indomitable sense of vocation. After this time, he continued to go off alone to pray from time to time.

—From *Spiritual Friend* by Tilden H. Edwards

✦ I spent many hours with Brother John in conversation and in silence and came to realize anew the truth that the closer one is to God the more deeply human one becomes. One of the first requests I made of John after we had become acquainted was to ask for a word, a blessing of his wisdom, some gift from his prayer, a share in his experience. His response to my request was a deep smile.

. . . After John and I had spent three days together he invited me to spend a few days in solitude in his hermitage. He, no doubt, needed a rest from me and I, too, was anxious to spend more time alone.

. . . John came to repossess his hermitage the third day. We celebrated Eucharist together quietly. When we had finished our thanksgiving John turned to me and said, "When you go back and talk with your people tell them to be patient with

God, to wait for Him." I had forgotten that I had asked John for "a word." When I had forgotten it was given to me.

—From *Surprised by the Spirit* by Edward J. Farrell

✦ As long as my mind is raging with thoughts, ideas, plans, and fears, I cannot listen significantly to God or any other dimension of reality. In his book *Doors of Perception* (Harper and Row, 1970), Aldous Huxley suggested that our sense organs, nervous systems, and brains are basically eliminative in nature. They are designed to help us survive on the surface of this particular planet, and so they cut down or tune out many other possible realms of experience. They rivet our attention on the physical realm and keep us from being confused and overwhelmed by much useless and irrelevant information. However, in the process they keep us out of touch with other dimensions of reality. We human beings can experience a spiritual dimension as well as a physical one. In quietness we find detachment and so untie ourselves from total attention to outer, physical reality. Then we sometimes find another kind of experience breaking through. Only those entirely brainwashed by Western materialism ignore this possibility.

—From *Adventure Inward* by Morton T. Kelsey

✦ How much prayer meant to Jesus! It was not only His regular habit, but His resort in every emergency, however slight or serious. When perplexed He prayed. When hard pressed by work He prayed. When hungry for fellowship He found it in prayer. He chose His associates and received His messages upon His knees. If tempted, He prayed. If criticised, He prayed. If fatigued in body or wearied in spirit, He had recourse to His one unfailing habit of prayer. Prayer brought Him unmeasured power at the beginning, and kept the flow unbroken and undiminished. There was no emergency, no difficulty, no necessity, no temptation that would not yield to prayer, as He practiced it. Shall not we, who have been tracing these steps in His prayer-life, go back over them again and again until we breathe in His very spirit of prayer? And shall we not, too, ask Him daily to teach us how to pray, and then plan to get alone with Him regularly that He may have opportunity to teach us, and we the opportunity to practice His teaching?

—From *Quiet Talks on Prayer* by S. D. Gordon

✦ Let him who cannot be alone beware of community. He will only do harm to himself and to the community. Alone you stood before God when he called you; alone you had to answer that call; alone you had to struggle and pray; and alone you will die and give an account to God. You cannot escape from yourself; for God has singled you out. If you refuse to be alone you are rejecting Christ's call to you, and you can have no part in the community of those who are called. "The challenge of death comes to us all, and no one can die for another. Everyone must fight his own battle with death by himself, alone . . . I will not be with you then, nor you with me" (Luther).

—From *Life Together* by Dietrich Bonhoeffer

✦ Exterior retirement is not sufficient to engage and satisfy a heart which would really withdraw itself from creatures to be occupied on itself alone, but interior retirement is likewise necessary, which is a spirit of recollection and prayer. A soul which is separated from all the amusements of the senses seeks and finds in God that pure satisfaction which it can never meet within creatures.

A respectful and frequent remembrance of the presence of God occupies the mind, and an ardent desire of pleasing Him and of becoming worthy of His love engages the heart. It is absorbed in Him alone. All things else dwindle into nothing. It buries itself in its dear solitude and dies to itself and all things in God. It breathes only His love. It forgets all but to remember only Him. Penetrated with grief for its infidelities it mourns incessantly in His presence. It sighs continually for the pleasure of seeing and possessing Him in heaven. It nourishes itself with reading good books and with the exercise of prayer. It is never tired of treating with God on the affairs of salvation. At least it humbly supports the irksomeness it may experience and with a view of honoring His sovereign dominion by the complete destruction of sin in itself, it renounces all desire of finding any other satisfaction than that of pleasing Him.

—From *Imitation of Christ* by Thomas à Kempis

✦ The desert initiates us into the life of the spirit by helping us to discover who we most deeply are. To follow Christ means that we must let go of excessive attachments to passing pleasures and possessions, to ploys of autonomous power, to tangible goods as if they were ultimate. Christ asks us to abandon our idols, whatever they may be, and to love Him with our entire being.

"Pray to thy Father which is in secret." God is a God who hides Himself to the carnal eye. As long as in our worship of God we are chiefly occupied with our own thoughts and exercises, we shall not meet Him who is a spirit, the unseen One. But to the man who withdraws himself from all that is of world and man, and prepares to wait upon God alone, the Father will reveal Himself. As he forsakes and gives up and shuts out the world, and the life of the world, and surrenders himself to be led of Christ into the secret of God's presence, the light of the Father's love will rise upon him. The secrecy of the inner chamber and the closed door, the entire separation from all around us, is an image of, and so a help to that inner spiritual sanctuary, the secret of God's tabernacle, within the veil, where our spirit truly comes into contact with the Invisible One.

—From *With Christ in the School of Prayer*
by Andrew Murray

7. Making Moments

INVOCATION

Father, give me eyes to see and a heart to respond to all which will come to me this day. Forbid that I should miss its graces by looking ahead to some tomorrow. Let me accept the newness each moment brings with awareness and gratitude. In the name of the one who makes all things new I pray. Amen.

PSALM 81

DAILY SCRIPTURE

Monday	Luke 24:13–35
Tuesday	Mark 9:2–8
Wednesday	1 Chronicles 28:10–30
Thursday	Revelation 3:14–22
Friday	1 Samuel 7:7–17
Saturday	Mark 14:1–9
Sunday	Matthew 17:1–13

SELECTIONS FOR MEDITATION

PERSONAL MEDITATION

PRAYER

Begin to pray this week that the moments of your life may themselves become prayers. Whether they are in the joy of a birthday party, in the weariness that comes from labor, in the majesty of the setting sun or in the pain that comes with tears. Pray that each in its turn will cause you to lift your voice to him.

HYMN   "This Is My Father's World"

> This is my Father's world,
> And to my listening ears,

All nature sings, and round me rings,
The music of the spheres.
. . . . .

This is my Father's world,
Oh, let me ne'er forget
That though the wrong seems oft so strong,
God is the Ruler yet.
This is my Father's world
The battle is not done;
Jesus who died shall be satisfied,
And earth and heav'n be one.

Maltbie D. Babcock

BENEDICTION

Father, so much of my life seems to be devoid of events that can be labeled important. Its content and quality will more likely be determined by my responses to the ordinary. Let me see your hand in the providences and circumstances of this day. Amen.

SELECTIONS FOR MEDITATION

✦ "To pray is to take notice of the wonder, to regain a sense of the mystery that animates all beings, the divine margin in all attainments." Prayer is "our" humble "answer" to the inconceivable surprise of living. It is all we can offer in return for the mystery by which we live. Who is worthy to be present at the constant unfolding of time? Amidst the meditation of mountains, the humility of flowers—wiser than all alphabets—clouds that die constantly for the sake of His glory, "we" are hating, hunting, hurting. Suddenly we feel ashamed for our clashes and complaints in the face of the tacit glory in nature. It is so embarrassing to live! How strange we are in the world, and how presumptuous our doings! Only one response can maintain us: gratefulness for witnessing the wonder, for the gift of our unearned right to serve, to adore, and to fulfill. It is gratefulness which makes the soul great.

—From *Man's Quest for God* by Abraham Joshua Heschel

◆ Temperance, then, is the teacher of that genial humility which is an essential of spiritual health. It makes us realize that the normal and moderate course is the only one we can handle successfully in our own power: that extraordinary practices, penances, spiritual efforts, with their corresponding graces, must never be deliberately sought. Some people appear to think that the "spiritual life" is a peculiar condition mainly supported by cream ices and corrected by powders. But the solid norm of the spiritual life should be like that of the natural life: a matter of porridge, bread and butter, and a cut off the joint. The extremes of joy, discipline, vision, are not in our hands but in the Hand of God. We can maintain the soul's house in order without any of these. It is not the best housekeeper who has the most ferocious spring-clean, or gets things from the confectioner when she is expecting guests. "If any man open the door, I will come in to him"; share his ordinary meal, and irradiate his ordinary life. The demand for temperance of soul, for acknowledgment of the sacred character of the normal, is based on that fact—the central Christian fact—of the humble entrance of God into our common human life. The supernatural can and does seek and find us, in and through our daily normal experience: the invisible in the visible. There is no need to be peculiar in order to find God. The Magi were taught by the heavens to follow a star; and it brought them, not to a paralyzing disclosure of the Transcendent, but to a little Boy on His mother's knee.
—From *The House of the Soul and Concerning the Inner Life*
by Evelyn Underhill

◆ Varied and rich are the methods used by individuals who have discovered the strength and the security that come from the practice of the Presence of God. Most often these practices are very private and are a part of the intimate resources of personal religious living. To talk about such things is like living one's private life in public. In the course of a lifetime a person may be privileged to share the testimony in most unexpected ways.

. . . There is a friend who is in her seventies now. In her

professional life she was a secretary. Each morning before breakfast she sits at her typewriter and writes a letter to God. No one else ever sees what she writes. It is part of her own private communion with Him.

There is another person well into the later years. For some months now she has been in uncertain health. Each morning when she awakes, she stops for a period of meditation. The phrase is the same each day: "This is the day that the Lord has made. I will rejoice and be glad in it." At night, as she turns out the light over her bed, she says it a little differently because "rejoice" and "be glad" are not very restful words. She says, "This is the night which the Lord has made. I will relax and rest in it." One day she had a fall, but managed to pull herself up without calling for help. She was quite shaken and was in much pain. She prepared herself for bed and with much discomfort was able to get in beneath the covers. As she turned out the light, she said, "This is the night which the Lord has made. I will relax and cry in it." Then she realized what she had said, and her tears were all mixed with her laughter.

Varied and rich indeed are the methods used by individuals who have discovered the strength and serenity that come from the "practice of the Presence of God."

—From *The Inward Journey* by Howard Thurman

◆ Well, I'm disappointed. Who wouldn't be? With socks, a Sunday school shirt, some handkerchiefs, a hand-me-down sweater and a year's subscription to a religious magazine for children. The Little Shepherd. It makes me boil. It really does.

My friend has a better haul. A sack of Satsumas, that's her best present. She is proudest, however, of a white wool shawl knitted by her married sister. But she "says" her favorite gift is the kite I built her. And it "is" very beautiful; though not as beautiful as the one she made me, which is blue and scattered with gold and green Good Conduct stars; moreover, my name is painted on it, "Buddy."

"Buddy, the wind is blowing."

The wind is blowing, and nothing will do till we've run to a pasture below the house where Queenie has scooted to bury her bone (and where, a winter hence, Queenie will be buried, too). There, plunging through the healthy waist-high grass, we unreel our kites, feel them twitching at the string like sky fish as they swim into the wind. Satisfied, sun-warmed, we sprawl in the grass and peel Satsumas and watch our kites cavort. Soon I forget the socks and hand-me-down sweater. I'm as happy as if we'd already won the fifty-thousand-dollar Grand Prize in that coffee-naming contest.

"My, how foolish I am!" my friend cries, suddenly alert, like a woman remembering too late she has biscuits in the oven. "You know what I've always thought?" she asks in a tone of discovery, and not smiling at me but a point beyond. "I've always thought a body would have to be sick and dying before they saw the Lord. And I imagined that when He came it would be like looking at the Baptist window: pretty as colored glass with the sun pouring through, such a shine you don't know it's getting dark. And it's been a comfort: to think of that shine taking away all the spooky feeling. But I'll wager it never happens. I'll wager at the very end a body realizes the Lord has already shown Himself. That things as they are"—her hand circles in a gesture that gathers clouds and kites and grass and Queenie pawing earth over her bone—"just what they've always been, was seeing Him. As for me, I could leave the world with today in my eyes."

—From *A Christmas Memory* by Truman Capote

◆ Alan Watts once used a royal comparison for our moving around. A king and queen are the center of "where it's at," so they move with easy, royal bearing. They have no place to "get." They have already "arrived." Looking deeply at our lineage, we see that we are of the highest royal line: the royal image of God is in us—covered over, but indestructibly there. We need rush nowhere else to get it. We mainly need to attentively relax and dissolve the amnesia that obscures our true identity.

—From *Living Simply Through the Day*
by Tilden H. Edwards

✦ This "dark night" of disbelief lasted four bleak and barren months. Then it happened. It was the beginning of the rest of my life, the pivotal religious experience of my own personal history. In the evenings, we novices had a fifteen-minute examination of conscience, during which we knelt on wooden blocks, our hands resting on our desks, our minds combing through the day for failures of commission and omission in thought, word, and deed. The only thing I did well, or at least so it seemed to me, was to get that wooden block in the right place. A well-adjusted kneeler, I used to say humorously to myself, was half the battle.

It happened on a definite Friday evening in the early spring, while I was kicking that kneeler into place for the evening examination of conscience. With all the suddenness and jolt of a heart attack, I was filled with an experiential awareness of the presence of God within me. It has been said that no one can convey an experience to another, but can only offer his reflections on the experience. I am sure that this is true. I can only say, in trying to share my experience with you, that I felt like a balloon being blown up with the pure pleasure of God's loving presence, even to the point of discomfort and doubt that I could hold any more of this sudden ecstasy.

—From *He Touched Me* by John Powell

✦ Nothing is more reasonable, perfect or divine than the will of God. No difference in time, place or circumstance could add to its infinite worth, and if you have been granted the secret of how to discover it in every moment, you have found what is most precious and desirable. God is telling you, dear sisters, that if you abandon all restraint, carry your wishes to their furthest limits, open your heart boundlessly, there is not a single moment when you will not be shown everything you can possibly wish for.

The present moment holds infinite riches beyond your wildest dreams but you will only enjoy them to the extent of your faith and love. The more a soul loves, the more it longs, the more it hopes, the more it finds. The will of God is manifest in each moment, an immense ocean which the heart only fathoms insofar as it overflows with faith, trust and love. The whole of the rest of creation cannot fill your heart, which is larger than all that is not God; terrifying mountains are mere molehills to it. It is in his purpose, hidden in the cloud of all that happens to you in the present moment, that you must rely. You will find it always surpasses your own wishes. Woo no man, worship no shadows or fantasies; they have nothing to offer or accept from you. Only God's purpose can satisfy your longing and leave you nothing to wish for. Adore, walk close to it, see through and abandon all fantasy. Faith is death and destruction to the senses for they worship creatures, whereas faith worships the divine will of God. Discard idols, and the senses will cry like disappointed children, but faith triumphs for it can never be estranged from God's will. When the present moment terrifies, crushes, lays waste and overwhelms the senses, God nourishes, strengthens and revives faith, which, like a general in command of an impregnable position, scorns such useless defenses.

When the will of God is revealed to souls and has made them feel that they, for their part, have given themselves to him, they are aware of a powerful ally on every hand, for then they taste the happiness of the presence of God which they can only enjoy when they have learnt, through surrendering themselves, where they stand each moment in relation to his ever-loving will.

—From *The Sacrament of the Present Moment* by Jean-Pierre de Caussade. Translated by Kitty Muggeridge

8. Silence

INVOCATION

O God, God, my Father, I have no words, no words by which I dare express the things that stir within me. I lay bare myself, my world, before you in the quietness. Brood over my spirit with your great tenderness and understanding and judgment, so that I will find, in some strange new way, strength for my weakness, health for my illness, guidance for my journey. This is the stirring of my heart, O God, my Father. Amen.

Howard Thurman in The Growing Edge

PSALM 8

DAILY SCRIPTURE

Monday	Revelation 3:20–22
Tuesday	James 3:1–12
Wednesday	Ecclesiastes 5:1–3
Thursday	1 Kings 19:9–13
Friday	Psalm 46
Saturday	John 10:1–15
Sunday	Habakkuk 2:20

SELECTIONS FOR MEDITATION

PERSONAL MEDITATION

PRAYER

There is much to be said in the Christian life; but it is God who is to do the speaking. Pray for silence both in mind and spirit so that you may hear his voice. If he spoke to you in a whisper, would you be quiet enough to hear him?

HYMN   "Still, Still with Thee"

Still, still with Thee,

When purple morning breaketh,
When the bird waketh,
And the shadows flee;
Fairer than morning,
lovelier than the daylight,
Dawns the sweet consciousness,
I am with Thee.

. . . . .

So shall it be
at last,
in that bright morning
When the soul waketh,
and life's shadows flee;
Oh, in that hour,
fairer than day-light dawning,
Shall rise the glorious thought—
I am with Thee.

Harriet Beecher Stowe

BENEDICTION

Come, Lord, and speak to my heart. Communicate to it your holy will, and mercifully work within it both to will and to do according to your good pleasure. Alas! how long shall my exile be prolonged? When shall the veil be removed which separates time from eternity? When shall I see that which I now believe? When shall I find what I seek? When shall I possess what I love, which is you, O my God! Grant, O Jesus, that these holy desires with which you now inspire me, may be followed by that eternal happiness which I hope for from your infinite mercy. Amen.

Thomas à Kempis

SELECTIONS FOR MEDITATION

✦ Unfortunately, in seeing ourselves as we truly are, not all that we see is beautiful and attractive. This is undoubtedly part of the reason we flee silence. We do not want to be confronted with our hypocrisy, our phoniness. We see how false and fragile is the false self we project. We have to go through this painful experience to come to our true self. It is a harrowing journey, a death to self—the false self—and no one wants to die. But it is the only path to life, to freedom, to peace, to true love. And it begins with silence. We cannot give ourselves in love if we do not know and possess ourselves. This is the great value of silence. It is the pathway to all we truly want. This is why Saint Benedict speaks of silence as if it were a value in itself: for the sake of silence.

—From *A Place Apart* by M. Basil Pennington

✦ By the grace You grant me
   of silence without loneliness,
   give me the right to plead,
   to clamour
   for my brothers
   imprisoned in
   a loneliness without silence!

—From *A Thousand Reasons for Living*
by Dom Helder Camara

✦ Silence is the very presence of God—always there. But activity hides it. We need to leave activity long enough to discover the Presence—then we can return to activity with it.

Stillness is present throughout the run at every point. But if one only runs, he never knows stillness.

God is present in all beings, but we will never be aware of him if we never stop and leave behind all beings to be to him.

—From *O Holy Mountain!* by M. Basil Pennington

✦ Not long ago the religion instructor at a Christian high school decided to introduce silent meditation into one of his classes. He gave the students instructions simply to "be" during the silence: to be relaxed and awake, open to life as it is, with nothing to do but appreciate whatever comes. Week by week he slowly increased the amount of time to a maximum of ten minutes.

The student response was very revealing. One boy summarized a general feeling of the class: "It is the only time in my day when I am not expected to achieve something." The response of several irate parents was equally revealing: "It isn't Christian," said one. "I'm not paying all that tuition for my child to sit there and do nothing," proclaimed another.

How is it that ten minutes of silence can be so special and so threatening?

—From *Spiritual Friend* by Tilden H. Edwards

◆ As there are definite hours in the Christian's day for the Word, particularly the time of common worship and prayer, so the day also needs definite times of silence, silence under the Word and silence that comes out of the Word. These will be especially the times before and after hearing the Word. The Word comes not to the chatterer but to him that holds his tongue. The stillness of the temple is the sign of the holy presence of God in His Word.

There is an indifferent, or even negative, attitude toward silence which sees in it a disparagement of God's revelation in the Word. This is the view which misinterprets silence as a ceremonial gesture, as a mystical desire to get beyond the Word. This is to miss the essential relationship of silence to the Word. Silence is the simple stillness of the individual under the Word of God. We are silent before hearing the Word because our thoughts are already directed to the Word, as a child is quiet when he enters his father's room. We are silent after hearing the Word because the Word is still speaking and dwelling within us. We are silent at the beginning of the day because God should have the first word, and we are silent before going to sleep because the last word also belongs to God. We keep silence solely for the sake of the Word, and therefore not in order to show disregard for the Word but rather to honor and receive it.

Silence is nothing else but waiting for God's Word and coming from God's Word with a blessing. But everybody knows that this is something that needs to be practiced and learned, in these days when talkativeness prevails. Real silence, real stillness, really holding one's tongue comes only as the sober consequence of spiritual stillness.

—From *Life Together* by Dietrich Bonhoeffer

✦ It is God who wishes to establish communication. He is more anxious to speak to us than we are to hear him. He is incredibly persistent in trying to get through. Our real problem is that we tend to avoid hearing him.

—From *The Fight* by John White

✦ The disciplined person is the person who can do what needs to be done when it needs to be done. The mark of a championship basketball team is a team that can score the points when they are needed. Most of us can get the ball in the hoop eventually but we can't do it when it is needed. Likewise a person who is under the Discipline of silence is a person who can say what needs to be said when it needs to be said. "A word fitly spoken is like apples of gold in a setting of silver" (Proverbs 25:11). If we are silent when we should speak, we are not living in the Discipline of silence. If we speak when we should be silent, we again miss the mark.

—From *Celebration of Discipline* by Richard J. Foster

✦ For as long as I can remember, I have not feared silence but welcomed it as a source of spiritual deepening. Like other people living in the world, I've grown accustomed to the noise in my place of work, to the raucous sounds of the city, to the inner disquiet stirred up by busy thoughts and earnest projects. Silence can be an escape from the functional responsibilities and physical demands of listening and conversing with colleagues, friends, and family members. But it can also be an opening to God.

—From *Pathways of Spiritual Living*
by Susan Annette Muto

✦ A common problem, related to why we may seek to escape silence, is the discovery that it evokes nameless misgivings, guilt feelings, strange, disquieting anxiety. Anything is better than this mess, and so we flick on the radio or pick up the phone and talk to a friend. If we can pass through these initial fears and remain silent, we may experience a gradual waning of inner chaos. Silence becomes like a cre-

ative space in which we regain perspective on the whole.
—From *Pathways of Spiritual Living*
by Susan Annette Muto

✦ Hasten unto Him who calls you in the silences of your heart.
—From *A Testament of Devotion* by Thomas R. Kelly

✦ It is necessary that we find the silence of God not only in ourselves but also in one another. Unless some other man speaks to us in words that spring from God and communicate with the silence of God in our souls, we remain isolated in our own silence, from which God tends to withdraw. For inner silence depends on a continual seeking, a continual crying in the night, a repeated bending over the abyss. If we cling to a silence we think we have found forever, we stop seeking God and the silence goes dead within us. A silence in which He is no longer sought ceases to speak to us of Him. A silence from which He does not seem to be absent, dangerously threatens His continued presence. For He is found when He is sought and when He is no longer sought He escapes us. He is heard only when we hope to hear Him, and if, thinking our hope to be fulfilled, we cease to listen, He ceases to speak, His silence ceases to be vivid and becomes dead, even though we recharge it with the echo of our own emotional noise.
—From *Thoughts in Solitude* by Thomas Merton

✦ Contradictions have always existed in the soul of man. But it is only when we prefer analysis to silence that they become a constant and insoluble problem. We are not meant to resolve all contradictions but to live with them and rise above them and see them in the light of exterior and objective values which make them trivial by comparison.

Silence, then, belongs to the substance of sanctity. In silence and hope are formed the strength of the Saints (Isaiah 30:15).
—From *Thoughts in Solitude* by Thomas Merton

✦ There are times when our silence pleads for forgiveness or acceptance; times when our wordlessness is gratitude or adoration. All of a sudden, one becomes aware that he actually believes in God with all his heart and that God neither ultimately disappoints nor decisively deserts man. Sometimes silence makes us appreciate the daring with which we say "Father" to God and consider ourselves his children. "Father" sometimes becomes the only word silence allows as we express inexpressibly all we feel and want and reach for.

—From *Dawn without Darkness* by Anthony Padovano

✦ A second, more positive, meaning of silence is that it protects the inner fire. Silence guards the inner heat of religious emotions. This inner heat is the life of the Holy Spirit within us. Thus, silence is the discipline by which the inner fire of God is tended and kept alive.

Diadochus of Photiki offers us a very concrete image: "When the door of the steambath is continually left open, the heat inside rapidly escapes through it; likewise the soul, in its desire to say many things, dissipates its remembrance of God through the door of speech, even though everything it says may be good. Thereafter the intellect, though lacking appropriate ideas, pours out a welter of confused thoughts to anyone it meets, as it no longer has the Holy Spirit to keep its understanding free from fantasy. Ideas of value always shun verbosity, being foreign to confusion and fantasy. Timely silence, then, is precious, for it is nothing less than the mother of the wisest thoughts."

—From *The Way of the Heart* by Henri J. Nouwen

9. Adoration

Eternal Father of my soul, let my first thought today be of You, let my first impulse be to worship You, let my first speech be Your name, let my first action be to kneel in prayer. Amen.

John Baillie in *A Diary of Private Prayer*

PSALM 150

DAILY SCRIPTURE

Monday	Deuteronomy 6:4–25
Tuesday	Isaiah 43:1–13
Wednesday	Genesis 1:1–31, 2:1–3
Thursday	1 Peter 1:3–9
Friday	Job 38:1–33, 42:1–6
Saturday	Revelation 21:1–7
Sunday	Luke 1:46–55

SELECTIONS FOR MEDITATION

PERSONAL MEDITATION

PRAYER

Try to make the first petitions of your prayer this week to be those of praise and adoration. Do not let yourself begin with your needs or from within the context of your life. Instead, begin your prayer against the backdrop of the greatness and majesty of God:

Our Father . . . hallowed be your name
Your kingdom come, your will be done. . . .

HYMN   "Joyful, Joyful, We Adore Thee"

Joyful, joyful, we adore Thee,

God of glory, Lord of love
Hearts unfold like flowers before Thee,
Opening to the sun above.
Melt the clouds of sin and sadness,
Drive the dark of doubt away:
Giver of immortal gladness,
Fill us with the light of day.

All Thy works with joy surround Thee
Earth and heav'n reflect Thy rays:
Stars and angels sing around Thee,
Center of unbroken praise.
Field and forest, vale and mountain,
Flowery meadow, flashing sea,
Chanting bird and flowing fountain,
Call us to rejoice in Thee.

Thou art giving and forgiving,
Ever blessing, ever blest,
Wellspring of the joy of living,
Ocean depth of happy rest.
Thou our Father, Christ our brother
All who live in love are Thine,
Teach us how to love each other,
Lift us to the joy divine.

Mortals join the mighty chorus,
Which the morning stars began,
Father love is reigning o'er us,
Brother love binds man to man.
Ever singing, march we onward,
Victors in the midst of strife,
Joyful music leads us onward,
In the triumph song of life.

Henry Van Dyke

BENEDICTION

Father, may my life make your great heart glad today. Let me live in adoration, praise and gratitude for who you are and all you have come to mean to me. Amen.

SELECTIONS FOR MEDITATION

✦ "Adoration" for the man of today is difficult. He is not al-together sure what it is, what it means. Yet, "adoration" is one of the great continuing words of the religious vocabulary, a vocabulary which is one of the richest, most retensive elements of our language. Words linger on long after the deep experience which they signified has been forgotten. Sometimes, even the capacity for the experience has become dimmed or lost, the meaning of the word blurred. We "adore" many things—the word is in common use, is used to describe lesser and often inane things or ideas. Thus "adoration" in its religious and original sense—the bowing down in awe and reverence, tinged with the fear of God—has become largely lost in superficial wonder and feeling.

—From *Surprised by the Spirit* by Edward J. Farrell

◆ . . . the highest adoration is not occupied with the recollection of favors received and mercies extended, though they do help one be aware of the true nature of God. There is still, in all such recollection, a remnant of that self-centeredness which it should be the purpose of prayer to escape. In it, we are still thinking of God in terms of something done to "me" and for "me." We never really adore Him, until we arrive at the moment when we worship Him for what He is in Himself, apart from any consideration of the impact of His Divine Selfhood upon our desires and our welfare. Then we love Him for Himself alone. Then we adore Him, regardless of whether any personal benefit is in anticipation or not. Then it is not what He has done for us or what we expect Him to do for us, but what He has been from eternity before we existed, and what He is now even if we were not here to need Him, and what He will be forever whether that "forever" includes us or not—it is that which captivates us and evokes from us the selfless offering of self in worship. That is pure adoration. Nothing less is worthy of the name.

—From *An Autobiography of Prayer* by Albert E. Day

◆ There is a place in the religious experience where we love God for Himself alone, with never a thought of His benefits. And there is a place where the heart does not reason from admiration to affection. True, it all may begin lower down, but it quickly rises to the height of blind adoration where reason is suspended and the heart worships in unreasoning blessedness. It can only exclaim, "Holy, holy, holy," while scarcely knowing what it means.

If this should seem too mystical, too unreal, we offer no proof and make no effort to defend our position. This can only be understood by those who have experienced it. By the rank and file of present day Christians it will be rejected or shrugged off as preposterous. So be it. Some will read and will recognize an accurate description of the sunlit peaks where they have been for at least brief periods and to which they long often to return. And such will need no proof.
—From *The Root of the Righteous* by A. W. Tozer

✦ The Mass has been building to this point, to the solemn saying of those few hushed phrases known as the Sanctus. We have confessed, in a low distinct murmur, our sins; we have become the people broken, and then the people made whole by our reluctant assent to the priest's proclamation of God's mercy. Now, as usual, we will, in the stillest voice, stunned, repeat the Sanctus, repeat why it is that we have come:

Holy, holy, holy Lord,
God of power and might,
heaven and earth are full of your glory. . . .
—From *Teaching a Stone to Talk* by Annie Dillard

✦ So we have come to the point at which, through discipline and silent waiting, prayer happens. We do not create prayer, but merely prepare the ground and clear away obstacles. Prayer is always a gift, a grace, the flame which ignites the wood; the Holy Spirit gives prayer. The human response is one of adoring love. It is this posture of adoration which is the central posture of worship. "Religion is adoration" wrote Von Hugel. As in meditation, adoring prayer calls for a concentration. But it is not a fierce mental concentration so much as a focusing of our love, an outpouring of wonder toward God. In meditation there was a simplifying of thought so that we came to think deeply around a single word or phrase or theme until thought gave way to prayer. Similarly in the prayer of adoration we focus ourselves. The mind becomes less active, and we allow ourselves, body and spirit, to rest in an attitude of outpoured offering to God.

—From *True Prayer* by Kenneth Leech

◆ Rabbi Zalman, one of the great successors to Hasidism's founder, the Baal Shem Tov, was said to have interrupted his prayers to say of the Lord: "I don't want your paradise. I do not want your coming world. I want you, and you only." This was in the spirit of his predecessor, who said, "If I love God, what need have I of a coming world?" Such language is not likely to satisfy moderns who wish a more open future. It is an important first word for those who have only utilitarian views of God. In the world of the practical, God is loved for the sake of one's self, for the self's purposes, and for the yield of this relation in the reward of eternal life. The ancient Hebrew loved God for the sake of a long life in which to enjoy creation, but he also was to love the Lord for the Lord's sake.

The Christian tradition in its vital years picked up something of this sense of the love of God and of trust in the divine ways wherever they lead. From the tradition of Bernard of Clairvaux in the Middle Ages there survives the story of a woman seen in a vision. She was carrying a pitcher and a torch. Why these? With the pitcher she would quench the fires of hell, and with the torch she would burn the pleasures of heaven. After these were gone, people would be able to love God for God's sake. Here, as so often in Hebrew thought, a regard for the intrinsic character of God and of divine trustworthiness shines through. A believer shifts away from a bartering concept in which one loves God for the sake of a transaction. Now there is a relation in which the trusting one is simply reposed in the divine will.

—From *A Cry of Absence* by Martin E. Marty

◆ Our children can teach us a great deal about ourselves. My daughter once came home with the not unusual remark for a nine-year-old, "I'll never speak to Elizabeth again." She was angry with Elizabeth but, either because of the latter's size or the restraining influence of a civilized image of a young lady, she refrained from scratching Elizabeth's eyes. Instead, she did the more civilized thing: she refused to speak.

To act as if another does not exist is a more hostile act than to slap his face. In the latter action one at least acknowledges his presence. The silent treatment is an extremely powerful weapon of aggression. With God, we are seemingly unable to hurt him in any other way. The only weapon we can use on him, as a vehicle for our anger at all the suffering he allows, is our silence. Like my daughter we can at least not speak to him.

—From *Guilt, Anger, and God* by C. Fitzsimons Allison

✦ And let it be observed, as this is the end, so it is the whole and sole end, for which every man upon the face of the earth, for which every one of you, were brought into the world and endued with a living soul. Remember! You are born for nothing else. Your life is continued to you upon earth for no other purpose than this, that you may know, love and serve God on earth, and enjoy him to all eternity. Consider! You were not created to please your senses, to gratify your imagination, to gain money, or the praise of men; to seek happiness in any created good, in anything under the sun. All this is "walking in a vain shadow"; it is leading a restless, miserable life, in order to avoid a miserable eternity. On the contrary, you were created for this and for no other purpose, by seeking and finding happiness in God on earth, to secure the glory of God in heaven. Therefore let your heart continually say, "This one thing I do"—having one thing in view, remembering why I was born, and why I am continued in life—"I press on to the mark." I aim at the one end of my begging, God; even at "God in Christ reconciling the world to himself." He shall be my God forever and ever, and my guide even until death!

—From *The Message of the Wesleys.*
Compiled by Philip S. Watson

◆ When the worst finally happens, or almost happens, a kind of peace comes. I had passed beyond grief, beyond terror, all but beyond hope, and it was there, in that wilderness, that for the first time in my life I caught sight of something of what it must be like to love God truly. It was only a glimpse, but it was like stumbling on fresh water in the desert, like remembering something so huge and extraordinary that my memory had been unable to contain it. Though God was nowhere to be clearly seen, nowhere to be clearly heard, I had to be near him—even in the elevator riding up to her floor, even walking down the corridor to the one door among all those doors that had her name taped on it. I loved him because there was nothing else left. I loved him because he seemed to have made himself as helpless in his might as I was in my helplessness. I loved him not so much in spite of there being nothing in it for me but almost because there was nothing in it for me. For the first time in my life, there in that wilderness, I caught what it must be like to love God truly, for his own sake, to love him no matter what. If I loved him with less than all my heart, soul, might, I loved him with at least as much of them as I had left for loving anything.

—From *A Room Called Remember* by Frederick Buechner

10. Confession

INVOCATION

Here in the presence of Almighty God, I kneel in silence, and with penitent and obedient heart confess my sins, so that I may obtain forgiveness by your infinite goodness and mercy. Amen.

The Book of Common Prayer

PSALM 32

DAILY SCRIPTURE

Monday	1 John 2:1–14
Tuesday	Hosea 1:1–11
Wednesday	Romans 10:1–13
Thursday	Leviticus 26:32–45
Friday	Nehemiah 9:1–3
Saturday	Proverbs 28:13
Sunday	Jeremiah 3:11–13

SELECTIONS FOR MEDITATION

PERSONAL MEDITATION

PRAYER

It is easier to confess some things than others. But it is usually the more difficult ones and the more personal problems that we need to confess for they are impeding our Christian growth. Quiet yourself before God this week and let him bring to your mind those things that you need to confess to him. He knows best what lies between the two of you.

HYMN   "Just As I Am"

Just as I am, without one plea,

But that Thy blood was shed for me
And that Thou bidd'st me come to Thee.
O Lamb of God, I come! I come!

Just as I am, and waiting not
To rid my soul of one dark blot.
To Thee whose blood can cleanse each spot,
O Lamb of God, I come! I come!

Just as I am, tho' tossed about,
With many a conflict, many a doubt.
Fightings within, and fears without,
O Lamb of God, I come! I come!
Charlotte Elliott

BENEDICTION

Dear Lord, grant me absolution and remission for all my sins, true repentance, amendment of life and the grace and consolation of your Holy Spirit. Amen.

SELECTIONS FOR MEDITATION

◆ This morning I had a pleasant discussion with David Molineau, the new director of Noticias Aliadas (Latin American Press). I mentioned to David how impressed I had been with the way the Peruvian people express their faith, their gratitude, their care, their hopes, and their love. I told him that it might be a special task for me to give words to much of the spiritual richness that I saw, but of which the people themselves are hardly aware. David agreed, but added: "Living with the poor not only makes you see the good more clearly, but the evil as well." He told me some stories from his own experience in a Peruvian parish, and illustrated the truth that in a world of poverty, the lines between darkness and light, good and evil, destructiveness and creativity, are much more distinct than in a world of wealth.

One of the temptations of the upper-middle-class is to create large gray areas between good and evil. Wealth takes away the sharp edges of our moral sensitivities and allows a comfortable confusion about sin and virtue. The difference between rich and poor is not that the rich sin more than the poor, but that the rich find it easier to call sin a virtue. When the poor sin, they call it a sin; when they see holiness, they identify it as such. This intuitive clarity is often absent from the wealthy, and that absence easily leads to the atrophy of the moral sense.

David helped me see that living with the poor does not keep me away from evil, but it does allow me to see evil in sharper, clearer ways. It does not lead me automatically to the good either, but will help me see good in a brighter light, less hidden and more convincing. Once I can see sin and virtue with this clarity, I will also see sadness and joy, hatred and forgiveness, resentment and gratitude in less nebulous ways.

—From *Gracias!* by Henri J. Nouwen

◆ "Confess your faults one to another" (James 5:16). He who is alone with his sin is utterly alone. It may be that Christians, not withstanding corporate worship, common prayer, and all their fellowship in service, may still be left to their loneliness. The final break-through to fellowship does not occur, because, though they have fellowship with one another as believers and as devout people, they do not have fellowship as the undevout, as sinners. The pious fellowship permits no one to be a sinner. So everyone must conceal his sin from himself and from the fellowship. We dare not be sinners. Many Christians are unthinkably horrified when a real sinner is suddenly discovered among the righteous. So we remain alone with our sin, living in lies and hypocrisy. The fact is that we are sinners!

—From *Life Together* by Dietrich Bonhoeffer

◆ There are two dangers that a Christian community which practices confession must guard against. The first concerns the one who hears confessions. It is not a good thing for one person to be the confessor for all the others. All too easily this one person will be overburdened; thus confession will become for him an empty routine, and this will give rise to the disastrous misuse of the confessional for the exercise of spiritual domination of souls. In order that he may not succumb to this sinister danger of the confessional every person should refrain from listening to confession who does not himself practice it. Only the person who has so humbled himself can hear a brother's confession without harm.

The second danger concerns the confessant. For the salvation of his soul let him guard against ever making a pious work of his confession. If he does so, it will become the final, most abominable, vicious, and impure prostitution of the heart; the act becomes an idle, lustful babbling. Confession as a pious work is an invention of the devil. It is only God's offer of grace, help, and forgiveness that could make us dare to enter the abyss of confession. We can confess solely for the sake of the promise of absolution. Confession as a routine duty is spiritual death; confession in reliance upon the promise is life. The forgiveness of sins is the sole ground and goal of confession.

—From *Life Together* by Dietrich Bonhoeffer

✦ Confession is so difficult a Discipline for us partly because we view the believing community as a fellowship of saints before we see it as a fellowship of sinners. We come to feel that everyone else has advanced so far into holiness that we are isolated and alone in our sin. We could not bear to reveal our failures and shortcomings to others. We imagine that we are the only ones who have not stepped onto the high road to heaven. Therefore we hide ourselves from one another and live in veiled lies and hypocrisy.

But if we know that the people of God are first a fellowship of sinners we are freed to hear the unconditional call of God's love and to confess our need openly before our brothers and sisters. We know we are not alone in our sin. The fear and pride which cling to us like barnacles cling to others also. We are sinners together. In acts of mutual confession we release the power that heals. Our humanity is no longer denied but transformed.

—From *Celebration of Discipline* by Richard J. Foster

✦ The discipline of confession brings an end to pretense.

God is calling into being a church that can openly confess its frail humanity and know the forgiving and empowering graces of Christ. Honesty leads to confession, and confession leads to change. May God give grace to the church once again to recover the Discipline of confession.

—From *Celebration of Discipline* by Richard J. Foster

✦ Complete sincerity is an unattainable ideal. But what is attainable is the periodic moment of sincerity, the moment, in fact, when we confess that we are not as we have sought to appear; and it is at those moments that we find contact with God once more. The progress of our spiritual life is made up of these successive discoveries, in which we perceive that we have turned away from God instead of going towards him. That is what makes a great saint like St. Francis of Assisi declare himself chief among sinners. We cannot, indeed, be content with this fluctuating condition, any more than we can resign ourself to always rediscovering discordances between our personage and our person. We hear Christ's command: "Be ye therefore perfect, even as your Father which is in heaven is perfect" (Matthew 5:48). We find this intuitive aspiration towards perfection in unbelievers as well as in believers. It implies especially a complete concordance between personage and person. Now it is precisely because we feel the impossibility of following this call that we recognize our need of God and his grace, of Jesus Christ and his atonement. If we thought we did not need God, should we still have a spiritual life?

—From *Reflections* by Paul Tournier

✦ We may trust God with our past as heartily as with our future. It will not hurt us so long as we do not try to hide things, so long as we are ready to bow our heads in hearty shame where it is fit we should be ashamed. For to be ashamed is a holy and blessed thing. Shame is a thing to shame only those who want to appear, not those who want to be. Shame is to shame those who want to pass their examination, not those who would get into the heart of things. . . . To be humbly ashamed is to be plunged in the cleansing bath of truth.

—From *An Anthology of George MacDonald.*
Edited by C. S. Lewis

✦ Shall I not tell Him my troubles—how He, even He, has troubled me by making me?—how unfit I am to be that which I am?—that my being is not to me a good thing yet?—that I need a law that shall account to me for it in righteousness— reveal to me how I am to make it a good—how I am to be a good and not an evil?

—From *An Anthology of George MacDonald.*
Edited by C. S. Lewis

✦ Misunderstanding, then, on this point of known or con- scious sin, opens the way for great dangers in the higher Christian life. When a believer, who has as he trusts entered upon the highway of holiness, finds himself surprised into sin, he is tempted either to be utterly discouraged, and to give everything up as lost; or else, in order to preserve the doc- trine untouched, he feels it necessary to cover his sin up, call- ing it infirmity, and refusing to be honest and aboveboard about it. Either of these courses is equally fatal to any real growth and progress in the life of holiness. The only way is to face the sad fact at once, call the thing by its right name, and discover, if possible, the reason and the remedy. This life of union with God requires the utmost honesty with Him and with ourselves. The blessing which the sin itself would only momentarily disturb, is sure to be lost by any dishonest deal- ing with it. A sudden failure is no reason for being dis- couraged and giving up all as lost. Neither is the integrity of our doctrine touched by it. We are not preaching a state, but a walk. The highway of holiness is not a place, but a way.

—From *The Christian's Secret of a Happy Life*
by Hannah Whitall Smith

✦ The fact is that the same moment which brings the consciousness of having sinned, ought to bring also the consciousness of being forgiven. This is especially essential to an unwavering walk in the highway of holiness, for no separation from God can be tolerated here for an instant.

We can only walk in this path by looking continually unto Jesus, moment by moment; and if our eyes are taken off of Him to look upon our own sin and our own weakness, we shall leave the path at once. The believer, therefore, who has, as he trusts, entered upon this highway, if he finds himself overcome by sin must flee with it instantly to Jesus. He must act on 1 John 1:9, "If we confess our sins, He is faithful and just to forgive us our sins, and to cleanse us from all unrighteousness." He must not hide his sin and seek to salve it over with excuses, or to push it out of his memory by the lapse of time. But he must do as the children of Israel did, rise up "early in the morning," and "run" to the place where the evil thing is hidden, and take it out of its hiding place, and lay it "out before the Lord." He must confess his sin.

—From *The Christian's Secret of a Happy Life*
by Hannah Whitall Smith

11. Petition

Lord, teach me to pray, with a faith in your goodness that believes for the answers; with a love for your will that cleanses my askings. Amen.

PSALM 5

DAILY SCRIPTURE

Monday	2 Thessalonians 1:1–12
Tuesday	Colossians 1:1–13
Wednesday	Matthew 7:7–12
Thursday	James 5:13–20
Friday	Genesis 18:16–33
Saturday	John 14:1–14
Sunday	1 John 5:13–21

SELECTIONS FOR MEDITATION

PERSONAL MEDITATION

PRAYER

Jesus reminded us to bring our needs to the Father, bread for today, forgiveness for past trespasses, guidance and deliverance for the days that are ahead. Bring those needs, for yourself and others, to him this week. Remember also to pray for your requests to grow out of a deep desire to be in his will.

HYMN   "My Faith Looks Up to Thee"

> My faith looks up to Thee,
> Thou Lamb of Calvary,
> Saviour divine;
> Now hear me while I pray,

Take all my sin away,
O let me from this day,
Be wholly Thine!

May Thy rich grace impart,
Strength to my fainting heart,
My zeal impart;
As Thou hast died for me,
O may my love to Thee,
Pure, warm and spotless be,
—a living fire!

While life's dark maze I tread,
And griefs around me spread,
Be Thou my Guide;
Bid darkness turn to day,
Wipe sorrow's tears away,
Nor let me ever stray,
From Thee aside.

                                        Ray Palmer

BENEDICTION

Grant me, O Lord, heavenly wisdom, that I may learn to seek you above all things, and to understand all other things as they are according to the order of your wisdom. Amen.

                                        Thomas à Kempis

SELECTIONS FOR MEDITATION

✦ True, the New Testament says, "What things soever ye desire, when ye pray, believe that ye receive them, and ye shall have them." That surely does not mean that anything we desire, we may have. There is a limitation in the passage itself which is usually overlooked; "What things soever ye desire, when ye pray." There are many things we naturally desire when we are on holiday, or are worried with our work, or are walking the streets, or are just daydreaming. But those same desires disappear when we begin to pray. They and prayer just do not seem to go together. The moment we begin to talk to God, we begin to be ashamed to talk about them. And when talking to God becomes talking with God, we forget those desires altogether. As one man said to me once: "I remember something I very much wanted. It seemed the answer to a long-felt and almost intolerable hunger. Every time I thought about it, and that was often, my heart was on fire and my pulse raced. So I tried to pray for it. But I couldn't. The words choked me. My God-directed thought could not tolerate it."

Another word of Jesus is often misinterpreted: "If ye abide in me, and my words abide in you, ye shall ask what ye will, and it shall be done unto you." That seems at first an unlimited guarantee of an affirmative answer to any desire— "what ye will." But it is not what anybody wills, that is assured of the answer. It is what is willed by a particular kind of person, one who is abiding in Christ. When a man truly abides in Christ there are many, many things he never wills to ask: he does not want them. And if Christ's words are abiding in a man—all of Christ's words—you can be sure that man will not ask for a whole category of events. When Christ's words are in the soul, a wish that the secular heart grasps after is no longer even interesting! When we truly abide in Christ, when our union with Him is complete, then His desires and ours are one. Having no will but His, it is right that that will should find expression in our prayers. Here is where the difficulty arises. Most of us are far from such unity with Him. We still will things which God must veto. Therefore, our desires should always be suspect—our preferences should not become petitions. Jesus' counsel, "Ask and ye shall receive," should always be understood to mean the asking sanctioned in another of the Master's words, "But seek ye first the kingdom of God, and his righteousness; and all these things shall be added unto you." So petition is now for the unfolding of His will, guidance, and power for its fulfillment.

—From *An Autobiography of Prayer* by Albert E. Day

◆ There can be no doubt that petition is a dominant part of prayer. How dominant it ought to be, and what petitions ought to be offered, are questions calling for further examination.

In many discussions of prayer, petition if not ruled out is

placed on the lower rounds of the ladder. I have many times heard and read that the true end of prayer is to cultivate fellowship with God, seeking not to have anything from his hand but only to be in his presence. As has earlier been suggested, this seems to me to rest on a false antithesis.

Certainly to be in fellowship with God and in right relations with him is a higher aspiration than to possess anything else we may desire. But does this discredit the prayer of petition? On the contrary, it calls for discrimination in petitioning. All prayer springs from a sense of need. What is required is not to eliminate petition, which would eliminate the expression of desire, but to purge and redirect desire until we pray for the right things.

—From *Prayer and the Common Life* by Georgia Harkness

✦ For several months, I'd been attempting to absorb the truth of this Scripture: Seek God first. Why do we tend to seek other things first . . . and want God to be added later?

We seek success . . .
    and want God to endorse our goals.
We seek acceptance . . .
    and want God to provide the cheering section.
We seek increased income . . .
    and want God to be the bonus.
We seek vindication . . .
    and want God to take our side.
We seek happiness . . .
    and want God's smile of approval.
We seek health . . .
    and want God to dispense an instant cure.

As we mature in our relationship with the Lord, our goals change. But we don't realize that our pattern often remains the same!

We seek to be useful . . .
    and want God to bless our busy activities.
We seek to be helpful to others . . .
    and want God to tag along.
We seek to be spiritual . . .

and want God to applaud.

We tend to use God instead of seek Him. We want God to do our bidding more than we want Him.

What percentage of our prayers are for our own comfort? To fulfill our fantasies? Where do we ask for God's will? Isn't it usually at the end of the prayer . . . as a closing benediction . . . sometimes almost as an afterthought?

I wonder how this all-wise God of ours feels about being brought in at the conclusion and asked to bless the plan? What a waste to rely on our wisdom, when God's wisdom is available!

—From *When the Pieces Don't Fit* by Glaphre Gilliland

✦ Another element in Jesus' prayers was petition. We have seen already that asking for God's gifts was certainly not the whole or even the main part of the Master's prayer life, but we must be careful not to go to the other extreme and imagine that such petitionary prayers found no place at all. It is particularly necessary at the present time to emphasize this, for there is a dangerous tendency today, even among good Christian people, to speak disparagingly of petitionary prayers and to say that asking for definite things from God is prayer of such a rudimentary and childish form that it ought to have no place in the religion of the mature and fully developed believer. This we must quite definitely deny. The idea that it is expedient to outgrow petitionary prayer goes to pieces on one clear fact—Jesus never outgrew it.

—From *The Life and Teaching of Jesus Christ*
by James Stewart

✦ "Teach us to pray."

And he did. "Do it this way," he told them.

"When you pray say, 'Our Father.'" Dear Abba. The first tentative and informal sound made at the baby's first taste of wheat.

Father. KINFOLKS!

Not "Our God." Gods aren't kin to folks. "Our Father." No doubt they had heard God referred to as Father before, but not very often. Most often the image they heard the rabbis use was of King. Or Lord. The idea of sonship, of actual kinship had not been developed. Fathers are kinfolks! God is God and a human is a human. God has claims and designs on us but we have no claims and designs on God. God is God. But kinfolks have claims and designs on each other. Kinfolks ask each other for things: Give us some bread, something to eat. Don't hold things against us. Forgive us. Excuse and understand. Comfort and accept us. Protect and defend us. Keep us away from the Evil One. Keep the Evil One away from us.

Kinfolks is a good idea.

—From *God on Earth* by Will Campbell

✦ Somehow I feel sure that the most direct route to religious experience is to ask for the grace to give, to share, to console another, to bandage a hurting wound, to lift a fallen human spirit, to mend a quarrel, to search out a forgotten friend, to dismiss a suspicion and replace it with trust, to encourage someone who has lost faith, to let someone who feels helpless do a favor for me, to keep a promise, to bury an old grudge, to reduce my demands on others, to fight for a principle, to express gratitude, to overcome a fear, to appreciate the beauty of nature, to tell someone I love him and then to tell him again.

There is a haunting possibility that I have not heard the voice of God speaking to me in all circumstances and persons in my life because I have been asking the wrong questions, making the wrong requests. I have been too busy speaking to listen. The Psalmist prays: "Create in me, O God, a loving and listening heart!" Maybe I should pray for such a heart.

—From *A Reason to Live! A Reason to Die!* by John Powell

✦ The prayer of faith, like some plant rooted in a fruitful soil, draws its virtue from a disposition which has been brought into conformity with the mind of Christ.

1. It is subject to the Divine will—"This is the confidence that we have in Him, that, if we ask anything according to His will, He heareth us" (1 John 5:14).

2. It is restrained within the interest of Christ—"Whatsoever ye shall ask in My name, that will I do, that the Father may be glorified in the Son" (John 14:13).

3. It is instructed in the truth—"If ye abide in Me, and My words abide in you, ye shall ask what you will, and it shall be done unto you" (John 15:7).

4. It is energized by the Spirit—"Able to do exceeding abundantly above all that we ask or think, according to the power that worketh in us" (Eph. 3:20).

5. It is interwoven with love and mercy—"And when ye stand praying, forgive, if ye have ought against any; that your Father also which is in heaven may forgive you your trespasses" (Mark 11:25).

6. It is accompanied with obedience—"Whatsoever we ask, we receive of Him, because we keep His commandments, and do those things that are pleasing in His sight" (1 John 3:22).

7. It is so earnest that it will not accept denial—"Ask, and it shall be given you; seek, and ye shall find; knock, and it shall be opened unto you" (Luke 11:9).

8. It goes out to look for, and to hasten its answer—"The supplication of a righteous man availeth much its working" (James 5:16, R.V.).

—From *The Hidden Life of Prayer* by D. M. M'Intyre

12. Intercession

O Lord, You lover of souls, in whose hand is the life of every living thing, I bring before You in my prayers all those who are lonely in this world. Yours they are, and none can pluck them out of Your hand. In Your pitiful mercy let my remembrance reach them and comfort their hearts. For Your love's sake. Amen.

Little Book of Prayers

PSALM 20

DAILY SCRIPTURE

Monday	Numbers 14:11–20
Tuesday	1 Samuel 12:12–25
Wednesday	Psalm 106:1–48
Thursday	Genesis 18:16–33
Friday	Hebrews 7:23–25
Saturday	Romans 8:28–39
Sunday	1 Timothy 2:1–8

SELECTIONS FOR MEDITATION

PERSONAL MEDITATION

PRAYER

Lift up to God those persons who have asked you to pray for them. Try to visualize your becoming strength in their weakness, courage in their fear, freedom in their guilt and hope in their despair.

HYMN   "Lord, As to Thy Dear Cross We Flee"

Lord, as to thy dear Cross we flee.

And plead to be forgiven,
So let thy life our pattern be,
And form our souls for heaven.

Help us, through good report and ill,
Our daily cross to bear;
Like thee, to do our Father's will,
Our brethren's griefs to share.

Let grace our selfishness expell,
Our earthliness refine,
And in our hearts let kindness dwell,
As free and true as thine.

If joy shall at thy bidding fly,
And grief's dark day come on,
We in our turn would meekly cry,
"Father, thy will be done."

       C. M. Windsor

BENEDICTION

Grant my Savior, that your patience in bearing with me and suffering for me may be the model and principle of my patience in suffering for you, and that, entering into your designs of my salvation, which you would secure for me by the good use I make of afflictions, I may receive all things with humble submission to your holy will. Amen.

SELECTIONS FOR MEDITATION

✦ When I was minister in residence of The Church for the Fellowship of All Peoples in San Francisco, I experienced this in a human relationship. For several weeks, every day, I visited a member of my church who was very ill. She had a disease for which there was no cure. For one-half hour every day, for several weeks, I read to her. Finally I stopped reading to her. I would simply go and sit. We would sit and "is" together. When I had to leave the city for several weeks, we entered into a very interesting little agreement. I worked out a timetable of the difference in the time between the Pacific coast and the various spots at which I would be stopping until I arrived in New York. At the same hour every morning, we met. For seven weeks every day with from two thousand to three thousand six hundred miles separating us, we touched each other outside of time.

—From *The Growing Edge* by Howard Thurman

◆ And why should the good of anyone depend on the prayer of another? I can only answer with the return question, "Why should my love be powerless to help another?"

—From *An Anthology of George MacDonald.*
Edited by C. S. Lewis

◆ A Christian fellowship lives and exists by the intercession of its members for one another, or it collapses. I can no longer condemn or hate a brother for whom I pray, no matter how much trouble he causes me. His face, that hitherto may have been strange and intolerable to me, is transformed in intercession into the countenance of a brother for whom Christ died, the face of a forgiven sinner. This is a happy discovery for the Christian who begins to pray for others. There is no dislike, no personal tension, no estrangement that cannot be overcome by intercession as far as our side of it is concerned. Intercessory prayer is the purifying bath into which the individual and the fellowship must enter every day. The struggle we undergo with our brother in intercession may be a hard one, but that struggle has the promise that it will gain its goal.

How does this happen? Intercession means no more than to bring our brother into the presence of God, to see him under the Cross of Jesus as a poor human being and sinner in need of grace. Then everything in him that repels us falls away; we see him in all his destruction and need. His need and his sin become so heavy and oppressive that we feel them as our own, and we can do nothing else but pray: Lord, do Thou, Thou alone, deal with him according to Thy severity and Thy goodness. To make intercession means to grant our brother the same right that we have received, namely, to stand before Christ and share in his mercy.

—From *Life Together* by Dietrich Bonhoeffer

✦ How excellent a means of sanctifying us and of fitting us for heaven is the exercise of that charity by which we support in ourselves and in others those weaknesses which we cannot correct! For nothing can humble us and confound us before God more than a sense of our own miseries, and nothing can be more just than that we should bear in others those things which we would have them support in ourselves. We should, therefore, bear with the tempers of others and endeavor to give no cause of uneasiness to anyone on account of our own. It is thus, according to St. Paul, we shall carry one another's burdens and fulfil the law of Jesus Christ, which is a law of charity, meekness and patience.

—From *Imitation of Christ* by Thomas à Kempis

✦ What requests did Paul make for his Ephesian friends (Eph. 1:17–21)? Pause a moment. You are writing a letter to a friend for whom you pray fairly regularly. What will you tell him? "I do pray for you, Jack. I'm asking God to bless you and to lead you. I really pray. I pray he'll bless you richly."

What do the words mean? What does bless mean? Is the word an excuse on your part for not being specific? Is it too much trouble to think out a specific request? It is easier of course if Jack has pneumonia or if Jack's girl friend has just been killed in a car accident. You can get your teeth into prayer under such circumstances. But if nothing dramatic is happening to Jack and if he's a Christian who's getting along reasonably well in his Christian walk, how are you supposed to pray? Bless comes in handy. You probably use it at different times to mean such things as, "Do whatever is best for Jack and make things work out for him. Make him a better Christian in some way or another. Make him happy," and so on.

Are these the things God wants for Jack? What does God want? Remember God has his own goals for Jack's life. God will share those goals with you if you are willing to get involved with him in a partnership of prayer. You may need to begin praying something like this, "Lord, I don't know how to pray for Jack. I thank you for bringing him to yourself. I know you have been working in his life. What is it he most needs?

What are you trying to do in him?" God still has the initiative in Jack's life. Play it God's way. That is what partnership in prayer is all about.

—From *Daring to Draw Near* by John White

✦ The thought of our fellowship in the intercession of Jesus reminds us of what He has taught us more than once before, how all these wonderful prayer-promises have as their aim and justification, the glory of God in the manifestation of His kingdom and the salvation of sinners. As long as we only or chiefly pray for ourselves, the promises of the last night must remain a sealed book to us. It is to the fruit-bearing branches of the Vine; it is to disciples sent into the world as the Father sent Him, to live for perishing men; it is to His faithful servants and intimate friends who take up the work He leaves behind, who have like their Lord become as the seed-corn, losing its life to multiply it manifold—it is to such that the promises are given. Let us each find out what the work is, and who the souls are entrusted to our special prayers; let us make our intercession for them our life of fellowship with God, and we shall not only find the promises of power in prayer made true to us, but we shall then first begin to realize how our abiding in Christ and His abiding in us make us share in His own joy of blessing and saving men.

—From *With Christ in the School of Prayer* by Andrew Murray

✦ Prayer does not occur in the heart of a man who thinks God will do it all or who supposes he himself can do nothing. Prayer is a willingness to admit we can do something even if not everything and that, although nothing is done without God, God does nothing without us. So often in our theology of prayer we have articulated half-truths. We have emphasized the vertical dimension of prayer and neglected its horizontal character. We have used prayer to make too much of God, too little of ourselves. We have turned away from life in the foolish notion that one could, thereby, discover the God of life. We have judged the value of prayer by the amount of time given to it rather than by its intensity.

—From *Dawn Without Darkness* by Anthony Padovano

✦ Today I imagined my inner self as a place crowded with pins and needles. How could I receive anyone in my prayer when there is no real place for them to be free and relaxed? When I am still so full of preoccupations, jealousies, angry feelings, anyone who enters will get hurt. I had a very vivid realization that I must create some free space in my innermost self so that I may indeed invite others to enter and be healed. To pray for others means to offer others a hospitable place where I can really listen to their needs and pains. Compassion, therefore, calls for a self-scrutiny that can lead to inner gentleness.

If I could have a gentle "interiority"—a heart of flesh and not of stone, a room with some spots on which one might walk barefooted—then God and my fellow humans could meet each other there. Then the center of my heart can become the place where God can hear the prayer for my neighbors and embrace them with his love.

—From *The Genesee Diary* by Henri J. Nouwen

✦ A final characteristic of the prayer of the heart is that it includes all our concerns. When we enter with our mind into our heart and there stand in the presence of God, then all our mental preoccupations become prayer. The power of the prayer of the heart is precisely that through it all that which is on our mind becomes prayer.

When we say to people, "I will pray for you," we make a very important commitment. The sad thing is that this remark often remains nothing but a well-meant expression of concern. But when we learn to descend with our mind into our heart, then all those who have become part of our lives are led into the healing presence of God and touched by him in the very center of our being. We are speaking here about a mystery for which words are inadequate. It is the mystery that the heart, which is the center of our being, is transformed by God into his own heart, a heart large enough to embrace the entire universe. Through prayer we can carry in our heart all human pain and sorrow, all conflicts and agonies, all torture and war, all hunger, loneliness, and misery, not because of some great psychological or emotional capacity, but because God's heart has become one with ours.

Here we catch sight of the meaning of Jesus' words, "Shoulder my yoke and learn from me, for I am gentle and humble in heart, and you will find rest for your souls. Yes, my yoke is easy and my burden light" (Matthew 11:29–30). Jesus invites us to accept his burden, which is the burden of the whole world, a burden that includes human suffering in all times and places. But this divine burden is light, and we can carry it when our heart has been transformed into the gentle and humble heart of our Lord.

—From *The Way of the Heart* by Henri J. Nouwen

13. Meditation

INVOCATION

My Father of infinite love, enter and fill me and take control of every area of my life. Let my mind be as transparent as a window for letting Your truth shine through me. Let my heart be as the widow's cruse, ever brimming over with Your compassion for men. Let the threads of my life be interwoven with the tapestry of Your eternal purposes. For Yours is the Kingdom, and the power, and the glory forever and ever. Amen.

Glenn Clark in *Daily Prayer Companion*

PSALM 27

DAILY SCRIPTURE

Monday	Ecclesiastes 12:1–7
Tuesday	Colossians 4:4–9
Wednesday	Luke 16:19–31
Thursday	Deuteronomy 10:12–22
Friday	Psalm 119:97–104
Saturday	Joshua 1:1–9
Sunday	Luke 20:41–47

SELECTIONS FOR MEDITATION

PERSONAL MEDITATION

PRAYER

Ask God this week to help you to keep your mind fixed on his greatness and wonder. Begin in your devotional times and practice such meditation with short affirmations woven into the fabric of your everyday life.

HYMN   "O Thou in Whose Presence"

O Thou in whose presence; my soul takes delight,

On whom in affliction I call,
My comfort by day and my song in the night,
My hope, my salvation, my all.

Where dost Thou, dear Shepherd, resort with Thy sheep,
To feed them in pastures of love?
Say, why in the valley of death should I weep,
Or alone in this wilderness rove?

He looks! and ten thousands of angels rejoice,
And myriads wait for His word.
He speaks! and eternity, filled with His voice,
Reechoes the praise of the Lord.

Dear Shepherd! I hear and will follow Thy call;
I know the sweet sound of Thy voice.
Restore and defend me, for Thou art my all,
And in Thee I will ever rejoice.

Joseph Swain

BENEDICTION

May the strength of God pilot me. May the power of God preserve me. May the wisdom of God instruct me. May the hand of God protect me. May the way of God direct me. May the shield of God defend me. Amen.

St. Patrick in *Little Book of Prayers*

SELECTIONS FOR MEDITATION

✦ Listening means being released from willfulness, arrogance, and self-assertiveness. It calls for respectful presence to the mystery we are meditating, for humble openness to its meaning. Such listening or apprehending is prior to our appraisal of these meanings and our decision to incorporate them into our spiritual development, should God give us the grace for this growth. . . . Listening is only possible to the degree that we let go of the grip of our egotistic will and become inwardly and outwardly silent, alert, receptive, attentive. Then we may be able to think clearly or meditate; it becomes possible to reflect on our lives as a whole or on a text we are reading. What we hear sinks from our minds into our hearts. Ideas are not exploited to serve our purposes but to direct us to deeper wisdom, to a revelation of persons, events, and things as they are in themselves. We become the servants rather than the masters of the word.

—From *Pathways of Spiritual Living*
by Susan Annette Muto

◆ We have some idea, perhaps, what prayer is, but what is meditation? Well may we ask; for meditation is a lost art today, and Christian people suffer grievously from their ignorance of the practice. Meditation is the activity of calling to mind, and thinking over, and dwelling on, and applying to oneself, the various things that one knows about the works and ways and purposes and promises of God. It is an activity of holy thought, consciously performed in the presence of God, under the eye of God, by the help of God; as a means of communion with God. Its purpose is to clear one's mental and spiritual vision of God, and to let His truth make its full and proper impact on one's mind and heart. It is a matter of talking to oneself about oneself; it is, indeed, often a matter of arguing with oneself, reasoning oneself out of moods of doubt and unbelief into a clear apprehension of God's power and grace. Its effect is ever to humble us, as we contemplate God's greatness and glory, and our own littleness and sinfulness, and to encourage and reassure us—"comfort" us, in the old, strong, Bible sense of the word—as we contemplate the unsearchable riches of divine mercy displayed in the Lord Jesus Christ. . . . as we enter more and more deeply into this experience of being humbled and exalted, our knowledge of God increases, and with it our peace, our strength, and our joy.

—From *Knowing God* by J. I. Packer

◆ The late-medieval German mystics speak of a necessity for the soul to achieve a "departure" from the world, from the body and the self. This departure is nothing other than what Laing calls the inward journey. To set out on this journey means for us to go away from the familiar traveled roads of our association with the world, because all these ways of the world and our self are subject to the basic law of the age to produce and consume. It is not enough to change things. In his free time the sales manager of a shoe factory will not be able to accomplish this "departure" from the world . . . because his experience of the world has conditioned him to look upon everything in terms of being saleable or of having no value at all. Capitalism is everywhere and in everything; we cannot escape it. Capitalism rules not only our economy and politics but our whole way of thinking. We think in terms of end result, of bottom line, of time as money. We even ask if there is not a faster method of meditation! Can't we learn more and produce more at the same time we are meditating?

It is of this kind of total dominance of society that we must think when in ancient writings we find the word "flesh." That word expressed the power of this world, a power which is irresistible because it is so deeply rooted in our nature. For us the irresistible and inescapable power is no longer nature but the society that has become second nature to us. We remain in the flesh and cannot get out of it so long as we cannot question within ourselves the presuppositions of our methods of production and distribution.

Meditative association not only with words or tests but with ourselves helps us to just such questioning. To meditate means neither to produce or consume. Nor does it mean to make oneself fit for further production and consumption— even if one could market meditation like everything else in this world. Whenever we try to make it serve a purpose, the practice of meditation destroys the "contemplation," to use a word of which the mystics were fond. If I contemplate a rose or a pond or a human face and ask myself the question that cannot be evaded on our level, "Why should I do this?" then in that very moment I cease to contemplate. I begin playing my old game of becoming master of things through knowledge and use. I make the rose, the pond, and the human face subject to myself; I use them as aesthetic or psychological objects. Consciously or unconsciously I select. The capitalist in me has won out.

—From *Death by Bread Alone* by Dorothee Soelle

✦ The creation of a framework, an atmosphere, a structure, is not prayer, but it is a necessary preliminary to prayer. It is within the atmosphere of inner discipline and simplicity that prayer can begin to grow. The eastern church, in its teaching on prayer, focuses on the constant use of the Name of Jesus. The first recorded teaching about the invocation of the Name of Jesus comes in the mid-fifth century writer Diadochus. He recommended the prayer "Lord Jesus Christ have mercy on me" as a way of cleansing the mind of its sickness, and he recommended this to beginners. The Prayer of Jesus was to be used inwardly and secretly at all times—when dropping off to sleep, when waking, when eating or drinking, while talking. It is seen as a prayer which both binds the mind and unifies the personality. Thus Philotheus of Sinai in the tenth century says: "By the memory of Jesus Christ gather together your mind that is scattered abroad. Through the Fall this disintegration has happened, but memory of God restores primal wholeness."

One of the essential aspects of the use of the Name of Jesus then is the "binding of the mind." This is an expression used by the nineteenth-century eastern spiritual teacher Theophan the Recluse. He advises his disciples to "bind the mind with one thought—or the thought of One only." It is this process of binding which is the purpose of meditation. What is meant by meditation? In Christian spirituality, the term "meditation" has generally been used to describe a way of disciplined thinking, an ascetical exercise marked by discipline and sobriety. It involves pursuing one line of thought and renouncing all others. It is therefore a method of reducing the range of activity of the mind, allowing it to center on one point, to focus.

—From *True Prayer* by Kenneth Leech

✦ Today we will have a primer talk. What is confusing to you I imagine is that you have not quite understood what takes place when you have a new thought, a sun-thought, in the galaxy which makes your identity, especially such powerful ones as you have been given. You do not take, as it were, a new concept in your hands, place it in the midst of the familiar galaxy and expect a sudden radiance, an immediate change, although I do not forget that instant revelation and realization have come to some of the great ones who have walked this way. No, like all good things this work begins humbly. It is like planting a seed that grows and grows for a time in the dark. Ideas that have been given to you in these communions are in movement and as they grow larger and larger they push out into oblivion the older ideas which were foolish and out of proportion. This is difficult to put into words, but it may help you not to be too introspective.

When you meditate or abide in your quiet times of communion, you do not charge in and do something, like saying, "I will now be good and move mountains by my act of faith." No, you water your garden, knowing that these ideas are growing into a heavenly garden; the indwelling spirit doeth the work, not you: you merely water it. Do you not see the comfort there is in that? I can tell you in primer language that a very gentle, calm, unemotional, selfless, and patient attitude toward your spiritual growth is essential—such as all old gardeners know. They know that patience, hoeing, watering, and a certain order, a quiet rhythm, bring to birth a heavenly beauty.

—From *Letters of the Scattered Brotherhood.*
Edited by Mary Strong

✦ Living things need an appropriate climate in order to grow and bear fruit. If they are to develop to completion, they require an environment that allows their potential to be realized. The seed will not grow unless there is soil that can feed it, light to draw it forth, warmth to nurture and moisture that unlocks its vitality. Time is also required for its growth to unfold.

. . . Meditation is the attempt to provide the soul with the proper environment in which to grow and become. In the lives of people like St. Francis or St. Catherine of Genoa one gets a glimpse of what the soul is able to become. Often this is seen as the result of heroic action lying beyond the possibility of ordinary people. The flowering of the human soul, however, is more a matter of the proper psychological and spiritual environment than of particular gifts or disposition or heroism. How seldom we wonder at the growth of the great redwood from a tiny seed dropped at random on the littered floor of the forest. From one seed is grown enough wood to frame several hundred houses. The human soul has seed potential like this if it has the right environment. Remember that only in a few mountain valleys were the conditions right for the Sequoia gigantea, the mighty redwood, to grow.

. . . For both the seed and the soul, these things all take time. In both cases there is need for patience. Most of us know enough not to poke at the seed to see if it is sprouting, or to try to hurry it along with too much water or fertilizer or cultivation. The same respect must be shown for the soul as its growth starts to take place. Growth can seldom be forced in nature. Whether it is producing a tree or a human personality, nature unfolds its growth slowly, silently.

. . . Where meditation is concerned, we need to realize two things. Meditation is simple and natural, like a seed growing and becoming a tree. At the same time it requires the right conditions, conditions not provided by the secular world today. If meditation is to touch reality, we must seek out the right climate.

—From *The Other Side of Silence* by Morton T. Kelsey

✦ Meditation is one of the ways in which the spiritual man keeps himself awake. It is not really a paradox that it is precisely in meditation that most aspirants for religious perfection grow dull and fall asleep. Meditative prayer is a stern discipline, and one which cannot be learned by violence. It requires unending courage and perseverance, and those who are not willing to work at it patiently will finally end in compromise. Here, as elsewhere, compromise is only another name for failure.

To meditate is to think. And yet successful meditation is much more than reasoning or thinking. It is much more than "affections," much more than a series of prepared "acts" which one goes through.

In meditative prayer, one thinks and speaks not only with his mind and lips, but in a certain sense with his whole being. Prayer is then not just a formula of words, or a series of desires springing up in the heart—it is the orientation of our whole body, mind, and spirit to God in silence, attention, and adoration. All good meditative prayer is a conversion of our entire self to God.

—From *Thoughts in Solitude* by Thomas Merton

14. Study

INVOCATION

O you who are the Source and Ground of all truth, guide me today, I beseech you, in my hours of reading. Give me wisdom to abstain as well as to persevere. Let the Bible have proper place; and grant that as I read I may be alive to the stirrings of the Holy Spirit in my soul. Amen.

John Baillie in *A Diary of Private Prayer*

PSALM 119:1–16

DAILY SCRIPTURE

Monday	Philippians 4:8–9
Tuesday	1 Timothy 4:6–16
Wednesday	Deuteronomy 17:18–20
Thursday	2 Peter 1:3–8
Friday	Psalm 119:97–104
Saturday	Luke 8:16–18
Sunday	Proverbs 2:1–22

SELECTIONS FOR MEDITATION

PERSONAL MEDITATION

PRAYER

Jesus said, "You will know the truth and the truth will set you free." Our problem is not in believing his statement, but in knowing the truth. Pray that your capacity to receive the truth is not blocked by pride or by the ungodly thought that you already know enough truth.

HYMN   "How Blest Are They Who Hear God's Word"

How blest are they who hear God's word,

Who keep in faith what they have heard,
Who daily grow in learning;
From light to light shall they increase,
And tread life's weary path in peace,
The balm of joy discerning
To soothe the spirit's yearning.

Through sorrow's night my sun shall be
God's word—a treasure dear to me,
My shield and buckler ever.
My title as his child and heir
The Father's hand hath written there,
His promise failing never:
"Thou shalt be mine forever."

Today his voice with joy I heard,
And, nourished by his holy word,
That bread so freely given,
May stronger faith through grace prevail,
And may its fruits for me avail,
That, after I have striven,
I rest with him in heaven.

Johan Nordahl Brun

BENEDICTION

Grant me grace to desire ardently all that is pleasing to you, and to examine it prudently, to acknowledge it truthfully, and to accomplish it perfectly, for the praise and glory of your name. Amen.

SELECTIONS FOR MEDITATION

✦ So there is need for some sort of prayer which is not spontaneous but which is truly rooted in conviction. To find this you can draw from a great many of the existing prayers. We already have a rich panoply of prayers which were wrought in the throes of faith, by the Holy Spirit. For example, we have the psalms, we have so many short and long prayers in the liturgical wealth of all the Churches from which we can draw. What matters is that you should learn and know enough of such prayers so that at the right moment you are able to find the right prayers. It is a question of learning by heart enough meaningful passages, from the psalms or from the prayers of the saints. Each of us is sensitive to certain particular passages. Mark these passages that go deep into your heart, that move you deeply, that make sense, that express something which is already within your experience, either of sin, or of bliss in God, or of struggle. Learn those passages, because one day when you are so completely low, so profoundly desperate that you cannot call out of your soul any spontaneous expression, any spontaneous wording, you will discover that these words come up and offer themselves to you as a gift of God, as a gift of the Church, as a gift of holiness, helping our simple lack of strength. And then you really need the prayers you have learnt and made a part of yourself.

—From *Beginning to Pray* by Anthony Bloom

✦ The question of the proper feeding of our own devotional life must of course include the rightful use of spiritual reading. And with spiritual reading we may include formal or informal meditation upon Scripture or religious truth: the brooding consideration, the savouring—as it were the chewing of the cud—in which we digest that which we have absorbed, and apply it to our own needs. Spiritual reading is, or at least can be, second only to prayer as a developer and support of the inner life. In it we have access to all the hoarded supernatural treasure of the race: all that it has found out about God. It should not be confined to Scripture, but should also include at least the lives and the writings of the canonized and uncanonized saints: for in religion variety of nourishment is far better than a dyspeptic or fastidious monotony of diet. If we do it properly, such reading is a truly social act. It gives us not only information, but communion; real intercourse with the great souls of the past, who are the pride and glory of the Christian family. Studying their lives and work slowly and with sympathy; reading the family history, the family letters; trying to grasp the family point of view; we gradually discover these people to be in origin though not in achievement much like ourselves. They are people who are devoted to the same service, handicapped often by the very same difficulties; and yet whose victories and insights humble and convict us, and who can tell us more and more, as we learn to love more and more, of the relation of the soul to Reality.

—From *The House of the Soul and Concerning the Inner Life* by Evelyn Underhill

✦ Formative reading thus involves a shift, in Adrian van Kaam's terms, from "form-giving," in which we are inclined to impose our meaning on the text, to "form-receiving," in which we let its meaning influence us. We move from a mainly argumentative, rationalistic, faultfinding mentality to an appreciative, meditative, confirming mood. Our spiritual life is refreshed whenever we take time to savor these timeless values. They become a living part of who we are. The text is like a bridge between the limits of our life here and now and the possibilities awaiting us if we open our minds and hearts to God.

—From *Pathways of Spiritual Living* by Susan Annette Muto

✦ Many Christians remain in bondage to fears and anxieties simply because they do not avail themselves of the Discipline of study. They may be faithful in church attendance and earnest in fulfilling their religious duties and still they are not changed. . . . They may sing with gusto; pray in the Spirit, live as obediently as they know, even receive divine visions and revelations; and yet the tenor of their lives remains unchanged. Why? Because they have never taken up one of the central ways God uses to change us: study. Jesus made it unmistakably clear that it is the knowledge of the truth that will set us free.

—From *Celebration of Discipline* by Richard J. Foster

✦ I have learned to distrust speed reading and instant knowledge. Few joys of the mind can compare with the experience of lingering over deft character description, or hovering over a well-wrought passage. "Some people," said Alexander Pope, "will never learn anything . . . because they understand everything too soon."

—From *Human Options* by Norman Cousins

✦ Countless writings underlie the urgency for our modern world, with all its bustle and noise, of rediscovering the value of meditation, of silence, of prayer, of devotion. I preached it before I practised it. If one is to help the world towards this rediscovery, one must practice it oneself. The religious life must be fed. We devote years to studying a trade or profession. Ought we to show less perseverance in acquiring the experience of God? The least player of billiards or chess knows how long he has to spend in order to learn to play, and how many games he had to lose before winning one. The scientist, when an experiment fails, instead of abandoning it, asks himself whether there has not slipped into his arrangements or his calculations some cause of error. One of my patients had a dream. She was given the task of keeping alight the fire under the boiler. A voice kept saying to her: "Put coal on regularly. Don't let the fire go out." Recently I saw a young woman who after several years of great spiritual adventure, was swamped in overwhelming difficulties. I happened to mention to her that during the last twelve years, I could count the days on which I had neglected to write down during meditation what I thought God had expected of me. A few days later she wrote me: "I am grateful for what you said. It is a long time since I gave up the habit of written meditation. Someone told me that after a time one had made sufficient spiritual progress to be able to keep contact with God all day long, without having to reserve any special time for listening to Him!"

Everything is habit in biology, and habits are created only by means of repetition. Experiments have shown how much of our behavior is determined by the mental images to which our minds are constantly returning. If we bring our minds back again and again to God, we shall by the same inevitable law be gradually giving the central place to God, not only in our inner selves, but also in our practical everyday lives.
—From *Reflections* by Paul Tournier

✦ Spiritual life is not mental life. It is not thoughts alone. Nor is it, of course, a life of sensation, a life of feeling—"feeling" and experiencing the things of the spirit, and the things of God.

Nor does the spiritual life exclude thought and feeling. It needs both. It is not just a life concentrated at the "high point" of the soul, a life from which the mind and the imagination and the body are excluded. If it were so few people could lead it. And again, if that were the spiritual life, it would not be a life at all. If man is to live, he must be all alive, body, soul, mind, heart, spirit. Everything must be elevated and transformed by the action of God, in love and faith.

—From *Thoughts in Solitude* by Thomas Merton

◆ Without hesitation, without inner debate, I entered into the inheritance of every modern Russian writer intent on the truth: I must write simply to ensure that it was not all forgotten, that posterity might someday come to know of it. Publication in my own lifetime I must shut out of my mind, out of my dreams.

I put away my idle dream. And in its place there was only the surety that my work would not be in vain, that it would someday smite the heads I had in my sights and that those who received its invisible emanations would understand. I no more rebelled against lifelong silence than against the lifelong impossibility of freeing my feet from the pull of gravity. As I finished one piece after another, at first in the camps, then in exile, then after rehabilitation, first verses, then plays, and later prose works too, I had only one desire: to keep all these things out of sight and myself with them.

In the camp this meant committing my verse—many thousands of lines—to memory. To help me with this I improvised decimal counting beads and, in transit prisons, broke up matchsticks and used the fragments as tallies. As I approached the end of my sentence I grew more confident of my powers of memory, and began writing down and memorizing prose—dialogue at first, but then, bit by bit, whole densely written passages. My memory found room for them! It worked. But more and more of my time—in the end as much as one week every month—went into the regular repetition of all I had memorized.

—From *The Oak and the Calf* by Aleksandr Solzhenitsyn

✦ One simple and somewhat obvious technique is memorization. The expression "to know by heart" already suggests its value. Personally I regret the fact that I know so few prayers and psalms by heart. Often I need a book to pray, and without one I tend to fall back on the poor spontaneous creations of my mind. Part of the reason, I think, that it is so hard to pray "without ceasing" is that few prayers are available to me outside church settings. Yet I believe that prayers which I know by heart could carry me through very painful crises. The Methodist minister Fred Morris told me how Psalm 23 ("The Lord is my shepherd") had carried him through the gruesome hours in the Brazilian torture chamber and had given him peace in his darkest hour. And I keep wondering which words I can take with me in the hour when I have to survive without books. I fear that in crisis situations I will have to depend on my own unredeemed ramblings and not have the word of God to guide me.

—From *The Living Reminder* by Henri J. Nouwen

✦ It cannot be that the people should grow in grace unless they give themselves to reading. A reading people will always be a knowing people. A people who talk much will know little. Press this upon them with your might, and you will soon see the fruit of your labours.

. . . You can never be deep . . . without it any more than a thorough Christian. O begin! Fix some part of every day for private exercises. You may acquire the taste which you have not; what is tedious at first will afterwards be pleasant. Whether you like it or not, read and pray daily. It is for your life; there is no other way; else you will be a trifler all your days. . . .

—From *The Message of the Wesleys.*
Compiled by Philip S. Watson

15. Bible Reading

Father, let your word be a lamp to my feet, and a light to my path. Let me hide it in my heart that I might not sin against you. Amen.

Psalm 119:105, 11

PSALM 19

DAILY SCRIPTURE

Monday	John 8:31–32
Tuesday	Hebrews 4:12–13
Wednesday	1 Peter 1:13–25
Thursday	Deuteronomy 30:11–14
Friday	John 5:31–47
Saturday	2 Peter 1:3–21
Sunday	2 Timothy 3:10–17

SELECTIONS FOR MEDITATION

PERSONAL MEDITATION

PRAYER

Spend part of your prayer time in asking for a deeper understanding of the Word of God and for a renewed love for all that it speaks to you.

HYMN   "Lamp of Our Feet"

Lamp of our feet, whereby we trace
Our path when wont to stray:
Stream from the fount of heav'nly grace,
Brook by the trav'lers' way.

Bread of our souls, whereon we feed;
True manna from on high;

Our guide and chart, wherein we read
Of realms beyond the sky.

Pillar of fire, thro' watches dark,
Or radiant cloud by day;
When waves o'erwhelm our tossing bark,
Our anchor and our stay.

Word of the ever living God;
Will of His glorious Son,
Without thee how could earth be trod,
Or heav'n be won?

Lord, grant us all aright to learn
The wisdom it imparts,
And to its heav'nly teaching turn
With simple, childlike hearts.

Bernard D. Barton

BENEDICTION

Dear Jesus, this day do not let me forget that I cannot live by bread alone, that like you I must have words from the mouth of the Father. Amen.

SELECTIONS FOR MEDITATION

✦ For in the sacred books, the Father who is in heaven meets His children with great love and speaks with them; and the force and power in the word of God is so great that it remains the support and energy of the Church, the strength of faith for her children, the food of the soul, the pure and perennial source of spiritual life.

—From *Christian Mysticism Today* by William Johnston

✦ It has long been repeated that prayer is a loving conversation with one whom you know loves you. Yet not a few today ask how do I know that I am not talking to myself, in an ongoing dialogue between me, myself and I? Is it really an I-Thou encounter or just more I-me? . . . It is Scripture, the Word of God that is the reality-depth of our prayer, for "we speak to Him when we pray: we hear Him when we read the divine sayings." From the Hassidim, the Jewish mystics, there is the beautiful legend of the rabbi who would go into ecstasy every time he would utter the words "and God spoke. . . ." He would become totally overwhelmed with the realization that God spoke to man!

What would happen to us if we would more deeply believe the truth—God speaks! God speaks to me! This is the heart of prayer, this is the power behind the prayer revolution of to-day—that God is speaking directly to me in Scripture.

—From *Prayer Is a Hunger* by Edward J. Farrell

✦ Known primarily as an educator, Frank Gaebelein was the founding headmaster at the Stony Brook School, a Christian college preparatory school in Long Island, which has become a prototype. He held the post for 41 years and considered his work there his most important accomplishment.

When once asked what counsel he wished to pass on to the next generation of Christians, Gaebelein replied: "Maintain at all costs a daily time of Scripture reading and prayer. As I look back, I see that the most formative influence in my life and thought has been my daily contact with Scripture over 60 years."

—From "Frank Gaebelein: Character Before Career,"
Christianity Today by Gretchen Gaebelein Hull

✦ I had read here and there in the Bible before, the way people do—dutifully, haphazardly, far from sure either what I was looking for or what I was supposed to find. I was aware that there was said to be great treasure buried somewhere among all those unpromising, double-columned pages, but I had never had anybody point me very adequately to a place to start digging. I must have already been through a fair sampling of the Gospels, some of the psalms, some of Genesis, of Job; and though I have no specific memories of it, I remember having been moved and having sensed that there was something deeper down than I had ever gone to move me more deeply still. But it all seemed very hazy and elusive.

What I began to see was that the Bible is not essentially, as I had always more or less supposed, a book of ethical principles, of moral exhortations, of cautionary tales about exemplary people, of uplifting thoughts—in fact, not really a religious book at all in the sense that most of the books you would be apt to find in a minister's study or reviewed in a special religion issue of the *New York Times* book section are religious. I saw it instead as a great, tattered compendium of writings, the underlying and unifying purpose of all of which is to show how God works through the Jacobs and Jabboks of history to make himself known to the world and to draw the world back to himself.

For all its vast diversity and unevenness, it is a book with a plot and a plot that can be readily stated. God makes the world in love. For one reason or another the world chooses to reject God. God will not reject the world but continues his mysterious and relentless pursuit of it to the end of time. That is what he is doing by choosing Israel to be his special people. That is what he is doing through all the passion and poetry and invective of the prophets. That is why history plays such a crucial part in the Old Testament—all those kings and renegades and battles and invasions and apostasies—because it was precisely through people like that and events like those that God was at work, as, later, in the New Testament, he was supremely at work in the person and event of Jesus Christ. Only "is at work" would be the more accurate way of putting it because if there is a God who works at all, his work goes on still, of course, and at one and the same time the Biblical past not only illumines the present but becomes itself part of that present, part of our own individual pasts. Until you can read the story of Adam and Eve, of Abraham and Sarah, of David and Bathsheba, as your own story, you have not really understood it. The Bible is a book finally about ourselves, our own apostasies, our own battles and blessings; and it was the discovery of that . . . that constituted the real reward. . . .

—From *Now and Then* by Frederick Buechner

◆ In this context, God's word whether written or spoken may be compared to a mirror. Spiritually, the eyes of your soul are your reason, your consciousness is your spiritual face.

And just as it is so that if you have a dirty spot on your physical face your eyes cannot see that spot nor know where it is without a mirror or someone else to tell you so; so it is spiritually in the same way that without reading or hearing God's word it is not possible for a soul blinded by habitual sin to see the foul spot upon his consciousness.

—From *The Cloud of Unknowing* translated by Ira Progoff

✦ How does one go about it? One cannot avoid beginning with those memory impressions in the Gospel, set against the history of Judaism in the whole Bible. A few years ago, it would have been necessary for me to apologize at length for recommending that people would do well to read the Bible. Today, however, a new generation at least comprehends how and why it is that such texts have to be pored over.

Critic Leslie Fiedler observed that young people living in communes read in a different way than the detached scholars did. They might read the novels of Herman Hesse or Ken Kesey, or they might probe *The Whole Earth Catalogue*. In any case, they have read these "scripturally." That is, they have drawn the signals for their community from them. They ransacked and searched these sources and measured their way of life by what they read. The Bible has to be plundered and searched for what has to do with one's promise.

—From *You Are Promise* by Martin E. Marty

✦ ... this word which sets us at once to work and obedience, is the rock on which to build our house. The only proper response to this word which Jesus brings with him from eternity is simply to do it. Jesus has spoken: his is the word, ours the obedience. Only in the doing of it does the word of Jesus retain its honor, might, and power among us. Now the storm can rage over the house, but it cannot shatter that union with him, which his word has created.

There is only one other possibility, that of failing to do it. It is impossible to want to do it and yet not do it. To deal with the word of Jesus otherwise than by doing it is to give him the lie. It is to deny the Sermon on the Mount and say No to his word. If we start asking questions, posing problems, and offering interpretations, we are not doing his word. Once again the shades of the rich young man and the lawyer of Luke 10 are raising their heads. However vehemently we assert our faith, and our fundamental recognition of his word, Jesus still calls it "not doing." But the word which we fail to do is no rock to build a house on. There can then be no union with Jesus. He has never known us. That is why as soon as the hurricane begins we lose the word, and find that we have never really believed it. The word we had was not Christ's, but a word we had wrested from him and made our own by reflecting on it instead of doing it. So our house crashes in ruins, because it is not founded on the word of Jesus Christ.

—From *The Cost of Discipleship* by Dietrich Bonhoeffer

✦ The Bible is the record of those divine breakthroughs into human history. "God's search for man," it is described, rather than being our search for God. And its accents are considered a key for discerning the continuing divine activity in the present. Unlike most religious literature, it is not chiefly a collection of noble sayings, but a drumroll of events, people, struggles, great and terrible, of frailty, doubts, and heroism, of the ultimate might of right. Scripture isn't meant as scientific exposition or as mere history. It is "salvation history," a universal spiritual drama of an overarching compassion and concern for human integrity, of an unwavering love that seeks an answering affirmation. It is a vivid, sometimes parabolic account of God's persistent, unrelenting quest for us and our stumbling, often faithless response.

—From *The Untamed God* by George Cornell

✦ To candid, reasonable men, I am not afraid to lay open what have been the inmost thoughts of my heart. I have thought, I am a creature of a day, passing through life as an arrow through the air. I am a spirit come from God, and returning to God: just hovering over the great gulf; till, a few moments hence, I am no more seen; I drop into an unchangeable eternity! I want to know one thing—the way to heaven: how to land safe on that happy shore. God Himself has condescended to teach the way; for this very end He came from heaven. He hath written it down in a book. O give me that book! At any price, give me the book of God! I have it: here is knowledge enough for me.

—From *A Compend of Wesley's Theology*.
Edited by Robert W. Burtner and Robert E. Chiles

✦ We are to hear. All of us are. That is what the whole Bible is calling out. "Hear, O Israel!"

But hear what? Hear what? The Bible is hundreds upon hundreds of voices all calling at once out of the past and clamoring for our attention like barkers at a fair, like air-raid sirens, like a whole barnyard of cockcrows as the first long shafts of dawn fan out across the sky. Some of the voices are shouting, like Moses' voice, so all Israel, all the world, can hear, and some are so soft and halting that you can hardly hear them at all, like Job with ashes on his head and his heart broken, like old Simeon whispering, "Lord, now lettest thou thy servant depart in peace." The prophets shrill out in their frustration, their rage, their holy hope and madness; and the priests drone on and on about the dimensions and furniture of the Temple; and the lawgivers spell out what to eat and what not to eat; and the historians list the kings, the battles, the tragic lessons of Israel's history. And somewhere in the midst of them all one particular voice speaks out that is unlike any other voice because it speaks so directly to the deepest privacy and longing and weariness of each of us that there are times when the centuries are blown away like mist, and it is as if we stand with no shelter of time at all between ourselves and the one who speaks our secret name. Come, the voice says. Unto me. All ye. Every last one.

—From *A Room Called Remember*
by Frederick Buechner

16. Journaling

INVOCATION

O God, what can we do of ourselves if you support us not but fall into sin and offend you? Leave us not, therefore, to ourselves, but strengthen us in the inward man, that so we may at all times and in all things renounce our evil inclinations, which are incessantly endeavoring to withdraw our hearts from you. Complete your conquest and make us all your own both now and forever. Amen.

PSALM 44

DAILY SCRIPTURE

Monday	Ephesians 6:10–18
Tuesday	Jeremiah 17:5–10
Wednesday	2 Corinthians 4:7–5:5
Thursday	2 Corinthians 10:11
Friday	1 Chronicles 16:8–16
Saturday	Luke 2:8–19
Sunday	Luke 1:1–4

SELECTIONS FOR MEDITATION

PERSONAL MEDITATION

PRAYER

Being open and honest with your feelings is never easy and almost always painful. But God gives courage in the midst of both. Ask him for the desire to be transparent in his sight.

HYMN   "I Must Tell Jesus"

> I must tell Jesus all of my trials;
> I cannot bear these burdens alone.

In my distress He kindly will help me;
He ever loves and cares for His own.

. . . . .

Tempted and tried, I need a great Saviour,
One who can help my burdens to bear.
I must tell Jesus, I must tell Jesus;
He all my cares and sorrows will share.

Elisha A. Hoffman

BENEDICTION

Almighty and eternal God, so draw our hearts to you, so
guide our minds, so fill our imaginations, so control our wills,
that we may be wholly yours, utterly dedicated to you; and
then use us, we pray, as you will, and always to your glory and
the welfare of your people; through our Lord and Savior Jesus
Christ. Amen.

SELECTIONS FOR MEDITATION

◆ Prayer is a hunger, a hunger that is not easily quieted. Today the cry "teach us to pray" echoes and reverberates from
many directions. One of the ways I have learned to pray is by
writing. I began by copying favorite passages from reading,
then thoughts and ideas of others and finally by jotting down
my own insights and reflections from prayer and experiences
of each day. This prayer journal at times seems like my own
biography of Christ, a kind of Fifth Gospel. Writing makes me
think of the Evangelists' experience. Why and how did Matthew, Mark, Luke and John begin their writing? What happened in them? What kind of grace was affecting them?
Certainly their experience in writing was a prayer, an entering into the mind and heart of Christ. I wonder if the evangelist's experience is not to be a more common experience for
many Christians.

—From *Prayer Is a Hunger* by Edward J. Farrell

◆ A help to me in working things out has been to keep an
honest—as honest as the human being can be—unpublish-
able journal. Granted, much of my non-fiction work is lifted

directly from my journals, but what I use is only a small fraction of these numerous, bulky volumes. If I can write things out I can see them, and they are not trapped within my own subjectivity. I have been keeping these notebooks of thoughts and questions and sometimes just garbage (which "needs" to be dumped somewhere) since I was about nine, and they are, I think, my free psychiatrist's couch.

Not long ago someone I love said something which wounded me grievously, and I was desolate that this person could have made such a comment to me.

So, in great pain, I crawled to my journal and wrote it all out in a great burst of self-pity. And when I had set it down, when I had it before me, I saw that something I myself had said had called forth the words which had hurt me so. It had, in fact, been my own fault. But I would never have seen it if I had not written it out.

—From *Walking on Water* by Madeleine L'Engle

◆ There is yet another and quite different reason for keeping a journal. The goal here is not simply that of achieving my own potential, but rather of deepening my relationship with that center of spiritual reality of which all the great religions of humankind speak. Here the goal of keeping the record of my life and struggle is not so much to forge the chain of growth as to bring my inner being to the blacksmith. The journal is not so much an integral part of the building as a scaffolding which is needed to construct the building and then needed later to repair the structure.

But the size of the building one can construct without scaffolding is limited indeed. The deep relationship with God which can be received and integrated in many men and women is limited by the amount of effort and time and discipline they will take to keep some record of their encounters with religious reality. Journals record these encounters and are also useful tools for keeping at the process of developing the relationship. They can also point out new ways to open one's being to God's transforming power. I doubt whether those who can read and write are able to come to the deep relationship with the divine lover which is possible for them if they do not keep a journal.

—From *Adventure Inward* by Morton T. Kelsey

✦ Journaling is one of the most helpful exercises we can do to increase our capacity for meditation and prayer. Pausing daily or a few times a week to jot down our thoughts has a way of quieting and uncluttering our overactive, decentered lives. Writing helps us to work through detected obstacles to spiritual living. . . . A journal is not only a record of events that touch and transform us; it is a private space in which we can meet ourselves in relation to others and God.

—From *Pathways of Spiritual Living*
by Susan Annette Muto

✦ Once we decide to start, are there any concrete aids to journal writing a practitioner may suggest? What incentives can we find to keep going? It is first of all fascinating to realize that the act of writing fixates on paper the stream of experience constantly slipping away from us. It helps us to remember a few important events among the mass of happenings we experience. Writing stops the flow of experience so that we can look at it again and gain insight into what was really occurring in this meeting or in the presence of such a text or during our pause for prayer and presence to the transcendent. Journaling in this regard could be compared to the construction of a dam on a river. The dam stops the rush of water for the sake of rechanneling it for higher yields of power. Similarly, writing channels our attention so that we can see more clearly the mystery of God's directing will in daily events.

—From *Pathways of Spiritual Living*
by Susan Annette Muto

✦ It is a comforting reality that there is not a right way or wrong way to keep a journal. If we will, ourselves, become readers of journals—aware of the different types—we will be helped in the keeping of our own. We can draw on one form or another to suit our needs, as we do in prayer. We cannot use the contemplative way of prayer when we want to cry for mercy or rage against our enemies. Writing in our journals seems to me to be very close to praying, if indeed it is not prayer. We cannot write our spiritual insights about the world when we have ourselves "on our hands." One inner condition may be a helpful guide in our choice of a form of journal writing for a given day or period in our life.

—From *Letters to Scattered Pilgrims*
by Elizabeth O'Connor

✦ The keeping of a pilgrim journal requires a conscious, un-swerving commitment to honesty with one's self . . . the first requirement for growth in self-understanding. No one can break our chains for us. We have to do this for ourselves. We may have some help along the way, but we are the only ones that can set ourselves free, and this we do by coming into possession of truth—by routing out lies and deceits. This takes a lot of courage, a lot of endurance, a commitment to press on when we want to shrink back. The goal is to make Jesus Christ the Lord of our life.

—From *Letters to Scattered Pilgrims*
by Elizabeth O'Connor

✦ Among our primary tools for growth are reflection, self-observation and self-questioning. The journal is one of the most helpful vehicles we have for cultivating these great powers in ourselves. We all have these powers but we need structures that encourage us to use and practice them. Journal writing is enforced reflection. When we commit our observations to writing we are taking what is inside us and placing it outside us. We are holding a piece of our life in our hands where we can look at it, and meditate on it, and deepen our understanding of it.

—From *Letters to Scattered Pilgrims*
by Elizabeth O'Connor

✦ Having developed the habit of reflection I discovered that on occasion something of a deeper nature emerged out of the depth of me. For instance, one day I felt that my life and everything around me was dull and uninteresting. I stopped in the church and quietly sat in the "grayness" with my journal open before me. After some time the thought popped into my head that grayness means that the sun is shining somewhere, and it is much better than blackness. After I had meditated quietly in the grayness for about twenty minutes, gradually the gray fog lifted, and I found myself bathed in the bright light of God's presence. I remember writing this down. I also discovered that the insights that I recorded stuck with me and were more likely to be integrated into my life than those ideas and experiences that were not written down.

—From *Companions on the Inner Way*
by Morton T. Kelsey

◆ The journal not only gives us a safe way of dealing with the feelings that are often ready to burst out of us, but offers us objectivity about them as well. How different ideas seem as they lie naked on the page before us than in the moment of "inspiration." Sometimes they appear less and sometimes even more inspired. How much less powerful the emotions that consumed us on one day are when we look at them with a calmer disposition the next day. I have found that writing my fears down one by one can often remove the panic I feel when they are invading me like a hostile army. When we look at them lying helpless in black and white on the pages of our journal, they often assume their proper size.

—From *Companions on the Inner Way*
by Morton T. Kelsey

◆ The work in the comparative study of lives brought another type of evidence in favor of using a personal journal as the basic instrument for personal growth. It was impressive to observe the number of persons in other cultures and other periods of history who have spontaneously kept a journal of some sort to meet various needs in their lives. These journals are primarily a chronological record of events. They are diaries elaborated to a greater or less degree depending on the temperament of the person and his life situation. Sometimes they are focused on a particular area of experience or a particular task, as is often the case of artists and novelists. In those cases a journal serves as the spontaneous psychological tool that makes it possible for the inner creative side of work in progress to be carried through.

The keeping of private journals has played a particularly important role in the history of religion, wherever the reality of inner experience has been valued in the religious life. From St. Augustine to Pascal to the Society of Friends, some form of personal journal has been called upon. Sometimes these journals deal with the full range of personal experience including all the intimacies of life from marital quarrels and sexuality to the visionary moments when a person feels himself to be hovering precariously between prophecy and insanity. Those, of course, are the dramatic journals. But more often the journals deal with an area of religious behavior that is specifically defined by the particular religious group to which the individual belongs. In those cases, the goals set by the sect's beliefs are the basis of keeping the journals. The individual uses the journal as a means of measuring his progress along the particular religious path that he has chosen.

That use of a private journal is exceedingly common, not only in the religious life but wherever a person has a fixed goal toward which he is trying to direct himself. Journals are used especially in those situations where a person is having difficulty in attaining his goal. A private journal is then drawn upon first as an instrument for recording and then for evaluating how far he has attained his goals and to what degree he has failed. Such a use of a journal becomes a self-testing device. It is helpful up to a point in providing a means of reflection for the contents of the life.

—From *At a Journal Workshop* by Ira Progoff

17. Spiritual Partners

O God, you have made us for fellowship, and have given us the power both to help and harm our fellows, grant us the wisdom to know what is their good, and the ready will to help them to attain it. Heal those we have wounded, strengthen those whom we have failed, grant us all your healing grace, and make our fellowship to be your family, through Jesus Christ our Lord, Amen.

Norman B. Nash in *Daily Prayer Companion*

PSALM 133

DAILY SCRIPTURE

Monday	John 13:1–35
Tuesday	1 Timothy 3:1–7
Wednesday	Philemon 1–25
Thursday	Philippians 2:19–30
Friday	1 Samuel 20:16–42
Saturday	Acts 9:10–19
Sunday	1 Thessalonians 5:12–28

SELECTIONS FOR MEDITATION

PERSONAL MEDITATION

PRAYER

Begin to pray that God will lead you to someone with whom you can be open and prayerful about both the efforts and progress in the spiritual life. For someone with whom you can begin to be mutually accountable for each other's journey in faith.

HYMN   "I've Found a Friend, O Such a Friend"

I've found a Friend, O such a Friend!
He loved me ere I knew Him;
He drew me with cords of love,
And thus He bound me to Him.
And 'round my heart still closely twine
Those ties which can't be severed.
For I am His, and He is mine,
Forever and ever.

I've found a Friend, O such a Friend!
He bled, He died to save me:
And not alone the gift of life,
But His own self He gave me.
Naught that I have my own to call,
I hold it for the Giver;
My heart, my strength, my life, my all
Are His, and His forever.

I've found a Friend, O such a Friend!
So kind, and true, and tender,
So wise a Counselor and Guide,
So mighty a Defender!
From Him who loves me now so well,
What power my soul can sever?
Shall life or death, shall earth or hell?
No! I am His forever.

James G. Small

BENEDICTION

Lord, you know I am not particularly heroic or saintly; that I
need someone who will be my friend on this spiritual journey. Let them find me through my willingness to be a spiritual
friend. Amen.

SELECTIONS FOR MEDITATION

✦ The rigorous demands of true friendship, the gift of
oneself, one's time, one's preferences, the nakedness and honesty, are beyond the price many are willing to pay—those
who have not yet experienced what is purchased by such a
price. Anyone who has been graced with true friendship
knows the cost and knows the worth. And he knows, too, the

ridiculousness of the fear that such friendship will undermine community.

—From *A Place Apart* by M. Basil Pennington

✦ Unless we are particularly heroic or saintly persons, each of us needs a relationship with at least one other person who also seeks and trusts the simple way, the Simple Presence. Such a "spiritual friend" can be enormously supportive to us, and we to them. Even if you meet or write to each other only once a month, it can be enough. Just knowing that someone else is struggling for the simple day with you, whether or not you speak together often, is encouraging. You feel a little less alone, a little less tempted to fall mindlessly into complicating traps. Someone else is there who knows whether or not you are trying to pay attention to the simple way; that brings a kind of accountability that is important. When someone else knows and cares, then we pay that much more attention to what we're doing.

—From *Living Simply Through the Day* by Tilden H. Edwards

✦ Whom you should see or respond to will depend on many things, including your age, sex, experience, personality, spiritual path, . . . faith tradition. . . . Let's look at each of these in turn.

Age

Normally I believe it is best to choose someone in the second half of life: roughly thirty-five or older.

Carl Jung believed that every person who came to him over thirty-five essentially brought a spiritual concern, regardless of the presenting problem. There is something new that usually begins to happen in mid-life: a sense of finitude, a sorting out of what is and isn't important in life, a fresh spiritual search or appreciation.

Sex

What difference does it make whether you choose someone of the same or opposite sex for a spiritual companion?

Over the past seven years some of us in Shalem have paid

particular attention to this question. There is not one answer for all people in all situations. However, where there is a choice between two good people of different sexes, with each of whom you are equally comfortable, in most situations I think it is best to choose a person of the same sex.

EXPERIENCE

If you have never been in a serious spiritual friendship before, and your own sense of spiritual life and experience seems thin, then you probably have little spiritual self-confidence and much vulnerability in approaching such a relationship.

In such circumstance I think it is important to seek out someone who is confident in experience yet humble in it. The confidence will free you to relax and be vulnerable. The humility will give you room for letting your own confidence rise; you won't be so intimidated by your own sense of spiritual distance. On the other hand, such humility will mean your friend will be less likely subtly, probably unconsciously, to exploit your "newness" by lording it over you with superior sounding, overconfident advice which you mistake for wisdom. Your friend will listen, gently evoking from you the light of the Spirit within.

PERSONALITY

If we can trust the work of Carl Jung in personality typing and development, then you might find it valuable to look for complementarity. If you are very analytical, seek someone more of a "feeling" type; if you are a feeler, seek more of a thinker; if you are more intuitive, seek a more concrete, detail-conscious, sensate person; if you are more sensate, seek an intuitive friend. However, be cautious of a person who is so extremely contrasting in personality type that he or she simply is not likely to be able to be in rapport with you.

SPIRITUAL PATH

Be aware of your dominant spiritual path now, a path influenced by your personality. It is important that your friend have some experience and sympathy with your path, even though he or she may not be traveling on it as centrally as you. In fact, someone with sympathetic yet critical experience of different paths is best of all: such a friend can help attune you to different possibilities you may be ready for, and call attention to possible deceptions.

FAITH TRADITION

Particular Christian faith traditions as expressed in a given place tend to emphasize certain paths more than others, sometimes explicitly over others. If your tradition weights a particular path, that is fine, as long as it truly is your path.

If it is not, and there is little room or understanding of the path you seem to be called to walk now, then you may have to find a spiritual companion from a more sympathetic tradition, or someone who shares your "minority views" within your own.

—From *Spiritual Friend* by Tilden H. Edwards

✦ Places are as full of mystery as times are, and almost from the start I knew that, of all places, it was the one that was right for me. The parish house seemed more part of the real working world than home ever had and thus made it easier to believe that maybe my work was real too. It was a place to put on a necktie for and to come home from. I could hear Bob Clayton and his wife, Betty, at work in the office downstairs, and the sounds of the typewriter, the telephone, and the comings and goings of the parish helped me believe in my more sanguine moments that, obscure and crackpot as my labors were, they might still have some remote, second-story connection at least with the church of Christ. And more perhaps than anything else, there were morning prayers.

Except on the rarest occasions, nobody ever came to them but Bob and me. The first thing every morning we would trudge across the grass to the church and ring the bell. On some days he would read the service and I the responses. On others we would reverse the procedure. The Lord be with you. And with thy spirit. O come let us sing. Let us pray. The psalms. The readings from the lectionary. The silences. At first I had the idea that my primary purpose in driving those fifteen miles every morning was to write and that the prayers were incidental, but later on I came to suspect that maybe the other way 'round was closer to the truth. And later on still, I was less sure than I had been that in the long run there was all that much difference between the writing and the praying anyway. In any case, most of what I wrote for the next ten years I wrote in that small, bare room, after those small, bare services, and on the few occasions when I have looked on the room since, I've realized that part of me will always be homesick for it.

—From *Now and Then* by Frederick Buechner

✦ Do you love the spirit of your friend, or do you just love the outside of him? If you love his clear complexion, his baritone voice, his straight Greek profile, his splendid figure, and stop there—then your love is not the true penetrating heavenly love. But if you love the deep wells of quietness, deep, deep down inside of him, if you love the Christlike quality of his compassion, or his yet unawakened capacity for intelligence, for endurance, for heroism, then you are beginning to get to the roots of him. Each person has a slightly different quality of personality, a different soul through which he expresses the great God Spirit. If you penetrate to that inner soul and love it—not some imaginary illusion or some imaginary pattern that you yourself place on him from without, but his own true soul, and love it—then he is really and truly your friend. You and he will be David and Jonathan for life, or Ruth and Naomi, as the case may be.

—From *I Will Lift Up Mine Eyes* by Glenn Clark

✦ Within the wider Fellowship emerges the special circle of a few on whom, for each of us, a particular emphasis of nearness has fallen. These are our special gift and task. These we "carry" by inward, wordless prayer. By an interior act and attitude we lift them repeatedly before the throne and hold them there in power. This is work, real labor of the soul. It takes energy but it is done in joy. But the membership of such special groups is different and overlapping. From each individual the bonds of special fellowship radiate near and far. The total effect, in a living Church, would be sufficient intersection of these bonds to form a supporting, carrying network of love for the whole of mankind. Where the Fellowship is lacking the Church invisible is lacking and the Kingdom of God has not yet come. For these bonds of divine love and "carrying" are the stuff of the Kingdom of God. He who is in the Fellowship is in the Kingdom.

Two people, three people, ten people may be in living touch with another through Him who underlies their separate lives. This is an astounding experience, which I can only describe but cannot explain in the language of science. But in vivid experience of divine Fellowship it is there. We know that these souls are with us, lifting their lives and ours continuously to God and opening themselves, with us, in steady and humble obedience to Him. It is as if the boundaries of our self were enlarged, as if we were within them and as if they were within us. Their strength, given to them by God, becomes our strength, and our joy, given to us by God, becomes their joy.

—From *A Testament of Devotion* by Thomas R. Kelly

✦ Christianity, after all, is a religion of love; and not of self-love but love of one's brethren and neighbors in Christ. "Fellowship" has therefore always been a key word in Methodism, and in original Methodism it was much more than a word. In order to make and keep it a living reality, Wesley divided his Societies up into Classes. These were groups of not more than a dozen members, who met together once a week under the leadership of one of their own number for conversation on the spiritual life.

The Class Meetings were not study circles, not discussion groups, and least of all were they debating societies. They were Christ-centered fellowships. Their members were taught to take seriously our Lord's promise that he would be present in the midst wherever two or three were gathered together in his name. Hence, when they met in Class, they would sing:

Jesus, we look to thee,
Thy promised presence claim!
Thou in the midst of us shalt be,

Assembled in thy name:
Thy name salvation is,
Which here we come to prove;
Thy name is life, and health, and peace,
And everlasting love.

Then they could go on to share their Christian experience with one another—their troubles and triumphs on the Christian way, or on their quest for that way. Sometimes they confessed their sins to one another, sometimes took one another to task, but always with the aim of helping one another grow in grace, in faith and hope and love.

—From *The Message of the Wesleys.*
Compiled by Philip S. Watson

18. Fasting

You know, O Lord, to how many sinful allurements, interior trials and dangers we are exposed, both from natural and violent inclinations to evil, our unceasing repugnance to good and the assaults of temptation. How shall we be able to resist so many and such powerful enemies bent as they are upon our destruction, if you in your bounty do not assist us? It is to you we raise up our hearts and our minds. It is to you we look for succor to keep us from yielding to temptation, to deliver us from the greatest of all evils, sin, and to preserve us from perishing everlastingly. Amen.

PSALM 54

DAILY SCRIPTURE

Monday	John 4:31–38
Tuesday	Matthew 9:14–17
Wednesday	Matthew 6:16–18
Thursday	Luke 4:1–13
Friday	Exodus 34:27–28
Saturday	Matthew 4:1–4
Sunday	Luke 5:33–39

SELECTIONS FOR MEDITATION

PERSONAL MEDITATION

PRAYER

I heard a godly man remark when asked if he got hungry while fasting, "Of course! But then I remember that I'm fasting for God and not for me, and the hunger goes away."

HYMN   "Fill Me Now"

> Hover o'er me, Holy Spirit,
> Bathe my trembling heart and brow;
> Fill me with Thy hallowed presence,
> Come, O come and fill me now.
>
> Thou canst fill me, gracious Spirit,
> Though I cannot tell Thee how;
> But I need Thee, greatly need Thee;
> Come, O come and fill me now.
>
> I am weakness, full of weakness;
> At Thy sacred feet I bow.
> Blest, divine, eternal Spirit,
> Fill with love, and fill me now.
>
> Cleanse and comfort, bless and save me;
> Bathe, O bathe my heart and brow.
> Thou art comforting and saving,
> Thou art sweetly filling now.
>
> Fill me now,
> Fill me now;
> Jesus, come and fill me now.
> Fill me with Thy hallowed presence;
> Come, O come and fill me now.
>
> Elwood Stokes

BENEDICTION

You have said, O Lord, that to become your disciples we must deny ourselves and take up our cross and follow you. You know our extreme repugnance to both one and the other. Suffer not our faith on this point to condemn us for not practicing what we believe to be necessary for salvation, but grant that as we believe so may we ever live as becomes Christians. Amen.

SELECTIONS FOR MEDITATION

✦ One issue that understandably concerns many people is whether or not Scripture makes fasting obligatory upon all Christians. . . . Although many passages of Scripture deal with this subject, two stand out in importance. The first is Jesus' startling teaching about fasting in the Sermon on the Mount. His teaching on fasting was directly in the context of His teaching on giving and praying. It is as if there is an almost unconscious assumption that giving, praying and fasting are all part of Christian devotion. Jesus stated, "When you fast . . ." (Matt. 6:16). He seemed to make the assumption that people would fast, and what was needed was instruction on how to do it properly.

. . . Having said this, however, we must go on to realize that those words of Jesus do not constitute a command. Jesus was giving instruction on the proper exercise of a common practice of His day. He did not speak a word about whether it was a right practice or if it should be continued. So although Jesus did not say "If you fast," neither did He say, "You must fast."

The second crucial statement of Jesus about fasting came in response to a question by the disciples of John the Baptist. Perplexed over the fact that both they and the Pharisees fasted but Jesus' disciples did not, they asked "Why?" Jesus replied, "Can the wedding guests mourn as long as the bridegroom is with them? The days will come, when the bridegroom is taken from them, and then they will fast" (Matt. 9:15). That is perhaps the most important statement in the New Testament on whether Christians should fast today.

The most natural interpretation of the days when Jesus' disciples will fast is the present church age, especially in light of its intricate connection with Jesus' statement on the new wineskins of the kingdom of God which follows immediately (Matt. 9:16–18). . . . Perhaps it is best to avoid the term "command" since in the strictest sense Jesus did not command fasting. But it is obvious that He proceeded on the principle that the children of the kingdom of God would fast. For the person longing for a more intimate walk with God, these statements of Jesus are drawing words.

—From *Celebration of Discipline* by Richard J. Foster

✦ Fasting also can simplify the compulsive, distracting, grasping nature of our appetites. When we fast intentionally, one of the first things we notice is how little food we really need, yet how much we have been wolfing down. The dull, bloated feeling from over-eating slowly vanishes. We become lighter and more lucid. We see that we really are capable of not responding to that grasping wave of appetite that clicks in our brain. That is a little realization of freedom. If we don't respond to that shallow, driving wave, we are free to flow in a simpler, deeper, more even-flowing stream.

This freedom can have a multiplier effect on our other appetites. We find that we need respond less to other waves of aggressive, grasping desire that shoot up. We become more and more simply present, able to see more clearly the concrete situation we are in, and care more gently and concertedly for it.

My own and others' experience leads me to recommend not a full fast, but a "juice fast": vegetable juice (preferably freshly made) and especially fruit juice (which will provide more energy sugar) three times a day. The juice provides a basic, simple, appropriate nourishment. It can save you from the complicating distractions of headaches and hunger pangs that more easily accompany total fasting. Take plenty of water in addition to the juice throughout the day to prevent dehydration.

If you want to undertake a fast, it is easiest to do so with others. You can do this, for example, during a weekend corporate retreat, or as a family during traditional fast days. When all fast together, it not only reinforces our sense of capacity for it, but it frees us a bit from the temptation to see what we are doing as something very "special." Such fantasies are "extra"—more than the act calls for.

—From *Living Simply Through the Day*
by Tilden H. Edwards

✦ On the matter of prayer and fasting, all you need to do is to follow the inner promptings of the Lord.

There is no set pattern in all this. It may be that for a day, or a longer period, you will want merely to pass up some part of a meal—dessert, or something else that you enjoy and you'd like to give it up. That's very good training for children.

It may be that God would only direct you to fast one meal. Or one day.

As you do these things, He then is more likely somewhere along the line to prompt you to fast for two or three days. Perhaps eventually longer than that.

The important thing is not just the fasting, but why you are fasting.

People often ask me, "Don't you get hungry when you fast?"

My response is, "Yes. Particularly the third day. After that it isn't too bad. But all I need to do to handle my problem of hunger, I have learned, is to remind myself of why I am fasting."

When I do that, handling the hunger is no big problem for me. Because I'm not fasting out of routine, or to make an impression, or to try to bargain with God. I am fasting because I feel the Holy Spirit has prompted me to fast for some reason, purpose, and sometimes even for no indicated purpose at all except to fast.

—Ponder Gilliland

◆ Physical pleasure is a sensual experience no different from pure seeing or the pure sensation with which a fine fruit fills the tongue; it is a great unending experience, which is given us, a knowing of the world, the fullness and the glory of all knowing. And not our acceptance of it is bad; the bad thing is that most people misuse and squander this experience and apply it as a stimulant at the tired spots of their lives and as a distraction instead of rallying toward exalted moments. Men have made even eating into something else: want on the one hand, superfluity upon the other, have dimmed the distinctness of this need, and all the deep, simple necessities in which life renews itself have become similarly dulled. But the individual can clarify them for himself and live them clearly. He can remember that all beauty in animals and plants is a quiet, enduring form of love and longing, and he can see animals, as he sees plants, patiently and willingly uniting and increasing and growing, not out of physical delight, not out of physical suffering, but bowing to necessities that are greater than pleasure and pain and more powerful than will and withstanding. O that man might take this secret, of which the world is full even to its littlest things, more humbly to himself and bear it.

—From *Letters to a Young Poet* by Rainer Maria Rilke

✦ The self is given to us that we may sacrifice it: it is ours, that we, like Christ, may have somewhat to offer—not that we should torment it, but that we should deny it; not that we should cross it, but we should abandon it utterly: then it can no more be vexed. "What can this mean?—we are not to thwart, but to abandon?" . . . It means this:—we must refuse, abandon, deny self altogether as a ruling, or determining, or originating element in us. It is to be no longer the regent of our action. We are no more to think "What should I like to do?" but "What would the Living One have me do?"

—From *An Anthology of George MacDonald.*
Edited by C. S. Lewis

✦ Prayer needs fasting for its full growth: this is the second lesson. Prayer is the one hand with which we grasp the invisible; fasting, the other, with which we let loose and cast away the visible. In nothing is man more closely connected with the world of sense than in his need of food, and his enjoyment of it. It was the fruit, good for food, with which man was tempted and fell in Paradise. It was with bread to be made of stones that Jesus, when hungered, was tempted in the wilderness, and in fasting that He triumphed. The body has been redeemed to be a temple of the Holy Spirit; it is in body as well as spirit, it is very specially, Scripture says, in eating and drinking, we are to glorify God. It is to be feared that there are many Christians to whom this eating to the glory of God, has not yet become a spiritual reality. And the first thought suggested by Jesus' words in regard to fasting and prayer is, that it is only in a life of moderation and temperance and self-denial that there will be the heart or the strength to pray much.

—From *With Christ in the School of Prayer*
by Andrew Murray

♦ Not that we are to imagine that performing the bare outward act will receive any blessing from God. If it be a mere external service, it is all but lost labour. Such a performance may possibly afflict the body; but as to the soul, it profiteth nothing.

. . . But let us take care to afflict our souls as well as our bodies. Let every season, either of public or private fasting, be a season of exercising all those holy affections which are implied in a broken and contrite heart. Let it be a season of devout mourning, of godly sorrow for sin.

And with fasting let us always join fervent prayer, pouring out our whole souls before God, confessing our sins with all their aggravations, humbling ourselves under his mighty hand, laying open before him all our wants, all our guiltiness and helplessness. This is a season for enlarging our prayers, both in behalf of ourselves and of our brethren. Let us now bewail the sins of our people; and cry aloud for the city of our God, that the Lord may build up Zion, and cause his face to shine on her desolations. Thus, may we observe, the man of God in ancient times always joined prayer and fasting together.

—From *The Message of the Wesleys.*
Compiled by Philip S. Watson

19. Faith in the Process

INVOCATION

Father, I thank you for this day, for what it shall bring, opportunities, life, hope, strength. And for what it may take away. Teach me to trust you in the comings and the goings of life. In the name of your Son, Jesus, I pray. Amen.

PSALM 107

DAILY SCRIPTURE

Monday	Hebrews 11:1–12:3
Tuesday	Genesis 22:1–19
Wednesday	1 Corinthians 10:1–13
Thursday	Nehemiah 6:1–9
Friday	Philippians 3:17–4:1
Saturday	1 Peter 5:1–11
Sunday	Romans 8:28–39

SELECTIONS FOR MEDITATION

PERSONAL MEDITATION

PRAYER

Ask God to reveal himself to you this week in his form or way. Promise him that you will not ask him to speak to you in any certain images; but that you want to be open to all of his entreaties to you. Ask him to show you that these experiences of today are part of his processes for your life.

HYMN   "Day by Day"

Day by day, and with each passing moment,
Strength I find to meet my trials here.
Trusting in my Father's wise bestowment,
I've no cause for worry or for fear.

He whose heart is kindness beyond measure
Gives unto each day what He deems best,
Lovingly its part of pain and pleasure,
Mingling toil with peace and rest.

Every day the Lord Himself is near me,
With a special mercy for each hour.
All my cares He fain would bear and cheer me,
He whose name is Counselor and Power.
The protection of His child and treasure
Is a charge that on Himself He laid.
"As thy days, thy strength shall be in measure,"
This the pledge to me He made.

Help me then in every tribulation,
So to trust Thy promises, O Lord.
That I lose not faith's sweet consolation,
Offered me within Thy holy Word.
Help me, Lord when toil and trouble meeting,
E'er to take, as from a Father's hand,
One by one, the days, the moments fleeting,
Till I reach the promised land.
Lina Sandell and Oscar Ahnfelt

BENEDICTION

O Lord, mercifully receive my prayer, and grant that I may know and understand what things I ought to do, and also grant the grace and power to faithfully accomplish them; through Jesus Christ our Lord. Amen.

SELECTIONS FOR MEDITATION

✦ "What can you do when you've failed and denied what you believe?" This question and others like it came out of the heart of a person who had stumbled badly. He felt he had no right to pray, and when he tried, he felt self-incrimination and condemnation. We all deny our Lord in so many little ways, but what do you do when the denial contradicts everything you've stood for and believed? Is there a way back? How does the Lord deal with failures?

The answer is vividly portrayed in the way Jesus Christ dealt with Simon Peter's denial. Peter could not handle the anguish of his cowardly denial. He had to block it out, try to forget; but his efforts were futile. Was that why he now could not bear to look Jesus in the eye?

What adventure Peter had known following the Master! He remembered with self-affirmation how on the road to Caesarea Philippi he felt the spirit rush within him. He had blurted out the conviction, "Thou art the Christ!" He would never forget the tone of the Lord's voice when he told him that the church would be built on the rock of his faith. A rock? The recollection reverberated with shock waves within him. "A rock that cracked!" he said to himself.

But the basic message of the story is this: the Lord's love does not fail however much we fail him. Peter had built his whole relationship with Jesus Christ on his assumed capacity to be adequate. That's why he took his denial of the Lord so hard. His strength, loyalty, and faithfulness were his self-generated assets of discipleship. The fallacy in Peter's mind was this: he believed his relationship was dependent on his consistency in producing the qualities he thought had earned him the Lord's approval.

Many of us face the same problem. We project onto the Lord our own measured standard of acceptance. Our whole understanding of him is based in a quid pro quo of bartered love. He will love us as if we are good, moral, and diligent. But we have turned the tables; we try to live so that he will love us, rather than living because he has already loved us.

—From *Ask Him Anything* by Lloyd Ogilvie

✦ During these days my eight-year-old daughter was diagnosed as having leukemia, and we have been called upon to shift very swiftly from the shock and numbness that first comes with such a disclosure to the task of learning to care for her and how to live with a degree of normalcy in the shadow of such an enormity.

Long before this happened to me, I had come to the conclusion that it was the nature of God to speak to us in the language of events, and that it was the nature of the Church for men to share with each other what they thought they heard God say in the things that had happened to them.

The first thing that I have to share may surprise you a bit, but I must in all honesty confess it, and that is: I have found no answers to the deepest questions of this experience. The enigma remains what it had been from the beginning—a dark mystery for which there is no satisfactory explanation. And while I have not found any total answer, I have found the challenge to go on living even though I have no answer or any complete explanation. The Bible arranges life and thought in just that sequence. We are called on to live passionately and openly and then to use our minds to try to understand and interpret what we have experienced. In this way life moves on and whatever insight is possible is born.

We do not first get all the answers and then live in light of our understanding. We must rather plunge into life—meeting what we have to meet and experiencing what we have to experience—and in the light of living try to understand. If insight comes at all, it will not be before, but only through and after experience.

—From *Tracks of a Fellow Struggler* by John Claypool

✦ And Enoch walked with God: and he was not, for God took him . . . Noah was a just man and perfect in his generations, and Noah walked with God (Genesis 5:24, 6:9).

How different is the case, how vast the preeminence, of those who "walk by faith!" . . .

Those who live by faith, walk by faith. But what is implied in this? They regulate all their judgments concerning good and evil, not with reference to visible and temporal things, but to things invisible and eternal. They think visible things to be of small value, because they pass away like a dream; but, on the contrary, they account invisible things to be of high value, because they will never pass away. . . . So the apostle: "The things that are seen are temporal; but the things that are not seen are eternal." Therefore, they who "walk by faith" do not desire the "things which are seen"; neither are they the object of their pursuit. They "set their affection on things above, not on things on the earth." . . . They regulate all their thoughts and designs, all their words and actions, so as to prepare them for that invisible and eternal world to which they are shortly going. They do not dwell but only sojourn here; not looking upon earth as their home, but only

> Travelling through Immanuel's ground,
> To fairer worlds on high.
> —From *The John Wesley Reader* by Al Bryant

✦ Many of us are willing to embark upon any adventure, except to go into stillness and to wait, to place all the wealth of wisdom in the secrecy of the soil, to sow our own soul for a seed in that tract of land allocated to every life which we call time—and to let the soul grow beyond itself. Faith is the fruit of a seed planted in the depth of a lifetime.
> —From *Man Is Not Alone: A Philosophy of Religion* by Abraham Joshua Heschel

✦ It is the bland and repetitious part of life at the center that seems its greatest defect; the reality of a life of care often seems as far from spirituality as possible. It is true that it is the greatest burden of this life, but it is not true that it is far from spirituality. . . . Spirituality is anything that reveals how close God is to us—as close as our hands, as close as our heart.
> —From *A Way in the World* by Ernest Boyer, Jr.

✦ I do not believe that we can always properly label the moments that come to us.

Last spring one of my close friends had a very serious heart attack. For a while it really didn't look like he would make it. But he grew better and was finally strong enough for the surgery which is supposed to give him a new lease on life. I was with him in the fall and he was still talking about the experience.

I call him Bo but since he is a District Superintendent and I never know when I might need a church, I'll at least say W. T. We had a conversation that ran something like this:

"W. T., how did you like your heart attack?"

"It scared me to death, almost."

"Would you like to do it again?"

"No!"

"Would you recommend it?"

"Definitely not."

"Does your life mean more to you than it did before?"

"Well, yes."

"You and Nell have always had a beautiful marriage, but now are you closer than ever?"

"Yes."

"How about that new granddaughter?"

"Yes. Did I show you her picture?"

"Do you have a new compassion for people—a deep understanding and sympathy?"

"Yes."

"Do you know the Lord in a richer, deeper fellowship than you had ever realized could be possible?"

"Yes."

"How'd you like your heart attack?"

Silence was his answer.

—From *Something's Going On Here* by Bob Benson

✦ By examining as closely and candidly as I could the life that had come to seem to me in many ways a kind of trap or dead-end street, I discovered that it really wasn't that at all. I discovered that if you really keep your eye peeled to it and your ears open, if you really pay attention to it, even such a limited and limiting life as the one I was living on Rupert Mountain opened up onto extraordinary vistas. Taking your children to school and kissing your wife goodbye. Eating lunch with a friend. Trying to do a decent day's work. Hearing the rain patter against the window. There is no event so commonplace but that God is present within it, always hiddenly, always leaving you room to recognize him, but all the more fascinatingly because of that, all the more compellingly and hauntingly. In writing those lectures and the book they later turned into, it came to seem to me that if I were called upon to state in a few words the essence of everything I was trying to say both as a novelist and as a preacher, it would be something like this: Listen to your life. See it for the fathomless mystery it is. In the boredom and pain of it no less than in the excitement and gladness: touch, taste, smell your way to the holy and hidden heart of it because in the last analysis all moments are key moments, and life itself is grace.

—From *Now and Then* by Frederick Buechner

✦ But when it comes to putting broken lives back together—when it comes, in religious terms, to the saving of souls—the human best tends to be at odds with the holy best. To do for yourself the best that you have it in you to do—to grit your teeth and clench your fists in order to survive the world at its harshest and worst—is, by that very act, to be unable to let something be done for you and in you that is more wonderful still. The trouble with steeling yourself against the harshness of reality is that the same steel that secures your life against being destroyed secures your life also against being opened up and transformed by the holy power that life itself comes from. You can survive on your own. You can grow strong on your own. You can even prevail on your own. But you cannot become human on your own. Surely that is why, in Jesus' sad joke, the rich man has as hard a time getting into Paradise as that camel through the needle's eye because with his credit card in his pocket, the rich man is so effective at getting for himself everything else he needs that he does not see that what he needs more than anything else in the world can be had only as a gift. He does not see that the one thing a clenched fist cannot do is accept, even from le bon Dieu himself, a helping hand.

—From *The Sacred Journey* by Frederick Buechner

SECTION TWO
obstacles to the inner life

The ten chapters that make up this section in the book have to do with the most common hindrances to communication with God and the development of the inner person.

One of the first things helpful for us to realize is that everyone who makes this spiritual pilgrimage encounters obstacles from time to time. They are not just your problems. And knowing that they are to be expected may help you in working through them as they come.

Probably the first area of your struggle will revolve around the difficulty in fixing the will to choose this inner way of living. There is a sense in which this is the cornerstone of your relationship to God. The determination that this is to become the habitual practice of your life will not be easy to make nor will it come effortlessly into being. One of the things that you are privileged to bring to him is your constancy, your faithfulness. For this to become a reality in your heart you will have to learn to deal with the hindrances that will beset you. Doubts, temptations, distractions, anxieties, a lack of wholeness and the seeming absence of God at times are some of the things that will have to be overcome.

A helpful word of counsel at this point is given to us by Anthony Bloom. Remember that what you are seeking is a relationship between you and God. It is an encounter that cannot be forced from either direction. Just as God respects your right to be absent or present you must not feel that you can mechanically draw him into meeting either. Do not complain if he does not seem to make himself present for the few minutes that you have put aside for him. Instead, regularly come into your place of prayer and faithfully wait for him to come and meet you. He will honor your steadfastness. Indeed you may often feel that a particular prayer time has been "useless," to use one of Henri Nouwen's phrases, only to realize at a later time that it actually had been a time of strength and insight for you.

Be diligent in your private times in spite of obstacles that seem to deny you immediate help and succor. Do not forget that he is "a rewarder of those that seek him." It is your duty to pray and his to reward. Do not let a period of distractions deter you from the practice of prayer the next day.

20. The Will

God unto whom all hearts are open and unto whom every will speaks, and from whom no secret thing is hidden, I pray You to cleanse the intent of my heart with the ineffable gift of Your grace, that I may perfectly love You, and worthily praise You. Amen.

The Prayer of the Prologue
The Cloud of the Unknowing

PSALM 71

DAILY SCRIPTURE

Monday	John 3:10–21
Tuesday	Luke 11:14–28
Wednesday	Matthew 26:36–46
Thursday	Luke 9:57–62
Friday	Mark 8:34–9:1
Saturday	Luke 5:1–11
Sunday	Luke 13:22–30

SELECTIONS FOR MEDITATION

PERSONAL MEDITATION

PRAYER

If Jesus believed that his life was to be spent doing "the will of the Father," then our task is to be no less. Pray for his will to be accomplished in your life; that you may bring glory to him as Jesus did.

HYMN   "My Jesus, As Thou Wilt"

My Jesus, as Thou wilt.
Oh, may Thy will be mine!

Into Thy hand of love
I would my all resign.
Thro' sorrow or thro' joy,
Conduct me as Thine own,
And help me still to say,
"My Lord, Thy will be done."

My Jesus, as Thou wilt.
Tho' seen thro' many a tear,
Let not my star of hope
Grow dim or disappear.
Since Thou on earth hast wept
And sorrowed oft alone,
If I must weep with Thee,
"My Lord, Thy will be done."

My Jesus, as Thou wilt.
All shall be well for me;
Each changing future scene
I gladly trust with Thee.
Straight to my home above,
I travel calmly on,
And sing in life or death,
"My Lord, Thy will be done."
Benjamin Schmolck

BENEDICTION

Lord, I am yours; I do yield myself up entirely to you, and I
believe that you do take me. I leave myself with you. Work in
me all the good pleasure of your will, and I will only lie still in
your hands and trust you. Amen.
—From *The Christian's Secret of a Happy Life*
by Hannah Whitall Smith

SELECTIONS FOR MEDITATION

✦ Our progress in holiness depends on God and ourselves—
on God's grace and on our will to be holy. We must have a real
living determination to reach holiness. "I will be a saint"
means I will despoil myself of all that is not God; I will strip
my heart of all created things; I will live in poverty and detachment; I will renounce my will, my inclinations, my whims

and fancies, and make myself a willing slave to the will of God.
—From *A Gift for God* by Mother Teresa of Calcutta

✦ There is a moment between intending to pray and actually praying that is as dark and silent as any moment in our lives. It is the split second between thinking about praying and really praying. For some of us, this split second may last for decades. It seems, then, that the greatest obstacle to prayer is the simple matter of beginning, the simple exertion of will, the starting, the acting, the doing. How easy it is, and yet—between us and the possibility of prayer there seems to be a great gulf fixed: an abyss of our own making that separates us from God.

To make matters worse, we can approach the abyss that lies between us and prayer and retreat from it under cover of being-too-busy or having-family-obligations or even serving-God-in-other-ways. This seemingly justified retreat makes the approach more difficult the next time until there is a last, before beginning, a beginning of beginning, and so on ad infinitum. A mud wall is built by the crawfish claws of our reluctance, hardened into clay, baked by the passage of time, till at last it seems too difficult to break down.
—From *Clinging—The Experience of Prayer*
by Emilie Griffin

✦ Unfree men are horrified by the suggestion of accepting a daily discipline. Confusing inner control with external tyranny, they prefer caprice to self-restraint. They would rather have ideals than norms, hopes than directions, faith than forms. But the goal and the way cannot long endure in separation. The days of the week, the food that we eat, the holidays of the year, the deeds that we do—these are the frontiers of faith. Unless the outer life expresses the inner world, piety stagnates and intention decays.

Man is constantly producing words and deeds, giving them over either to God or to the forces of evil. Every move, every detail, every act, every effort to match the spiritual and the material, is serious. The world is not a derelict; life is not a neutral ground. In this life of ours the undirected goes astray, the haphazard becomes chaotic, what is left to chance is abandoned.

We have said that prayer is the quintessence of the spiritual life, that is, the climax of aspirations. But faith cannot be satisfied with climaxes. It cannot rest content with essences. Faith knows no boundaries between the will of God and all of life. Therefore, we have been taught to care for the meaning that is found in deeds, to sense the holy that is available in the everyday, to be devoted to the daily as much as to the extraordinary, to be concerned for the cycle as much as for the special event.

—From *Man's Quest for God* by Abraham Joshua Heschel

◆ For in the governance of our natural lives, a genuine choice is left to us. We are neither dummies, nor the slaves of circumstance. We are living creatures possessed of a limited freedom, a power of initiative which increases every time we use it the right way; we are trained and developed by being confronted with alternatives, on which tremendous issues hang. It is typical of the completeness with which each essential factor of our human experience finds its rule and pattern in the Gospels, that this free choice between possible courses should form our Lord's actual preparation for His public ministry. Enlightened at baptism as to His divine Sonship, His unique commission, He did not at once rush off "in the power of the Spirit" to preach the good news. "He who believeth shall not make haste." Real power is the result of inner harmony, and requires perfect accord between the upper and the lower floors; impulse harnessed to obedience. Therefore the Spirit of Wisdom drove Him into the wilderness, to come to terms with His own human nature. More than one path lay open before Him. He might claim the privileges of an exceptional spirit, in the midst of a world which is not exceptional at all: turn the material world to His own purpose, transcend the common laws of nature, assume the position of the Father's pet child. He might follow the path disclosed by spiritual ambition, leading to obvious power and success: the most insidious of the three temptations, because it suggested that His mission of redemption and enlightenment could be fulfilled on a great scale, by entering into alliance with the spirit and methods of the world. People who think in numbers always mistake this for a call from God. Love, choosing what helped, rejected all these opportunities, and elected the humble career of a local prophet and evangelist: a limited scope, unrewarded service, an unappreciative public, a narrow path leading to the Cross.

—From *The House of the Soul* by Evelyn Underhill

♦ . . . most of our prayers ought to be for the enrichment and control of the spirit so that motives, desires, and the spirit's use of bodily powers will be in harmony with the will of God. If prayer did only this, it would do for us the most important thing that could be done.

—From *Prayer and the Common Life* by Georgia Harkness

♦ In a while I resolved totally to leave off some of my vanities, but there was a secret reserve in my heart of the more refined part of them, and I was not low enough to find true peace. Thus for some months I had great trouble, there remaining in me an unsubjected will which rendered my labors fruitless, till at length through the merciful continuance of heavenly visitations I was made to bow down in spirit before the Lord.

—From *Quaker Spirituality* by George Fox

♦ There is then no need for fret when faithfully turning to Him, if He leads us but slowly into His secret chambers. If He gives us increasing steadiness in the deeper sense of His presence, we can only quietly thank Him. If He holds us in the stage of alternation we can thank Him for His loving wisdom, and wait upon His guidance through the stages for which we are prepared. For we cannot take Him by storm. The strong man must become the little child, not understanding but trusting the Father.

—From *A Testament of Devotion* by Thomas R. Kelly

♦ I said that every Discipline has its corresponding freedom. What freedom corresponds to submission? It is the ability to lay down the terrible burden of always needing to get our own way. The obsession to demand that things go the way we want them to go is one of the greatest bondages in human society today. People will spend weeks, months, even years in a perpetual stew because some little thing did not go as they wished. They will fuss and fume. They will get mad about it. They will act as if their very life hangs on the issue. They may even get an ulcer over it.

In the Discipline of submission we are released to drop the matter, to forget it. Frankly, most things in life are not so nearly important as we think they are. Our lives will not come to an end if this or that does not happen.

If you will watch these things you will see, for example, that almost all church fights and splits occur because people do not have the freedom to give in to each other. We insist that a critical issue is at stake; we are fighting for a sacred principle. Perhaps that is true. Usually it is not. Often we cannot stand to give in simply because it would mean that we would not get things our own way. Only in submission are we enabled to bring that spirit to a place where it no longer controls us. Only submission can free us sufficiently to enable us to distinguish between genuine issues and stubborn self-will.

—From *Celebration of Discipline* by Richard J. Foster

✦ Self-denial conjures up in our minds all sorts of images of groveling and self-hatred. We imagine that it most certainly means the rejection of our individuality and will probably lead to various forms of self-mortification.

On the contrary, Jesus called us to self-denial without self-hatred. Self-denial is simply a way of coming to understand that we do not have to have our own way. Our happiness is not dependent upon getting what we want.

Self-denial does not mean the loss of our identity as some suppose. Without our identity we could not even be subject to each other. Did Jesus lose His identity when He set His face toward Golgotha? Did Peter lose his identity when he responded to Jesus' cross-bearing command, "Follow me" (John 21:19)? Did Paul lose his identity when he committed himself to the One who had said, "I will show him how much he must suffer for the sake of my name" (Acts 9:16)? Of course not. We know that the opposite was true. They found their identity in the act of self-denial.

Self-denial is not the same thing as self-contempt. Self-contempt claims that we have no worth, and even if we did have worth we should reject it. Self-denial declares that we are of infinite worth and shows us how to realize it. Self-contempt denies the goodness of the creation; self-denial affirms that it was indeed good. Jesus made the ability to love ourselves the prerequisite for our reaching out to others (Matt. 22:39).

—From *Celebration of Discpline* by Richard J. Foster

✦ Jesus in His prayers on earth, in His intercession in heaven, in His promise of an answer to our prayers from there, makes this His first objective—the glory of His Father. Is it so with us too? Or are not, in large measure, self-interest and self-will the strongest motives urging us to pray? Or, if we cannot see that this is the case, have we not to acknowledge that the distinct, conscious longing for the glory of the Father is not what animates our prayers? And yet it must be so.

Not as if the believer does not at times desire it. But he has to mourn that he has so little attained. And he knows the reason of his failure too. It was, because the separation between the spirit of daily life and the spirit of the hour of prayer was too wide. We begin to see that the desire for the glory of the Father is not something that we can awake and present to our Lord when we prepare ourselves to pray. No! It is only when the whole life, in all its parts, is given up to God's glory, that we can really pray to His glory too. "Do all to the glory of God," and, "Ask all to the glory of God"—these twin commands are inseparable: obedience to the former is the secret grace for the latter. A life to the glory of God is the condition of the prayers that Jesus can answer, "that the Father may be glorified."

—From *With Christ in the School of Prayer*
by Andrew Murray

21. Doubts

Almighty God, Lord of the storm and of the calm, of day and night, of life and death; grant to me so to have my heart stayed upon your faithfulness, your unchangingness and love, that whatsoever betides me, I may look upon you with untroubled eye. I ask it for thy mercy's sake. Amen.

George Dawson in *Little Book of Prayers*

PSALM 42

DAILY SCRIPTURE

Monday	Luke 7:1–10
Tuesday	Hebrews 10:19–25
Wednesday	Matthew 14:22–36
Thursday	Genesis 18:1–15
Friday	John 6:60–69
Saturday	Romans 4:1–25
Sunday	John 20:24–31

SELECTIONS FOR MEDITATION

PERSONAL MEDITATION

PRAYER

Sometimes we all are in need of praying as the father of the demon-possessed boy (Mark 9) who said to Jesus, "I do believe, help me overcome my unbelief." Do not be afraid to pray in this way if it reflects your needs.

HYMN   "Oh, for a Faith That Will Not Shrink"

Oh, for a faith that will not shrink,
Tho' pressed by ev'ry foe,

That will not tremble on the brink
Of any earthly woe.

That will not murmur nor complain
Beneath the chast'ning rod
But, in the hour of grief or pain,
Will lean upon its God.

A faith that shines more bright and clear
When tempests rage without;
That when in danger knows no fear,
In darkness feels no doubt.

Lord, give us such a faith as this;
And then, whate'er may come,
We'll taste, e'en here, the hallowed bliss
Of an eternal home.

William H. Bathurst

BENEDICTION

Father and God, you know the work, the worry, and the weariness which, day by day, even week after week, weigh so heavily upon my life. So often I grow faint and fearful, disturbed and doubtful. I long for rest and peace and full assurance of faith. May I so wait upon you in daily prayer and be renewed with spiritual might that I shall fight the good fight and keep the faith. For Jesus' sake I pray. Amen.

Orien W. Fifer in Daily Prayer Companion

SELECTIONS FOR MEDITATION

✦ Questions of faith are not like riddles or crossword puzzles: with things of this sort it may take one some time to find the solution, but once it's found, everything is clear and simple. It is completely different with faith. Here we have, not human truth which men can state and understand, but God's truth, which goes far beyond any statement or understanding of man's. The faith never becomes clear. The faith remains obscure. Not until we enter into glory will it be otherwise: "We see now through a glass in a dark manner: but then face to face. Now I know in part: but then I shall know even as I am known" (1 Cor. 13:12). Only when we are in glory will it be otherwise. Until then there will always be more difficulties coming up, more doubts coming up: there are bound to be. Doubt is the shadow cast by faith. One does not always notice it, but it is always there, though concealed. At any moment it may come into action. There is no mystery of the faith which is immune to doubt.

—From *That the World May Believe* by Hans Küng

◆ Whether one uses the words of the Bible or a traditional collection or formulates his own prayer is immaterial, provided what is expressed is the voice of the soul. Psychologically, the act of praying centers attention on the higher emotions, unifies the spirit, crystallizes motives, clarifies the judgment, releases latent powers, reinforces confidence that what needs to be done can be done. Religiously, the power of God who is ever waiting to bestow his strength on those who will receive it finds a channel.

The benefits of such praying are seldom disputed. But the question is often raised as to whether such benefits are not "all psychological." What is generally meant is whether they are not entirely subjective and self-induced. The answer lies in . . . the nature of God and his relations with men. If there is a personal God who has made us and sustains us, he hears and responds to prayer. Even if the response is wholly within the individual who prays and what happens can be described in psychological terms, it is still God's response. Unless there is such a God, no prayer has meaning. To deny that God acts to give us moral and spiritual help is an implicit atheism.

—From *Prayer and the Common Life* by Georgia Harkness

◆ A devoted Christian woman who conducted a large Bible class with zeal and success once came in trouble to her minister. In her earlier years she had enjoyed much blessing in the inner chamber, in fellowship with the Lord and His Word. But this had gradually been lost and, do what she would, she could not get it right. The Lord had blessed her work, but the joy had gone out of her life. The minister asked what she had done to regain the lost blessedness. "I have done everything," said she, "that I can think of, but all in vain."

He then questioned her about her experience in connection with her conversion. She gave an immediate and clear answer: "At first I spared no pains in my attempt to become better, and to free myself from sin, but it was all useless. At last I began to understand that I must lay aside all my efforts, and simply trust the Lord Jesus to bestow on me His life and peace, and He did it."

"Why then," said the minister, "do you not try this again? As you go to your inner chamber, however cold and dark your heart may be, do not try in your own might to force yourself into the right attitude. Bow before Him, and tell Him that He sees in what a sad state you are and that your only hope is in Him. Trust Him with a childlike trust to have mercy upon you, and wait upon Him. You have nothing—He has everything."

—From *The Prayer Life* by Andrew Murray

✦ I want to beg you to be patient toward all that is unsolved in your heart and to try to love the questions themselves like locked rooms and like books that are written in a very foreign tongue. Do not now seek the answers, which cannot be given you because you would not be able to live them. And the point is, to live everything. Live the questions now. Perhaps you will then gradually, without noticing it, live along some distant day into the answer.

—From *Letters to a Young Poet* by Rainer Maria Rilke

✦ Jesus never argued for the validity of prayer anymore than he argued for the existence of God. God was not something to be proved by argument; God was simply there, the beginning and the end of experience. Just so, prayer was not something to be proved by argument; prayer was there, the native breath of the soul. Prayer was man's instinctive tendency, wrought into the very constitution of his nature. Its well-springs lay deep down beneath the region of argument; they lay in hearts which God had made for fellowship with himself, which therefore (as Augustine at a later day expressed it) would always be restless until they found rest in him. Hence Jesus never argued the matter. But certainly there was a sense in which his own prayer life was the one unanswerable argument. Did any disciple—Thomas, for example—have doubts about prayer, genuine, honest doubts? Nothing was more likely to vanquish his doubts than the sight of Jesus upon his knees, for knowing Jesus and realizing what an utterly sure and reliable insight Jesus had into all the deepest things of life, such a disciple would feel it better to trust Jesus' certainty rather than his own uncertainty. He would think it wise to attach more importance to Christ's conviction than to his own doubts. In all matters of faith this is an enormously valuable principle, and certainly it carries weight here. Doubts are dispelled and dissolved before the shining prayer life of the Christ. The praying Christ is the supreme argument for prayer.

—From *The Life and Teaching of Jesus Christ*
by James Stewart

◆ For the word crisis, the Chinese use a combination of two characters. These two characters are those which designate "danger" and "opportunity." This disjunction seems to be true of every crisis. It is a turning point, and, depending on how one makes the turn, he can find danger or opportunity. The forks in the road of human life that demand decisions of us are always crossroads of danger and opportunity. As in the medical usage of this term, when a patient is pronounced "critical," the implication is that he can move either toward life or death.

In the process of faith, doubts and crises must occur. Paul Tillich points out that only through crises can faith mature. Doubt eats away the old relationship with God, but only so that a new one may be born. The same thing is true of our human, interpersonal relationships. They grow from initial fragility into permanence only through the tests of doubts and crisis. So Kahlil Gibran says that we can "forget those we have laughed with, but we can never forget those we have cried with."

There is something in older people that feels uneasy with, or even resents, crises of faith in the young. We lose sight of the fact that faith can mature only because of these crises. We forget that no one can say a meaningful "yes" of commitment until he has faced the alternate possibility of saying "no." The most destructive thing we can do to those passing through periods of crisis is to attempt to downplay these legitimate doubts and encourage their repression. Repressed doubts have a high rate of resurrection, and doubts that are plowed under will only grow new roots. One thing is certain, that passage through the darkness of doubts and crises, however painful they may be, is essential to growth in the process of faith.

—From *A Reason to Live! A Reason to Die!*
by John Powell

✦ One thing is sure: the Lord does want us to count most certainly on it that asking, seeking, knocking, cannot be in vain: receiving an answer, finding God, the opened heart and home of God, are the certain fruit of prayer.

That the Lord should have thought it needful in so many forms to repeat the truth, is a lesson of deep import. It proves that he knows our heart, how doubt and distrust toward God are natural to us, and how easily we are inclined to rest in prayer as a religious work without an answer. He knows too how, even when we believe that God is the Hearer of prayer, believing prayer that lays hold of the promise is something spiritual, too high and difficult for the half-hearted disciple. He therefore at the very outset of His instruction to those who would learn to pray, seeks to lodge this truth deep into their hearts: prayer does avail much; ask and ye shall receive; everyone that asketh, receiveth. This is the fixed, eternal law of the kingdom: if you ask and receive not, it must be because there is something amiss or wanting in the prayer.

—From *With Christ in the School of Prayer*
by Andrew Murray

✦ Then she turns toward me, reaches for me. "I'm scared. I'm scared."

I put my arms around her and hold her. I hold her as I held my children when they were small and afraid in the night; as, this summer, I hold my grandchildren. I hold her as she, once upon a time and long ago, held me. And I say the same words, the classic, maternal, instinctive words of reassurance. "Don't be afraid. I'm here. It's all right."

"Something's wrong. I'm scared. I'm scared."

I cradle her and repeat, "It's all right."

What's all right? What am I promising her? I'm scared too. I don't know what will happen when Hugh goes to the neurologist. I don't know what's going to happen to my mother this summer. I don't know what the message may be the next time the phone rings. What's all right? How can I say it?

But I do. I hold her close, and kiss her, and murmur, "It's all right, Mother. It's all right."

I mean these words. I do not understand them, but I mean them. Perhaps one day I will find out what I mean. They are implicit in everything I write. I caught a hint of them during that lecture, even as I was cautioning against false promises. They are behind everything, the cooking of meals, walking the dogs, talking with the girls. I may never find out with my intellectual self what I mean, but if I am given enough glimpses perhaps these will add up to enough so that my heart will understand. It does not; not yet.

—From *The Summer of the Great-Grandmother*
by Madeleine L'Engle

◆ But joy is only one of the gifts of this life. Another is that of consolation and courage. A mysterious strength and confidence—far greater than your own—comes with it. Then, too, you will find yourself more accepting of yourself and of others, since to discover that just as you are, you are loved, opens you to love others in the same way. And, finally, you may find that your faith itself has been transformed. For many people faith means nothing more than a set of beliefs to which they may either agree or disagree. To have faith is much like having an opinion, the only exception being that, where other opinions might concern politics or sports, this is an opinion on whether or not God exists. Living the presence of God, though, faith is transformed from an opinion to a relationship. God is not a belief to which you give your assent. God becomes a reality that you know intimately, meet every day, one whose strength becomes your strength, whose love, your love. Live this life of the presence of God long enough and when someone asks you, "Do you believe there is a God?" you may find yourself answering, "No, I do not believe there is a God. I know there is a God."

—From *A Way in the World* by Ernest Boyer, Jr.

22. Temptations

INVOCATION

My God, my Father, when I consider your greatness and your goodness, when my heart is bowed in adoration before the Holy One who inhabits eternity, my spirits sink as I remember that your thoughts have not been my thoughts and your ways have not been my ways. I have fallen far short of your glory. I have not been what I might have been; I have not done what I might have done. Have mercy on me, according to your loving-kindness in Christ Jesus, our Lord . . . In His Name. Amen.

Herbert Welch in *Daily Prayer Companion*

PSALM 141

DAILY SCRIPTURE

Monday	1 Corinthians 10:11–21
Tuesday	Matthew 4:1–11
Wednesday	James 1:2–4
Thursday	Mark 14:66–72
Friday	Matthew 16:21–24
Saturday	Hebrews 2:10–18
Sunday	1 Peter 2:19–25

SELECTIONS FOR MEDITATION

PERSONAL MEDITATION

PRAYER

To share his victory we must share in his suffering. And this includes sharing in his temptations. Temptations can serve to strengthen us as they strengthened Jesus. Inquire of him how you might benefit in such circumstances.

HYMN   "Yield Not to Temptation"

Yield not to temptation,
For yielding is sin.
Each victory will help you
Some other to win.
Fight manfully onward;
Dark passions subdue.
Look ever to Jesus;
He'll carry you through.

Shun evil companions;
Bad language disdain.
God's name hold in rev'rence,
Nor take it in vain.
Be thoughtful and earnest,
Kind-hearted and true.
Look ever to Jesus;
He'll carry you through.

To him that o'er-cometh
God giveth a crown.
Thro' faith we shall conquer,
Though often cast down.
He who is our Saviour
Our strength will renew.
Look ever to Jesus;
He'll carry you through.

Ask the Saviour to help you,
Comfort, strengthen, and keep you.
He is willing to aid you;
He will carry you through.
                        Horatio R. Palmer

BENEDICTION

We give thanks unto you, heavenly Father, through Jesus
Christ, your dear Son, that you have this day so graciously
protected us; and we beseech you to forgive us all our sins,
and by your great mercy defend us from all the perils and
dangers of this night.

Lutheran Service Book

SELECTIONS FOR MEDITATION

✦ We do not refuse to pray. We merely feel that our tongues are tied, our minds inert, our inner vision dim, when we are about to enter the door that leads to prayer. We do not refuse to pray; we abstain from it. We ring the hollow bell of selfishness rather than absorb the stillness that surrounds the world, hovering over all the restlessness and fear of life—the secret stillness that precedes our birth and succeeds our death. Futile self-indulgence brings us out of tune with the gentle song of nature's waiting, of mankind's striving for salvation. Is not listening to the pulse of wonder worth silence and abstinence from self-assertion? Why do we not set apart an hour of living for devotion to God by surrendering to stillness? We dwell on the edge of mystery and ignore it, wasting our souls, risking our stake in God. We constantly pour our inner light away from Him, setting up the thick screen of self between Him and us, adding more shadows to the darkness that already hovers between Him and our wayward reason. Accepting surmises as dogmas, and prejudices as solutions, we ridicule the evidence of life for what is more than life. Our mind has ceased to be sensitive to the wonder. Deprived of the power of devotion to what is more important than our individual fate, steeped in passionate anxiety to survive, we lose sight of what fate is, of what living is. Rushing through the ecstasies of ambition, we only awake when plunged into dread or grief. In darkness, then, we grope for solace, for meaning, for prayer.
—From *Man's Quest for God* by Abraham Joshua Heschel

✦ In the stories of the Desert Fathers, those men who, for several hundred years after Anthony, emulated his life in the desert, there is one concerning Abbot John the Dwarf who prayed to the Lord that his passion be taken from him. His prayer was granted so that he became impassable. And in this condition he went to one of the elders and said: You see before you a man who is completely at rest and has no more temptations. The elder said: Go and pray to the Lord to command some struggle to be stirred up in you, for the soul is matured only in battles. And when temptations started up again he did not pray that the struggle be taken from him, but only said: Lord, give me strength to get through the fight.

—From *A Way in the World* by Ernest Boyer, Jr.

✦ And one day when I had been walking solitarily abroad and was come home, I was taken up in the love of God, so that I could not but admire the greatness of his love. And while I was in that condition it was opened unto me by the eternal Light and power, and I therein saw clearly that all was done and to be done in and by Christ, and how he conquers and destroys this tempter, the Devil and all his works, and is atop of him, and that all these troubles were good for me, and temptations for the trial of my faith which Christ had given me. And the Lord opened me that I saw through all these troubles and temptations. My living faith was raised, that I saw all was done by Christ, the life, and my belief was in him. And when at any time my condition was veiled, my secret belief was stayed firm, and hope underneath held me, as an anchor in the bottom of the sea, and anchored my immortal soul to its Bishop, causing it to swim above the sea, the world where all the raging waves, foul weather, tempests, and temptations are. But oh, then did I see my troubles, trials, and temptations more than ever I had done!

—From *Quaker Spirituality* by George Fox

✦ We are programmed to see temptations as something evil: Lead us not into temptation. It comes as a bit of a surprise then when we read in St. Matthew's Gospel: "Jesus was led by the Spirit out into the wilderness to be tempted by the devil." This is not quite what we would expect the Holy Spirit to do. Temptation insofar as it is an act of the evil one arising out of his envy and hatred is certainly evil. Insofar as it is the good things of the world enticing our disintegrated nature to act in insubordination, it is not good. But for those who love God, all things work together unto good. The challenge can make us grow, give us fuller insight, make us more like our Lord and

Master, who struggled with temptation from the days in the wilderness till he hung naked on the cross and was buffeted with the cry: If you be the Son, come down.

—From *A Place Apart* by M. Basil Pennington

✦ These are moments God uses to put in the heart and the mouth the question, "Is there another way?" When that question is asked, one can begin to hear about the inward journey, or the "narrow gate." But from learning there are two ways— one that leads to death and one to life—it does not follow that we enter by the narrow gate. The facts about the gate are starkly simple.

One, it leads to life, but

Two, it is a hard way, and

Three, few find it.

For those who would be on the inward journey, these are three facts to ponder at the beginning and end of each day. We must cling to the first against temptations, and false prophets, and glittering goals. We must hold to the second lest we be too easily turned aside or corrupted by the illusion that something can be had for nothing. It is part of our sickness that we go after the high prize with so little understanding of the cost and so poorly equipped to meet and withstand the armies that will do battle against us. We do not ask for courage, because we do not know we have need of it. We are given over into the hands of the enemy without having discerned his shape on the horizon.

The man who would step out of the crowd and follow his own destiny, must keep before him the knowledge that the way is hard. But even if he is aware of this, he is still in danger. He must remember, also, that few find it. It will grow easy for him to imagine that he is on the way when he is not. This is where the religious lose out on the Kingdom. They assume that because they are aware of the two ways, and because they have chosen the second, they are on it. This is to fall comfortably into the sleep of the crowd again. It may well be a "religious" crowd, but it is nonetheless a crowd.

—From *Journey Inward, Journey Outward*
by Elizabeth O'Connor

✦ How did the story come to be in the Gospels at all? The Master's fight with Satan happened out in a desert, far from the beaten track and the eyes of men. During those forty days and nights Jesus was utterly alone, with not another soul anywhere near him, not a disciple or a friend or anyone to see what happened and tell the story afterward. Yet the evangelists are able to give a vivid and detailed account. How has that come about? Clearly there is only one explanation: the story came direct from the lips of Christ himself.

Why did Jesus tell it? That chapter of his life was closed; why did he go back and bring it to light? Certainly not to gratify anyone's curiosity. Certainly not to provide additional biographical materials for posterity or to supply an extra chapter in our Gospels. Probably there were two reasons. First, Jesus shared this experience with his disciples in order to help them through their own tempted hours. It does help greatly, as everyone who has ever been tempted knows, to hear of some other's fight and victory. And if that other should be Christ—how mightily it helps! But second, Jesus told this story because the titanic struggle of the desert days and nights had marked his soul forever, and he could never forget. He could see and feel it after months as plainly as if it happened only yesterday—the wild, desolate loneliness, the rocks and crags with the pitiless sun beating down on them by day and the biting wind moaning across them in the dark, the prowling beasts, the famishing hunger, the demon voices whispering to his heart, the grace of God and the angels that had brought him through. Jesus told his disciples of it because he could not help it. It would not hide.

—From *The Life and Teaching of Jesus Christ*
by James Stewart

✦ Why should I want to be rich, when You were poor? Why should I desire to be famous and powerful in the eyes of men, when the sons of those who exalted the false prophets and stoned the true rejected You and nailed You to the Cross? Why should I cherish in my heart a hope that devours me— the hope for perfect happiness in this life—when such hope, doomed to frustration, is nothing but despair?

My hope is in what the eye has never seen. Therefore, let me not trust in visible rewards. My hope is in what the heart of man cannot feel. Therefore let me not trust in the feelings of my heart. My hope is what the hand of man has never touched. Do not let me trust what I can grasp between my fingers. Death will loosen my grasp and my vain hope will be gone.

Let my trust be in Your mercy, not in myself. Let my hope be in Your love, not in health, or strength, or ability or human resources.

—From *Thoughts in Solitude* by Thomas Merton

✦ Christian life is to be throughout a warfare; and that especially when seated in heavenly places in Christ Jesus, we are to wrestle against spiritual enemies there, whose power and skill to tempt us must doubtless be far superior to any we have ever heretofore encountered. As a fact, temptations generally increase in strength tenfold after we have entered into the interior life, rather than decrease. And no amount or sort of them must ever for a moment lead us to suppose we have not really found the true abiding place. Strong temptations are generally a sign of great grace, rather than of little grace.

—From *The Christian's Secret of a Happy Life*
by Hannah Whitall Smith

✦ And the very power of your temptations, dear Christian, therefore, may perhaps be one of the strongest proofs that you really are in the land you have been seeking to enter, because they are temptations peculiar to that land. You must never allow them to cause you to question the fact of your having entered it.

—From *The Christian's Secret of a Happy Life*
by Hannah Whitall Smith

✦ We must not, therefore, despair when we are tempted but pray to God with so much the more fervor, that He may vouchsafe to help us in all tribulations, who, no doubt, according to the saying of St. Paul, will "make such issue with the temptation, that we may be able to bear it." (1 Cor. 10:13)

Let us, therefore, humble our souls under the hand of God in all temptations and tribulations, for the humble in spirit He will save and exalt.

—From *Imitation of Christ* by Thomas à Kempis

23. Distractions

INVOCATION

Lord, let me at least remain open to your initiative; let me wait patiently and attentively for that hour when you will come and break through all the walls I have erected. Teach me, O Lord, to pray. Amen.

Henri J. Nouwen in *A Cry for Mercy*

PSALM 64

DAILY SCRIPTURE

Monday	Luke 6:46–49
Tuesday	2 Timothy 1:1–14
Wednesday	Proverbs 3:1–18
Thursday	Ephesians 6:10–20
Friday	John 5:1–15
Saturday	James 3:13–18
Sunday	Luke 10:38–42

SELECTIONS FOR MEDITATION

PERSONAL MEDITATION

PRAYER

Try to use some of the ways of adoration and meditation to aid you in freeing your mind from all the things that would invade your mind as you would pray.

HYMN   "Sweetly Resting"

In the rifted Rock I'm resting,
Safely sheltered, I abide.
There no foes nor storms molest me,
While within the cleft I hide.

Long pursued by sin and Satan,
Weary, sad, I longed for rest.
Then I found this heavenly shelter
Opened in my Saviour's breast.

Peace which passeth understanding,
Joy the world can never give,
Now in Jesus I am finding;
In His smiles of love I live.
In the rifted Rock I'll hide me
Till the storms of life are past;
All secure in this blest refuge,
Heeding not the fiercest blast.

Now I'm resting, sweetly resting,
In the cleft once made for me.
Jesus, Blessed Rock of Ages,
I will hide myself in Thee.

Mary D. James

BENEDICTION

Father, you are full of compassion, I commit and commend myself unto you, in whom I am, and live, and know. Be the Goal of my pilgrimage, and my Rest by the way. Let my soul take refuge from the crowding turmoil of worldly thoughts beneath the shadow of your wings; let my heart, this sea of restless waves, find peace in you, O God. Amen.

St. Augustine in *Little Book of Prayers*

SELECTIONS FOR MEDITATION

✦ I have already spoken more than once about how this work is to be done. You must not allow your thoughts to wander at random, but as soon as they run away, you must immediately bring them back, reproaching yourself, regretting and deploring this straying of the mind. St. John of the Ladder says of this, "You must make a great effort to confine your mind within the words of prayer."

—From *The Art of Prayer* by Igumen Chariton of Valamo

✦ Most of our conflicts and difficulties come from trying to deal with the spiritual and practical aspects of our life separately instead of realising them as parts of one whole. If our practical life is centered on our own interests, cluttered up by possessions, distracted by ambitions, passions, wants and worries, beset by a sense of our own rights and importance, or anxieties for our own future, or longings for our own success, we need not expect that our spiritual life will be a contrast to all this. The soul's house is not built on such a convenient plan: there are few soundproof partitions in it. Only when the conviction—not merely the idea—that the demand of the Spirit, however inconvenient, comes first and IS first, rules the whole of it, will those objectionable noises die down which have a way of penetrating into the nicely furnished little oratory, and drowning all the quieter voices by their din.

—From *The Spiritual Life* by Evelyn Underhill

◆ Moods are worth attention. I am discovering during these first weeks in Genesee that I am subject to very different moods, often changing very quickly. Feelings of a depressive fatigue, of low self-esteem, of boredom, feelings also of anger, irritation, and direct hostility, and feelings of gratitude, joy, and excitement—they all can be there, sometimes even during one day.

I have the feeling that these quickly changing moods show how attached I really am to the many things given to me: a friendly gesture, pleasant work, a word of praise, a good book, etc. Little things can quickly change sadness into joy, disgust into contentment, and anger into understanding or compassion.

Somewhere during these weeks I read that sadness is the result of attachment. Detached people are not the easy victims of good or bad events in their surroundings and can experience a certain sense of equilibrium. I have the feeling that this is an important realization for me. When my manual work does not interest me, I become bored, then quickly irritated and sometimes even angry, telling myself that I am wasting my time. When I read a book that fascinates me, I become so involved that the time runs fast, people seem friendly, my stay here worthwhile, and everything one big happy event.

Of course, both "moods" are manifestations of false attachments and show how far I am from any healthy form of "indifference."

Thinking about all of this, I guess that my main problem still is that I have not really made prayer my priority. Still the only reason that I am here—I mean, the only reason I should be here—is to learn to pray. But, in fact, much of what I am doing is motivated by many other concerns: getting back in shape, learning some manual skills, knowing more about birds and trees, getting to know interesting people—such as John Eudes—and picking up many ideas and experiences for future teaching. But if prayer were my only concern, all these other laudable things could be received as free gifts. Now, however, I am obsessed by these desires which are false, not in themselves, but by their being in the wrong place in the hierarchy of values. That, I guess, is the cause of my moodiness. For the time being it seems so important to be at least aware of it.

—From *The Genesee Diary* by Henri J. Nouwen

◆ A great woman of the last century . . . was accustomed to say . . . : "Think glorious thoughts of God—and serve Him with a quiet mind!" And it is surely a fact that the more glorious and more spacious our thoughts of Him are, the greater the quietude and confidence with which we do our detailed work will be. Not controversial thoughts, or narrow conventional thoughts, or dry academic thoughts, or anxious worried thoughts. All these bring contraction instead of expansion to our souls; and we all know that this inner sense of contraction or expansion is an unfailing test of our spiritual state. But awed and delighted thoughts of a Reality and Holiness that is inconceivable to us, and yet that is Love. A Reality that pours itself out in and through the simplest forms and accidents, and makes itself known under the homeliest symbols; that is completely present in and with us, determining us at every moment of our lives. Such meditations as these keep our windows open towards Eternity; and preserve us from that insidious pious stuffiness which is the moth and rust of the dedicated life.

—From *The House of the Soul and Concerning the Inner Life* by Evelyn Underhill

✦ With this retreat has come the insight and will to act more effectively for the control of thoughts and purity of heart. Thank you, Lord. It seems strange now that the same "insight" and will was not previously present in me. It underlies the mystery of his grace and my weakness of mind and will coming from sin—original and personal. What before was perceived in a sort of vague way as not being all that it should be, but not clearly seen as something that should be effectively excluded, with the coming of grace is seen as wrong, contrary to what I really want, and is excluded with relative ease. Yet, with a clear consciousness that it is so by his grace, that without grace it would be as before, I would be letting these thoughts, this pesty swarm of flies, as William of Saint Thierry calls them, spoil the sweetness of the ointment, the devotion of mind and heart. How completely we are dependent on the coming and abiding presence of his grace.

—From *O Holy Mountain!* by M. Basil Pennington

✦ Many a one has turned to his inner chamber, under bitter self-accusation that he has prayed so little, and has resolved for the future to live in a different manner. Yet no blessing has come—there was not the strength to continue faithful, and the call to repentance had no power, because his eyes had not been fixed on the Lord Jesus. If he had only understood, he would have said: "Lord, Thou seest how cold and dark my heart is: I know that I must pray, but I feel that I can not do so; I lack the urgency and desire to pray."

He did not know that at that moment the Lord Jesus in His tender love was looking down upon him and saying: "You cannot pray; you feel that all is cold and dark: why not give yourself over into My hands? Only believe that I am ready to help you in prayer; I long greatly to shed abroad My love in your heart, so that you, in the consciousness of weakness, may confidently rely on Me to bestow the grace of prayer. Just as I will cleasne you from all other sins, so also will I deliver you from the sin of prayerlessness—only do not seek the victory in your own strength. Bow before Me as one who expects everything from his Saviour. Let your soul keep silence before Me, however sad you feel your state to be. Be assured of this—I will teach you how to pray."

—From *The Prayer Life* by Andrew Murray

✦ We have been speaking of the privilege of prayer, the supreme opportunity of friendship with God kept vital by deliberate communion, and we may well stop now to count the cost. Paul is typical of all Christian seers in discovering that the "excellency of the knowledge of Christ Jesus" is not arrived at without counting some things loss. It does cost to win a life that really can pray. Vasari says that Raphael used to wear a candle in a pasteboard cap, so that, while he was painting, his shadow would not fall upon his work. Many a man's prayers are spoiled by his own shadow. There are things in his life which must be given up if ever he is truly to pray. He must wear on his forehead the candle of renunciation for his work's sake. Consider the evil attitudes, cherished sins, bad tempers in your life that make praying in any deep and earnest way a difficult undertaking.

—From *The Meaning of Prayer* by Harry Emerson Fosdick

✦ Just as the silence seems complete, a noise or other sensation may intrude. Or an interruption may come purely from within, perhaps an idea about tomorrow's plans or a worry about a foolish remark or something one has forgotten to do. It does no good at all to get angry. This only adds to the activity that is trying to break in. With good-natured patience, one puts the cares of yesterday and tomorrow into the suspense file, much as St. Teresa told of doing. One day, trying to become still in the chapel, the saint noticed that the altar hangings were crooked. "How careless the sacristan is!" she said to herself. "I must. . . . No, I am here to pray, not to tell the sacristan what to do." With a smile she quieted down again, only to hear a sharp noise on the roof where some tiles were being replaced. "That careless workman!" she thought. "I had better get out there. No mere man could do it right. . . . No, not now." And once more she turned to rebuild the silence.

. . . This kind of silence cannot be hurried or forced; it does not come through effort. Instead, it must be allowed to happen. This is like eating an artichoke. It must be done one leaf at a time, down to the heart. If one tries to take it in a single bite, all he gets is a mouthful of thistles. One has to set aside time for silence and then turn toward it with composure, letting go of immediate things a little at a time in order to enter a world where dreams and also the energy for life are born.

—From *The Other Side of Silence* by Morton T. Kelsey

✦ It often seems to those in earnest about the right as if all things conspired to prevent their progress. This, of course, is but an appearance, arising in part from this, that the pilgrim must be headed back from the sidepaths into which he is constantly wandering.

—From *An Anthology of George MacDonald.*
Edited by C. S. Lewis

✦ You tell me nothing new; you are not the only one who is troubled with wandering thoughts. Our mind is extremely roving; but, as the will is the mistress of all our faculties, she must recall them, and carry them to God as their last end.

When the mind, for want of being sufficiently reduced by recollection at our first engaging in devotion, has contracted certain bad habits of wandering and dissipation, they are difficult to overcome, and commonly draw us, even against our wills, to the things of the earth.

I believe one remedy for this is to confess our faults and to humble ourselves before God. I do not advise you to use multiplicity of words in prayer, many words and long discourses being often the occasions of wandering. Hold yourself in prayer before God like a dumb or paralytic beggar at a rich man's gate. Let it be your business to keep your mind in the presence of the Lord. If it sometimes wanders and withdraws itself from Him, do not much disquiet yourself for that; trouble and disquiet serve rather to distract the mind than to recollect it; the will must bring it back in tranquillity. If you persevere in this manner, God will have pity on you.

—From *The Practice of the Presence of God*
by Brother Lawrence

24. Anxiety

O God! who is able and willing to assist me, what grounds have I not to place my whole confidence in you, to throw myself into the arms of your providence, and wait the effects of your bounty? You have care of all. I will therefore give myself up entirely to you, live always in your presence, and ever guide myself by your fear and love. It is this grace I now ask of you, the God of my heart, and my portion forever. Grant me to weigh well and to follow your admonition: "Be not solicitous, for your heavenly Father knoweth that you have need of all these things." Amen.

The Book of Common Prayer

PSALM 142

DAILY SCRIPTURE

Monday	Philippians 4:6–7
Tuesday	Matthew 5:25–34
Wednesday	Luke 12:1–12
Thursday	Matthew 13:1–23
Friday	Luke 11:38–42
Saturday	Luke 21:34–36
Sunday	1 Peter 5:6

SELECTIONS FOR MEDITATION

PERSONAL MEDITATION

PRAYER

Can you identify your greatest fear? And could you confess it to God? If you keep it hidden within you he can never cleanse it, much less use it to his glory. Offer your fears and anxieties to him this week.

HYMN   "Come, Thou Long-expected Jesus"

> Come, Thou long-expected Jesus,
> Born to set Thy people free.
> From our fears and sins release us;
> Let us find our rest in Thee.
> Israel's Strength and Consolation,
> Hope of all the earth Thou art;
> Dear Desire of every nation,
> Joy of every longing heart!
>
> Born Thy people to deliver,
> Born a child and yet a King,
> Born to reign in us forever,
> Now Thy gracious kingdom bring.
> By Thine own eternal Spirit
> Rule in all our heart alone;
> By Thine all sufficient merit,
> Raise us to Thy glorious throne.
>
> Charles Wesley

BENEDICTION

O God, who is the life of all who live, the light of the faithful, the strength of those who labor, and the repose of the dead: I thank you for the timely blessings of the day, and humbly beseech your merciful protection all the night. Bring me, I pray, in safety to the morning hours; through him who died for me and rose again, your Son my Savior Jesus Christ. Amen.

The Book of Common Prayer

SELECTIONS FOR MEDITATION

✦ There is a sense of wholeness at the core of man
  That must abound in all he does;
  That marks with reverence his ev'ry step;
  That has its sway when all else fails;
  That wearies out all evil things;
  That warms the depth of frozen fears
  Making friend of foe,
  Making love of hate,

And lasts beyond the living and the dead,
Beyond the goals of peace, the ends of war!
This man seeks through all his years:
To be complete and of one piece, within, without.
　　　　—From *The Inward Journey* by Howard Thurman

◆ I meant to accomplish a good bit today. Instead I keep thinking: Will the next generations of people remember to drain the pipes in the fall? I will leave them a note.
　　　　—From *Teaching a Stone to Talk* by Annie Dillard

◆ To preserve peace in time of trouble our will must remain firm in God and be ever directed towards Him, that is, we should be disposed to receive all things from the hand of God, from His justice, and from His bounty, with humble submission to His blessed will. Good and evil, health and sickness, prosperity and adversity, consolation and dryness, temptation and tranquility, interior sweetness, trials, and chastisements, all should be received by the soul with humility, patience, and resignation, as coming to us by the appointment of God. This is the only means of finding peace in the midst of great troubles and adversities.
　　　　—From *Imitation of Christ* by Thomas à Kempis

◆ The next hour, the next moment, is as much beyond our grasp and as much in God's care, as that a hundred years away. Care for the next minute is just as foolish as care for the morrow, or for a day in the next thousand years—in neither can we do anything, in both God is doing everything. Those claims only of the morrow which have to be repeated today are of the duty of today: the moment which coincides with work to be done, is the moment to be minded; the next is nowhere till God has made it.
　　　　—From *An Anthology of George MacDonald.*
　　　　Edited by C. S. Lewis

✦ Troubled soul, thou art not bound to feel but thou art bound to arise. God loves thee whether thou feelest or not. Thou canst not love when thou wilt, but thou art bound to fight the hatred in thee to the last. Try not to feel good when thou art not good, but to cry to Him who is good. He changes not because thou changest. Nay, He has an especial tenderness of love toward thee for that thou art in the dark and hast no light, and His heart is glad when thou doest arise and say, "I will go to my Father." . . . Fold the arms of thy faith, and wait in the quietness until light goes up in thy darkness. For the arms of thy Faith I say, but not of thy Action: bethink thee of something that thou oughtest to do, and go to do it, if it be but the sweeping of a room, or the preparing of a meal, or a visit to a friend. Heed not thy feeling: Do thy work.

—From *An Anthology of George MacDonald.*
Edited by C. S. Lewis

✦ All growth in the spiritual life is connected with the clearer insight into what Jesus is to us. The more I realize that Christ must be all to me and in me, that all in Christ is indeed for me, the more I learn to live the real life of faith, which, dying to self, lives wholly in Christ. The Christian life is no longer the vain struggle to live right, but the resting in Christ and finding strength in Him as our life, to fight the fight and gain the victory of faith.

—From *With Christ in the School of Prayer*
by Andrew Murray

✦ And remember, there are two things which are more utterly incompatible than even oil and water, and these two are trust and worry. Would you call it trust if you should give something into the hands of a friend to attend to for you, and then should spend your nights and days in anxious thought and worry as to whether it would be rightly and successfully done? And can you call it trust, when you have given the saving and keeping of your soul into the hands of the Lord, if day after day, and night after night you are spending hours of anxious thought and questionings about the matter? When a believer really trusts anything, he ceases to worry about that thing which he has trusted. And when he worries, it is plain proof that he does not trust.

—From *The Christian's Secret of a Happy Life*
by Hannah Whitall Smith

✦ You find no difficulty in trusting the Lord with the management of the universe, and all the outward creation, and can your case be any more complex or difficult than these, that you need to be anxious or troubled about His management of you? Away with such unworthy doubtings! Take your stand on the power and trustworthiness of your God, and see how quickly all difficulties will vanish before a steadfast determination to believe. Trust in the dark, trust in the light, trust at night and trust in the morning, and you will find that the faith which may begin by mighty effort, will end sooner or later by becoming the easy and natural habit of the soul.

—From *The Christian's Secret of a Happy Life*
by Hannah Whitall Smith

✦ The man who prays raises the question of what the limits of hope may be. Prayer is his way of declaring that the boundaries of life and the limits of hope cannot be drawn with the crayons of time and space. The man who prays pushes hope into areas where men who never dream never venture. And so it is not difficult for him to believe. He believes his prayer reaches God and that it influences reality although never in a strict cause-effect relationship. Prayer is successful not in terms of what it logically produces or pragmatically achieves but in terms of what it forces reality to experience.

—From *Dawn Without Darkness* by Anthony Padovano

✦ Once, as a young man full of exuberant fancy, I undertook to draw up a catalogue of the acknowledged "goods" of life. As other men sometimes tabulate lists of properties they own or would like to own, I set down my inventory of earthly desirables: health, love, beauty, talent, power, riches, and fame—together with several minor ingredients of what I considered man's perfect portion.

When my inventory was completed I proudly showed it to a wise elder who had been the mentor and spiritual model of my youth. Perhaps I was trying to impress him with my precocious wisdom and the universality of my interests. Anyway, I handed him the list. "This," I told him confidently, "is the sum of mortal goods. Could a man possess them all, he would be as a god."

At the corner of my friend's old eyes, I saw wrinkles of amusement gathering in a patient net. "An excellent list," he said, pondering it thoughtfully. "Well digested in content and set down in not-unreasonable order. But it appears, my young friend, that you have omitted the most important element of all. You have forgotten the one ingredient lacking which each possession becomes a hideous torment, and your list as a whole an intolerable burden."

"And what," I asked, peppering my voice with truculence, "is that missing ingredient?"

With a pencil stub he crossed out my entire schedule. Then, having demolished my adolescent dream structure at a single stroke, he wrote down three syllables: peace of mind.

"This is the gift that God reserves for His special proteges," he said. "Talent and beauty He gives to many. Wealth is commonplace, fame not rare. But peace of mind—that is His final guerdon of approval, the fondest sign of His love. He bestows it charily. Most men are never blessed with it; others wait all their lives—yes, far into advanced age—for this gift to descend upon them."

—From *Peace of Mind* by Joshua L. Liebman

✦ Be not anxious! Earthly possessions dazzle our eyes and delude us into thinking that they can provide security and freedom from anxiety. Yet all the time they are the very source of all anxiety. If our hearts are set on them, our reward is an anxiety whose burden is intolerable. Anxiety creates its own treasures and they in turn beget further care. When we seek for security in possessions we are trying to drive out care with care and the net result is the precise opposite of our anticipations. The fetters which bind us to our possessions prove to be cares themselves.

—From *The Cost of Discipleship* by Dietrich Bonhoeffer

✦ If then we add to the littleness of man the inexpressible shortness of his duration, is it any wonder that a man of reflection should sometimes feel a kind of fear, lest the great, eternal, infinite Governor of the universe should disregard so diminutive a creature as man—a creature so every way inconsiderable, when compared either with immensity or eternity?

. . . But how may we prevent this uneasy reflection, and effectually cure this fear? . . . by considering that the body is not the man; that man is not only a house of clay, but an immortal spirit; a spirit made in the image of God; a spirit that is of infinitely more value than the whole earth; yea, than the whole material creation. Consider that the spirit of man is not only of a higher order, of a more excellent nature, than any part of the visible world, but also more durable; not liable either to dissolution or decay.

—From *The Message of the Wesleys.*
Compiled by Philip S. Watson

✦ A few years ago I met an old professor at the University of Notre Dame. Looking back on his long life of teaching, he said with a funny wrinkle in his eyes: "I have always been complaining that my work was constantly interrupted, until I slowly discovered that my interruptions were my work."

That is the great conversion in our life: to recognize and believe that the many unexpected events are not just disturbing interruptions of our projects, but the way in which God molds our hearts and prepares us for his return. Our great temptations are boredom and bitterness. When our good plans are interrupted by poor weather, our well-organized careers by illness or bad luck, our peace of mind by inner turmoil, our hope for peace by a new war, our desire for a stable government by a constant changing of the guards, and our desire for immortality by real death, we are tempted to give in to a paralyzing boredom or to strike back in destructive bitterness. But when we believe that patience can make our expectations grow, then fate can be converted into a vocation, wounds into a call for deeper understanding, and sadness into a birthplace for joy.

—From *Out of Solitude* by Henri J. Nouwen

25. Consciousness

INVOCATION

Let me know you, O Lord, who knows me; let me know you as I am known. Enter into my soul and fit it for yourself so that you may have it and hold it without spot or wrinkle. This is my hope. Amen.

St. Augustine in *Confessions*

PSALM 104

DAILY SCRIPTURE

Monday	Isaiah 32:14–20
Tuesday	1 John 3:19–4:6
Wednesday	Philippians 4:2–9
Thursday	Romans 8:26–27
Friday	1 John 5:1–12
Saturday	1 Corinthians 2:6–16
Sunday	Acts 9:1–9

SELECTIONS FOR MEDITATION

PERSONAL MEDITATION

PRAYER

Everything is clamoring to become a part of you. You must carefully choose the things and thoughts you will allow to get inside. Ask God to begin to cleanse your consciousness. Then determine in prayer that you will guard the threshold of your mind.

HYMN   "Prayer Is the Soul's Sincere Desire"

Pray'r is the soul's sincere desire,
Uttered or unexpressed;
The motion of a hidden fire
That trembles in the breast.

Pray'r is the burden of a sigh,
The falling of a tear,
The upward glancing of an eye,
When none but God is near.

Pray'r is the simplest form of speech
That infant lips can try;
Pray'r the sublimest strains that reach
The majesty on high.
. . . . .
Pray'r is the Christian's vital breath,
The Christian's native air,
His watchword at the gates of death;
He enters heav'n with prayer.

James Montgomery

BENEDICTION

Father, protect me from the onslaught of things, both good and evil, that will bid for my attention this day. Make me to remember that all that I allow inside my heart will become some part of me as I pray. Let me come to you in singleness of heart and purity of desire. In the name of Christ. Amen.

SELECTIONS FOR MEDITATION

✦ . . . the consciousness of man can enter into a living, knowledge-communicating, life-transforming relationship with God. Obviously the consciousness of such a relationship would not be possible if the human consciousness can be aware only of what the eyes see and the ears hear and the hands touch and the tongue tastes and the nostrils smell. For no human eye has seen God, nor ear has heard His voice, no hands have touched the hand of God, no tongue has tasted Him, no nostril has breathed in His fragrance. Inside and outside the Bible, the language of religion employs terminology which suggests such experiences, but it is, as we all know, a metaphorical use of words. "No man hath seen God at any time."

God is a legitimate inference from events. That is why of late, especially, men declare that the method of revelation is in deeds, not in words. God acts and men interpret that action as divine and infer meanings which are divine.

But God may also be an immediate object of consciousness. That is what the great mystics and a multitude of humbler folk have declared. They have not merely studied events in history and concluded that God was in action there and reached a conclusion as to the meaning of that action. They have been as vividly aware of God as they were of any human with whom they have had fellowship. In that awareness they have had old ideas challenged and new ideas come to birth. They have been purged of old emotions and felt the surge of new and creative ones. They have become certain of inner transformations begun and carried on, as they have from time to time renewed their conscious contacts with God. They have become aware of an ever-deepening oneness with God which, among the greatest of them, made them affirm humbly but joyously, as did Teresa of Avila, "There is nothing in me that is not God: my 'me' is God."

—From *An Autobiography of Prayer* by Albert E. Day

✦ Prayer is the microcosm of the soul. It is the whole soul in one moment; the quintessence of all our acts; the climax of all our thoughts. It rises as high as our thoughts. Now, if the Torah is nothing but the national literature of the Jewish people; if the mystery of revelation is discarded as superstition, then prayer is hardly more than a soliloquy. If God does not have power to speak to us, how should we possess the power to speak to Him? Thus, prayer is part of a greater issue. It depends upon the total spiritual situation of man and upon a mind within which God is at home. Of course, if our lives are too barren to bring forth the spirit of worship; if all our thoughts and anxieties do not contain enough spiritual substance to be distilled into prayer, an inner transformation is a matter of emergency. And such an emergency we face today. "The issue of prayer is not prayer; the issue of prayer is God." One cannot pray unless he has faith in his own ability to accost the infinite, merciful, eternal God.

—From *Man's Quest for God* by Abraham Joshua Heschel

✦ It is a simple story, simply told. One day, a man walked into an antique shop and asked permission to look around. It was a rather exclusive shop frequented only by those who could afford to purchase articles made rare by their scarcity and age. The visitor seemed strangely out of place because he was poorly dressed though clean; indeed it was clear from his appearance that he was a laborer whose face had been etched by sun and rain and whose hands were rough and worn. After more than a half hour, he left. In about ten days he returned. This time he found a very beautiful piece of glass and asked if he could make a deposit on it. Each week he made a payment, until at last the article was his. With much curiosity, the owner of the shop engaged him in conversation to determine, if he could, the use to which such a man would put his new purchase. "I bought it for my little room. It isn't much, but I bring to it, from time to time, through the years, only the very best and beautiful things. You see, that is where I live." To bring to the place where you live only the best and most beautiful—what a plan for one's life! This is well within the reach of everyone. Think of using one's memory in that way. As one lives from day to day, there are all sorts of experiences, good, bad, beautiful, ugly, that become a part of one's past. To develop the ability to screen one's memory so that only the excellent is retained for one's own room! All kinds of ideas pass through one's mind, about oneself, about the world, about people. Which do you keep for your own room? Think it over now; which ideas do you keep for the place where you live? It is well within the mark to say that the oft-quoted words of Jesus, about laying up for yourself treasures in heaven, deal with this same basic idea. The place where you live is where your treasures are. Where your treasures are is where your heart is. Where your heart is, is where your God is.

    —From *Deep Is the Hunger* by Howard Thurman

✦ It is good to experience the quiet ministry of the living spirit of the living God. Again and again there are the little healings of silent breaches which sustain us in our contacts with the world and with one another. We are stunned by the little word, the unexpected silence, the smile off key; without quite knowing why, the balance is recovered and the rhythm of the hurt is stopped in its place. There is the sense of estrangement which overtakes the happiest human relations and the experience of recovery that makes the heart sing its old song with a new lilt. There are days when everything seems difficult, when the ordinary tasks become major undertakings, when one is sensitive and every moment is threatened by an explosion that does not quite come to pass; then without apparent cause, the whole picture changes and the spirit can breathe again with ease, the spring in the step comes back again. It is good to experience the quiet ministry of the living spirit of the living God.

Sometimes we are catapulted into disaster with a suddenness that paralyzes the mind and leaves the exposure to fear unshielded by courage or by strength. If there had been some warning, some intimation of what was to come, the wisdom of the years could have buttressed the life with a measured protection. But no, this was not the case. Often even before the full awareness of what has taken place can be felt, the realignment of one's powers begins to work and recovery is on the way. There are problems that meet us head-on in our journey. The issue of our spirit and the thing that confronts us is joined—we are engulfed in the great silence of fateful struggle. It seems that nowhere, in no place, can an answer be found. In vain we seek a clue, a key, even a little thing to give a fleeting respite, a second wind. Again and again it is apt to happen: the miracle of relief; a chance word from a casual conversation; a sentiment or a line in a letter; the refrain of an old song; an image from the past; a paragraph from a printed page; a stirring of prayer in the heart—the miracle of relief and we are released. The danger is passed, the conflict is over. It is good, so very good, to experience the quiet ministry of the living spirit of the living God.

—From *The Inward Journey* by Howard Thurman

✦ When a pond is greatly agitated by the breezes and the wind, one can throw in a pebble or even many pebbles and there is no noticeable effect. When a pond is perfectly at peace and one casts a pebble into it, the gentle waves spread in every direction till they reach even the farthest shore. When we are in the midst of a busy everyday life, so many thoughts go in and out of our minds and our hearts, we don't perceive the effect they are having upon us. But when we come to achieve a deeper inner quiet, then we are much more discerning. The way is open to follow even the most gentle leadings of the Spirit and to avoid even the most subtle deviations that are suggested either by the self or by the evil one.

—From *Centering Prayer* by M. Basil Pennington

✦ How, then, shall we lay hold of that Life and Power, and live the life of prayer without ceasing? By quiet, persistent practice in turning of all our being, day and night, in prayer and inward worship and surrender, toward Him who calls in the deeps of our souls. Mental habits of inward orientation must be established. An inner, secret turning to God can be made fairly steady, after weeks and months and years of practice and lapses and failures and returns. It is as simple an art as Brother Lawrence found it, but it may be long before we achieve any steadiness in the process. Begin now, as you read these words, as you sit in your chair, to offer your whole selves, utterly and in joyful abandon, in quiet, glad surrender to Him who is within.

—From *A Testament of Devotion* by Thomas R. Kelly

✦ "In the beginning," John Eudes said, "your thoughts will wander, but after a while you will discover that it becomes easier to stay quietly in the presence of the Lord. If your head seems filled with worries and concerns, you might like to start with some psalms or a Scripture reading that can help you to concentrate and then you will be better prepared for silent meditation. When you are faithful in this, you will slowly experience yourself in a deeper way. Because in this useless hour in which you do nothing 'important' or 'urgent,' you have come to terms with your basic powerlessness, you have to feel your fundamental inability to solve your or other people's problems or to change the world. When you do not avoid that experience but live through it, you will find out that your many projects, plans, and obligations become less urgent, crucial, and important and lose their power over you. They will leave you free during your time with God and take their appropriate place in your life."

— From *The Genesee Diary* by Henri J. Nouwen

◆ Thanks to modern psychology we know so much more than we once did about the nature of consciousness. We know, therefore, what is necessary to emancipate consciousness from the earthly and human tyrannies which keep it unaware of God.

We can now evolve our disciplines intelligently, with a relevance to the plight of our consciousness. We no longer need to strike out blindly in the hope of doing something now and then that will hasten our deliverance from "the world, the flesh, and the devil."

We know our consciousness, and knowing we can act wisely with reference to it. We know what keeps us from knowing God. We know what we can do to end that unknowing and to clear the way to the beatific vision.

— From *Discipline and Discovery* by Albert E. Day

26. Time Management

It is time, O Lord, I should cast myself on your mercy to obtain the pardon of my sins and your love, to follow all its attractions. Support me, O Lord, and strengthen me by your grace against the inclinations of nature and self-love, for of myself it is impossible to resist and conquer the motions of corrupt nature which is ever seeking its own gratification in direct opposition to your holy will. Amen.

PSALM 145

DAILY SCRIPTURE

Monday	Ecclesiastes 3:1–8
Tuesday	Psalm 90:12
Wednesday	2 Corinthians 5:18–6:2
Thursday	Job 7:1–10
Friday	Psalm 39:4–6
Saturday	James 4:13–17
Sunday	Ephesians 5:10–17

SELECTIONS FOR MEDITATION

PERSONAL MEDITATION

PRAYER

The hassle with being a better manager of your time is making the decisions about what is now most important and what is no longer as important. But if you will ask God what he'd remove if it were his life, he would gladly tell you.

HYMN   "Take Time to Be Holy"

> Take time to be holy.
> Speak oft with thy Lord;

Abide in Him always,
And feed on His Word.
Make friends with God's children;
Help those who are weak,
Forgetting in nothing
His blessing to seek. . . .
William D. Longstaff

BENEDICTION

O Christ, when I look at you I see that you were never in a hurry, never ran, but always had time for the pressing necessities of the day. Give me that disciplined, poised life with time always for the thing that matters. For I would be a disciplined person. Amen.

E. Stanley Jones in *The Way*

SELECTIONS FOR MEDITATION

✦ First of all I would like to draw your attention to something which we all know and we all discuss. There is absolutely no need to run after time to catch it. It does not run away from us, it runs towards us. Whether you are intent on the next minute coming your way, or whether you are completely unaware of it, it will come your way. The future, whatever you do about it, will become the present, and so there is no need to try to jump out of the present into the future. We can simply wait for it to be there, and in that respect we can perfectly well be completely stable and yet move in time, because it is time that moves. . . . The mistake we often make with our inner life is to imagine that if we hurry we will be in our future sooner—a little like the man who ran from the last carriage of the train to the first, hoping that the distance between London and Edinburgh would be shortened as a result. When it is that kind of example we see how absurd it is, but when we continually try to live an inch ahead of ourselves, we do not feel the absurdity of it. Yet that is what prevents us from being completely in the present moment, which I dare say is the only moment in which we can be, because even if we imagine that we are ahead of time or ahead of ourselves, we are not. The only thing is that we are in a hurry, but we are not moving more quickly for this. You must have seen that more than once. Someone with two heavy suitcases, trying to catch a bus, rushes: he is as quick as he can be, he runs as fast as the suitcases allow, and he is all intent on being where he is not.

But you know what happens when we take a walk on a holiday. We can walk briskly, gaily and quickly, or if we are of the right age and condition, we can even run, but we don't feel in a hurry at all, because what matters at that moment is the running, not the arriving. This is the kind of thing we must learn about prayer, to establish ourselves in the present.

—From *Beginning to Pray* by Anthony Bloom

✦ What can we do? This is the first exercise. It can be done at moments when you have absolutely nothing to do, when nothing pulls you either backward or forward and when you can use five minutes, three minutes or half an hour for leisure and for doing nothing. You sit down and say, "I am seated, I am doing nothing, I will do nothing for five minutes," and then relax, and continually throughout this time (one or two minutes is the most you will be able to endure to begin with) realise, "I am here in the presence of God, in my own presence and in the presence of all the furniture that is around me, just still, moving nowhere." There is, of course, one more thing you must do: you must decide that within these two minutes, five minutes, which you have assigned to learning that the present exists, you will not be pulled out of it by the telephone, by a knock on the door, or by a sudden upsurge of energy that prompts you to do at once what you have left undone for the past ten years. So you settle down and say "Here I am," and you are. If you learn to do this at lost moments of your life when you have learned not to fidget inwardly, but to be completely calm and happy, stable and serene, then extend the few minutes to a longer time and then to a little while longer still. A moment will come, of course, when you will require some defenses, because you can sit quietly for two minutes even if the telephone does ring or someone knocks at the door, whereas fifteen minutes may be too long for either the telephone to ring or for the person to stand at the door. But then make up your mind that if you were not at home you would not open the door, nor would you answer the telephone. Or, if you have more courage, or are more convinced of what you are doing, you can do what my father did. He had a little note on the door saying "Don't go to the trouble of knocking. I am at home but I will not open the door." This is a way which is much more decisive, because people understand it at once, whereas if you say "Kindly wait five minutes," the kindness usually dies out within two minutes!

Then when you have learned this stability, this serenity, you will have to learn to stop time not only at moments when it drags or has stopped anyway, but at moments when it rushes, when it puts forward claims. The way to do it is this. You are doing something which you feel is useful; you feel that unless this is done the world will falter on its course; and then if at a certain moment you say "I stop," you will discover many things. First you will discover that the world does not falter and that the whole world—if you can imagine it—can wait for five minutes while you are not busy with it. This is important, because we usually deceive ourselves, saying "Well, I must do it: it is charity, it is duty, I cannot leave it undone." You can, because at moments of sheer laziness you will leave it undone for much longer than the five minutes you have chosen. So the first thing to say is: "Whatever happens, I stop here." The simplest way to do it is to have an alarm clock. Wind it and say "Now I am working without looking at the clock until it rings." That is very important; one of the things which we must unlearn, is looking at the clock. If you are walking somewhere and are aware that you are late, you look at your watch. But you cannot walk as quickly while you look at your wrist as if you simply look straight ahead. And whether you are aware that it is seven minutes or five minutes or three minutes, you are nonetheless late. So add a starting time and you will be there on time, or else if you are late, walk as fast and as briskly as you can. When you are at the door, have a look to see how contrite you must look when the door is opened! Then, when the alarm clock goes off, you know that for the next five minutes the world has come to an end and you will not move from the spot. It is God's own time and you settle back in His own time quietly, silently and peacefully.

—From *Beginning to Pray* by Anthony Bloom

✦ We do not all have the flexibility in our lives to be able to make the time and establish the space for a weekly day of apartness. But, let's be very realistic here. There is in the lives of most of us a good bit more freedom and flexibility to organize such a dimension, if we really want to.

—From *A Place Apart* by M. Basil Pennington

✦ If we ask of the saints how they achieved spiritual effectiveness, they are only able to reply that, insofar as they did it themselves, they did it by love and prayer. A love that is very humble and homely; a prayer that is full of adoration and of confidence. Love and prayer, on their lips, are not mere nice words; they are the names of tremendous powers, able to transform in a literal sense human personality and make it more and more that which it is meant to be—the agent of the Holy Spirit in the world. Plainly then, it is essential to give time or to get time somehow for self-training in this love and this prayer, in order to develop those powers. It is true that in their essence they are "given," but the gift is only fully made our own by a patient and generous effort of the soul. Spiritual achievement costs much, though never as much as it is worth. It means at the very least the painful development and persevering, steady exercise of a faculty that most of us have allowed to get slack. It means an inward if not an outward asceticism: a virtual if not an actual mysticism.

—From *The House of the Soul and Concerning the Inner Life* by Evelyn Underhill

✦ Once we begin wisely allotting time for reading and reflection, wondering and writing, we shall soon notice the reward. Life becomes less pressured. Christ, not the clock on the wall, becomes the center of our lives. Amazingly, we seem to accomplish more because our energy is not siphoned into pockets of useless worry. What a joy it is to make time our servant instead of our becoming enslaved to time.

—From *Pathways of Spiritual Living*
by Susan Annette Muto

✦ Since meditation on the Scriptures, prayer, and intercession are a service we owe and because the grace of God is found in this service, we should train ourselves to set apart a regular hour for it, as we do for every other service we perform. This is not "legalism"; it is orderliness and fidelity. . . . We have a right to this time, even prior to the claims of other people, and we may insist upon having it as a completely undisturbed quiet time despite all external difficulties. . . . Who can really be faithful in great things if he has not learned to be faithful in the things of daily life?

—From *Life Together* by Dietrich Bonhoeffer

✦ Another thing which commonly stifles prayer is men's business. The days become so full that prayer gets crowded out. Sometimes when that happens, the plea is urged in extenuation that work itself is prayer, that honest work is indeed one of the highest kinds of prayer which can ever be offered, and that, therefore, the crowding out of the devotional hour does not really matter much. But look at Jesus. Busy and crowded as our days are, his were emphatically more so. Read the opening chapters of Mark's Gospel. There you have a number of pictures of typical days in Jesus' ministry, days that were quite usual and normal for Jesus; and as you study these pictures and see how one duty was heaped upon another, how sick people and broken sinners came clamoring for him until far into the night and none of them were sent away unhelped, you can almost see the virtue going out of him and can realize something of the strain and the drain of it; and yet the harder the days were, the more time did Jesus make for prayer.

—From *The Life and Teaching of Jesus Christ*
by James Stewart

✦ This morning I put this question to John Eudes: "How can I really develop a deeper prayer life when I am back again at my busy work? I have the tendency to finish small and large jobs as soon as possible, and as long as I remain surrounded by unfinished tasks, my prayer is nearly impossible since I use the time for prayer to wonder about the many things I still have to do. It always seems that there is something more urgent and more important than prayer."

John Eudes' answer was clear and simple: "The only solution is a prayer schedule that you will never break without consulting your spiritual director. Set a time that is reasonable, and once it is set, stick to it at all costs. Make it your most important task. Let everyone know that this is the only thing you will not change and pray at that time. One hour in the morning before work and a half hour before you go to bed might be a good start. Set the exact time and hold on to it. Leave a party when that time approaches. Simply make it an impossibility to do any type of work, even if it seems urgent, important, and crucial. When you remain faithful, you slowly discover that it is useless to think about your many problems since they won't be dealt with in that time anyhow. Then you start saying to yourself during these free hours, 'Since I have nothing to do now, I might just as well pray!' So praying becomes as important as eating and sleeping, and the time set free for it becomes a very liberating time to which you become attached in the good sense."
—From *The Genesee Diary* by Henri J. Nouwen

27. Place

Dear Father, let me seek and find you in this place of prayer. May your presence become so clear to me that I will also recognize you in all the places I may be today. Amen.

PSALM 11

DAILY SCRIPTURE

Monday	Hebrews 10:19–27
Tuesday	Mark 1:35–39
Wednesday	Acts 1:1–11
Thursday	Genesis 13:1–18
Friday	2 Samuel 24:18–25
Saturday	Luke 14:7–14
Sunday	Matthew 6:5–14

SELECTIONS FOR MEDITATION

PERSONAL MEDITATION

PRAYER

Let your prayers this week be that God will direct you to some particular place for your regular prayer and that he will make it a sacred and holy place for you.

HYMN   "Near to the Heart of God"

There is a place of quiet rest,
Near to the heart of God;
A place where sin cannot molest,
Near to the heart of God.

There is a place of comfort sweet,
Near to the heart of God;

A place where we our Savior meet,
Near to the heart of God.

There is a place of full release,
Near to the heart of God;
A place where all is joy and peace,
Near to the heart of God.

O Jesus, blest redeemer,
Sent from the heart of God,
Hold us, who wait before Thee,
Near to the heart of God.
C. B. McAfee

BENEDICTION

Father, teach me your Kingdom is all about me, teach me it is within me, teach me so that I may withdraw into it and so that I may live my life centered there. Amen.

SELECTIONS FOR MEDITATION

✦ Cells, as the monks call their rooms, have nothing to do with prison cells. "Cell" comes from the Latin word cella, related to the word coelum, heaven, the place where one enjoys God.
—From *A Place Apart* by M. Basil Pennington

✦ If you were to use yourself (as far as you can) to pray always in the same place; if you were to reserve that place for devotion, and not allow yourself to do anything common in it; if you were never to be there yourself, but in times of devotion; if any room, or (if that cannot be) if any particular part of a room was thus used, this kind of consecration of it as a place holy unto God, would have an effect upon your mind, and dispose you to such tempers, as would very much assist your devotion.
—From *A Serious Call to a Devout and Holy Life*
by William Law

✦ One way to express this is to say that in order to be a living reminder of the Lord, we must walk in his presence as Abraham did. To walk in the presence of the Lord means to move forward in life in such a way that all our desires, thoughts, and actions are constantly guided by him. When we walk in the Lord's presence, everything we see, hear, touch, or taste reminds us of him. This is what is meant by a prayerful life. It is not a life in which we say many prayers, but a life in which nothing, absolutely nothing, is done, said, or understood independently of him who is the origin and purpose of our existence.

—From *The Living Reminder* by Henri J. Nouwen

◆ The Holy Spirit came upon the waiting group not in the Temple nor in a synagogue but in the upper room. And the upper room was a home: "they went up to the upper room, where they were staying . . . All these . . . devoted themselves to prayer." (Acts 1:13, 14) The Holy Spirit came upon them when they were in the most common place—a place where we all live—a home. Under that apparently insignificant fact lies a deep significance. It was an amazing emancipation for religion. For up to this time religion had been associated with sacred places, sacred vestments, and sacred persons. Now the center of gravity in religion shifted from places to persons, from vestments to vitality, from services to service. It was a most important shift. It saved religion from sterility and saved man to vitality. Religion was put where it belongs—in the human heart. Paul, brought up under the spell of temple holiness, announced this extraordinary shift: "Do you not know that you are God's temple and that God's Spirit dwells in you? . . . For God's temple is holy, and that temple you are." (1 Cor. 3:16, 17) Her holiness had shifted from places to persons. And rightly so.

For there is no such thing as a holy place. A place has no moral qualities since it has no moral choice. "There is nothing good but a good will, and there is nothing bad but a bad will," said Kant. And we may add: There is nothing holy but a holy person; there is nothing unholy but an unholy person. Holy persons gathered together make a holy place, not the other way around.

This coming of the Holy Spirit on persons, rather than on places, was one of the most important happenings in history. It took religion out of the magical and put it in the moral. And in doing so universalized it. And further it saved the Temple. For the Temple was no longer the center—the persons in the Temple were. As such the Temple could be used.

—From *Mastery* by E. Stanley Jones

◆ Somehow we have gotten swept into a millrace, and it's nonstop flailing and thrashing just to keep ourselves from drowning. The sheer necessities of modern life sweep us farther and farther from any sense that it is all hallowed, really. What are we to do?

There are various things we could do no doubt. We could resign ourselves to the millrace and abandon any thought of anything but the flailing. Or we could take some drastic step like moving to a farm in Vermont or an island in the Aegean, hoping thereby to find some peace and quiet where we would be able to recollect ourselves and do things right. A third possibility would be to accept the fact that life comes tumbling at us nowadays but that it is nonetheless possible for us to see our ordinary daily routines as proceeding among the hallows, so to speak; and by stirring up in our minds the things that we vaguely acknowledge anyway, to begin to hallow those routines by doing once more what men have always done with things to hallow them; namely, offering them up in oblation to God, as literally as Abel offered up sacrifices from his ordinary routine of work.

. . . I would like to suggest that at least one place (among others) which may be hallowed anew as the place where the celebration of all the mysteries may occur, and where all of life may be offered up in oblation to the Most High, is the family household. Within these four walls, under this roof, the lamps are lighted. The offering is here, the vigil is here, the feast is here, the faithful are here. All the eating and drink-

ing, and the working and playing, and the discipline and serving and loving that go on here—they are all holy. For these
common routines of ordinary life are not only necessities and
functions: they are also messengers to us from the hallows.
Nay, more than messengers, they are those hallows, set hourly
before us in visible, touchable, light-of-day forms.

—From *Hallowed Be This House* by Thomas Howard

◆ "Enter into thy closet." Did you ever say anything like this
to yourself, "It is so difficult to select a place"? What about the
time when you were in love, was it impossible to select a
place to meet in? No, it was far from impossible; and beware
of self-indulgence. Think how long our Lord has waited for
you; you have seen Him in your visions, now pray to Him; get
a place, not a mood, but a definite material place and resort to
it constantly, and pray to God as His Spirit in you will help
you. Bring to the earth the promised life you have longed for,
curb your impulsive undisciplined wayward nature to His
use, and rule in your body like a king where now, even in
strength and honesty, you walked sentenced to be a prey to
baser and less spiritual things. Do not say, "If I only had so and
so"; you have not got so and so; but you can, if you will, select
a place where you are actually. We can always do what we
want to do if we want to do it sufficiently keenly. Do it now,
"enter into thy closet"; and remember, it is a place selected to
pray in, not to make little addresses in, or for any other purpose than to pray in, never forget that.

—From *Christian Discipline, Vol. 2* by Oswald Chambers

◆ The first problem is to find a place where the outer confusion can be shut off, where the bright lights and the telephone cannot break in, and where even religious discussion is
stilled. The purpose is not to create, or make something happen, but to allow it to happen, and where it takes place is an
individual matter. Some people find it easy to quiet down in a
church where the rule of silence is observed. For others it
may be in one's own room, or in a garden or near the water, or
on a mountain top.

. . . There is manna in certain places that can draw a person to silence, for instance in a room which has known the silence and listening of many people. This was the kind of power that Jacob felt when he awoke from dreaming of the ladder to heaven and cried out, "Truly, Yahweh is in this place and I never knew it!" Then he was afraid and said, "How awe-inspiring this place is! This is nothing less than a house of God; this is the gate of heaven!" And he made a sacred monument of the stone on which he had lain and poured oil on top of it, and he named the place Bethel (Genesis 28:10–19). We in the Western tradition are often reluctant to admit that there is reality behind an experience like this.

. . . Each of us can have a place like this, where stillness can take over and one becomes open to a reality beyond oneself.

—From *The Other Side of Silence* by Morton T. Kelsey

✦ My special place is a small brook in a green glade, a circle of quiet from which there is no visible sign of human beings. There's a natural stone bridge over the brook, and I sit there, dangling my legs and looking through the foliage at the sky reflected in the water, and things slowly come back into perspective. If the insects are biting me—and they usually are; no place is quite perfect—I use the pliable branch of a shadblow tree as a fan. The brook wanders through a tunnel of foliage, and the birds sing more sweetly there than anywhere else; or perhaps it is just that when I am at the brook I have time to be aware of them, and I move slowly into a kind of peace that is marvelous, "annihilating all that's made to a green thought in a green shade." If I sit for a while, then my impatience, crossness, frustration, are indeed annihilated, and my sense of humor returns.

—From *A Circle of Quiet* by Madeleine L'Engle

✦ . . . a sense of place . . . these days is not achieved easily. As Susanne Langer wrote in 1957, "Most people have no home that is a symbol of their childhood, not even a definite memory of one place to serve that purpose . . . all the old symbols are gone." Once I asked a roomful of supper guests who, if anyone, felt any strong pull to any certain spot on the face of the earth. Everyone was silent, except for a visitor from Bavaria.

... So what are we to do, those of us whose habit and pleasure and doom is our tendency, as a Georgia lady put it, to "fly off at every other whipstitch"? Think in terms of movable feasts, for a start. Live here, wherever here may be, as if we were going to belong here for the rest of our lives. Learn to hallow whatever ground we happen to stand on or land on. Like medieval knights who took their tapestries along on Crusades, like modern Afghanis with their yurts, we must pack such totems and icons as we can to make short-term quarters feel like home. Pillows, small rugs, watercolors can dispel much of the chilling anonymity of a sublet apartment or motel room. When we can, we should live with stoves or fireplaces or anyway candlelight. The ancient saying is still true: Extinguished hearth, extinguished family.

—From *Families* by Jane Howard

28. Guidance

O Lord My God, when the storm is loud, and the night is dark, and the soul is sad, and the heart oppressed; then, as a weary traveler, may I look to you; and beholding the light of your love, may it bear me on, until I learn to sing your song in the night. Amen.

George Dawson in *Little Book of Prayers*

PSALM 16

DAILY SCRIPTURE

Monday	1 Samuel 3:1–10
Tuesday	Exodus 13:17–22
Wednesday	John 10:1–15
Thursday	Genesis 24:1–67
Friday	1 Samuel 16:1–13
Saturday	Judges 6:11–40
Sunday	John 16:5–15

SELECTIONS FOR MEDITATION

PERSONAL MEDITATION

PRAYER

The Christian life has often been compared to the taking of a journey or pilgrimage. And this is so. There is a sense in which we are but "passing through this land." But we must always remember that we are never the Guide. We never blaze an uncut trail; Christ has gone before. In your prayer this week think of God as Guide, and ask him to direct your path.

HYMN   "Guide Me, O Thou Great Jehovah"

> Guide me, O Thou great Jehovah,
> Pilgrim thru this barren land;
> I am weak, but Thou art mighty;
> Hold me with Thy pow'rful hand;
> Bread of heaven, feed me till I want no more;
> Bread of heaven, feed me till I want no more.
>
> Open now the crystal fountain,
> Whence the healing waters flow;
> Let the fiery, cloudy pillar,
> Lead me all my journey thru;
> Strong deliv'rer, be Thou my strength and shield;
> Strong deliv'rer, be Thou my strength and shield. . . .
>
> William Williams

BENEDICTION

Father, you alone know what lies before me this day, grant that in every hour of it I may stay close to you. Let me today embark on no undertaking that is not in line with your will for my life, nor shrink from any sacrifice which your will may demand. Suggest, direct, control every movement of my mind; for my Lord Christ's sake. Amen.

John Baillie in A Diary of Private Prayer

SELECTIONS FOR MEDITATION

◆ Guidance of life by the Light within is not exhausted as is too frequently supposed, in special leadings toward particular tasks. It begins first of all in a mass revision of our total reaction to the world. Worshipping in the light we become new creatures, making wholly new and astonishing responses to the entire outer setting of life. These responses are not reasoned out. They are, in large measure, spontaneous reactions of felt incompatibility between "the world's judgments of value and the Supreme Value we adore deep in the Center. There is a total Instruction as well as specific instructions from the Light within. The dynamic illumination from the deeper level is shed upon the judgments of the surface level, and lo, the "former things are passed away, behold, they are become new."

Paradoxically, this total Instruction proceeds in two opposing directions at once. We are torn loose from earthly attachments and ambitions—*contemptus mundi.* And we are quickened to a divine but painful concern for this world—*amor mundi.* He plucks the world out of our hearts, loosening the chains of attachment. And He hurls the world into our hearts, where we and He together carry it in infinitely tender love.

The second half of the paradox is more readily accepted today than the first. For we fear it means world-withdrawal, world-flight. We fear a life of wallowing in ecstasies of spiritual sensuality while cries of a needy world go unheeded. And some pages of history seem to fortify our fears.

But there is a sound and valid *contemptus mundi* which the Inner Light works within the utterly dedicated soul. Positions of prominence, eminences of social recognition which we once meant to attain—how puny and trifling they become! Our old ambitions and heroic dreams—what years we have wasted in feeding our own insatiable self-pride, when only His will truly matters! Our wealth and property, security now and in old age—upon what broken reeds have we leaned, when He is "the rock of our heart, and our portion forever!"

—From *A Testament of Devotion* by Thomas R. Kelly

✦ God guides us, despite our uncertainties and our vagueness, even through our failings and mistakes. He often starts us off to the left, only to bring us up in the end to the right; or else he brings us back to the right, after a long detour, because we started off by mistake to the left in the belief that we were obeying him. He leads us step by step, from event to event. Only afterwards, as we look back over the way we have come and reconsider certain important moments in our lives in the light of all that has followed them, or when we survey the whole progress of our lives, do we experience the feeling of having been led without knowing it, the feeling that God has mysteriously guided us.

It was he who made us meet this man, made us hear that remark, read that book, with all the decisive consequences they have had on our lives. We did not perhaps know it at the time. Time has had to elapse to enable us to see it. Thus, the disciples on the Emmaus road talked with Jesus without recognizing him (Luke 24:13–35). It was he who brought us up short by means of a dream which at first we did not understand, a serious illness, a strange hesitation, or a painful failure. It was he also who guided us by means of a success, and so opened up a new and unexpected horizon to us. Ah, that is the true answer to our perplexing problem of success and failure!

—From *Reflections* by Paul Tournier

✦ One of the most delightful examples comes from "the poor little man of Assisi," St. Francis. Francis, it seems, was in "great agony of doubt" about whether he should devote himself only to prayer and meditation, which was a common practice in those days, or whether he should also engage in preaching missions. Wisely Francis sought out counsel. "As the holy humility that was in him did not allow him to trust in himself or in his own prayers, he humbly turned to others in order to know God's will in this matter."

He sent messages to two of his most trusted friends, Sister Clare and Brother Silvester, asking them to gather one of their "purer and more spiritual companions" with them and seek the will of God in the matter. Immediately they went to prayer and both Sister Clare and Brother Silvester returned with the same answer.

When the messenger returned, St. Francis first washed his feet and prepared him a meal. Then, kneeling down before the messenger, St. Francis asked him, "What does my Lord Jesus Christ order me to do?" The messenger replied that Christ had revealed that "He wants you to go about the world preaching, because God did not call you for yourself alone but also for the salvation of others." Receiving the message as the undisputed word of Christ, St. Francis jumped up saying, "So let's go—in the name of the Lord."

—From *Celebration of Discipline* by Richard J. Foster

✦ As a child I remember being fascinated with those fairy tales that centered around a lost throne.

They followed a basic pattern: A boy or girl is raised in poverty in some obscure place. However, the child really was born in the royal household; some wicked relative who wanted the throne for himself saw to it that at birth the real prince was banished to a distant place.

When the child grows up, he stumbles onto his true heritage at a particularly graced time, through sudden revelation with someone who knows the truth. Scales fall from the newly discovered one's eyes; a new dignity and purpose are born.

Finally, there is a period of struggle with the entrenched forces of evil (within and without); after much suffering and loss, the royal inheritor ascends his rightful throne, and rules with compassion, equity, and wisdom.

These stories reflect the intuition and experience of many people. They can be interpreted on many levels. Spiritually, for me, they express that basic insight found scattered throughout Christian literature that each of us is a child of royal lineage. Royal means a status that cannot be earned, only given. It is a gifted right and responsibility from the beginning, not a goal that is earned at the end, though there is struggle along the way to realize the full truth.

Those who would grasp for their own kingdom, however, are ignorant of the gift, or hostile toward recognition of its royal Source beyond themselves and its broad responsibilities. Such people forcefully spread their blindness and isolating self-importance. The gift is hidden from view. Yet it cannot be destroyed; it shows itself as an inner gnawing, a yearning that cannot be satisfied by our confused and willful efforts—until the time is ripe, and the giftedness is revealed, for those who have eyes to see.

There, in broadstroke Christian terms, is the human condition. Christian spiritual guidance in all its forms exists to reveal this condition in us and encourage our reconciliation with transforming power to our royal Source, whose hidden Realm is one of connectedness and compassion. That reconciliation, to Christian faith, is unfolded in the mystery of God's gift of a royal son, Jesus Christ, through whom we inherit the Kingdom.

—From *Spiritual Friend* by Tilden H. Edwards

✦ Next, you must remember that our God has all knowledge and all wisdom, and that therefore it is very possible He may guide you into paths wherein He knows great blessings are awaiting you, but which to the shortsighted human eyes around you seem sure to result in confusion and loss. You must recognize the fact that God's thoughts are not as man's thoughts, nor His ways as man's ways; and that He who knows the end of things from the beginning alone can judge of what the results of any course of action may be. You must therefore realize that His very love for you may perhaps lead you to run counter to the loving wishes of even your dearest friends.

—From *The Christian's Secret of a Happy Life*
by Hannah Whitall Smith

✦ There are four ways in which He reveals His will to us— through the Scriptures,—through providential circumstances,—through the convictions of our own higher judgment,—and through the inward impressions of the Holy Spirit on our minds.

The Scriptures come first. If you are in doubt upon any subject you must first of all consult the Bible about it, and see whether there is any law there to direct you. Until you have found and obeyed God's will as it is there revealed, you must not ask nor expect a separate direct personal revelation. . . . Where our Father has written out for us a plain direction about anything, He will not of course make an especial revelation to us about that thing. And if we fail to search out and obey the Scripture rule, where there is one, and look instead for an inward voice, we shall open ourselves to the deceptions of Satan, and shall almost inevitably get into error.

. . . But if, upon searching, you do not find in the Bible any directions upon your point of difficulty, or if the directions given do not reach into all the especial details of the case, then you must seek guidance in the other ways mentioned; and God will voice Himself to you either by conviction of your judgment, or by providential circumstances, or by a clear inward impression. And in all true guidance these four voices will necessarily harmonize, for God cannot say in one voice that which He contradicts in another. . . . If either one of these tests fail, it is not safe to proceed, but you must wait in quiet trust until the Lord shows you the point of harmony, which He surely will, sooner or later, if it is His voice that is speaking. Anything, therefore, which is out of this divine harmony must be rejected as not from God. For we must never forget that Satan can make impressions upon our minds as well as the blessed Spirit of God, and in this matter of guidance it is especially necessary not to be ignorant of his devices.

—From *The Christian's Secret of a Happy Life*
by Hannah Whitall Smith

✦ God's promise is, that He will work in us to will as well as to do of His good pleasure. This of course means that He will take possession of our will and work it for us, and that His suggestions will come to us, not so much commands from the outside, as desires springing up within. They will originate in our will; we shall feel as though we wanted to do so and so, not as though we must. And this makes it a service of perfect liberty; for it is always easy to do what we desire to do, let the accompanying circumstances be as difficult as they may.

. . . The way in which the Holy Spirit, therefore, usually works in this direct guidance is to impress upon the mind a wish or desire to do or to leave undone certain things.

—From *The Christian's Secret of a Happy Life*
by Hannah Whitall Smith

29. God's Absence

My Father, I know that you are present with me, but my knowledge is but a figure and shadow of truth and has little of the spiritual savor and inward sweetness such knowledge should afford. This is for me a great loss and the cause of much weakness of heart. Help me to make at once such amendment of life as is necessary before I can experience the true meaning of the words "In your presence is fulness of joy." Amen.

A. W. Tozer in *The Knowledge of the Holy*

PSALM 13

DAILY SCRIPTURE

Monday	2 Corinthians 1:1–11
Tuesday	Deuteronomy 7:1–9
Wednesday	Hebrews 12:1–13
Thursday	Job 19:1–27
Friday	1 Peter 4:1–19
Saturday	Job 23:1–17
Sunday	Isaiah 40:12–31

SELECTIONS FOR MEDITATION

PERSONAL MEDITATION

PRAYER

Rest your prayers in the love of an ever-present God. Remember that he is not present because you feel he is present nor is he absent because you feel he is absent. He is always present because he has promised to be. Speak to him because he is there.

HYMN   "Under His Wings"

Under his wings, I am safely abiding.
Tho' the night deepens and tempests are wild,
Still I can trust him; I know he will keep me.
He has redeemed me and I am his child.

Under his wings, what a refuge in sorrow!
How the heart yearningly turns to his rest!
Often when earth has no balm for my healing,
There I find comfort, and there I am blest.

Under his wings, oh, what precious enjoyment!
There will I hide till life's trials are o'er;
Sheltered, protected, no evil can harm me.
Resting in Jesus, I'm safe evermore.

Under his wings, under his wings,
Who from his love can sever?
Under his wings my soul shall abide,
Safely abide forever.

William O. Cushing

BENEDICTION

Almighty God, you are ever present in the world without me,
in my spirit within me, and in the unseen world above me, let
me carry with me through this day's life a most real sense of
your power and your glory. Hallowed be your name. Amen.

John Baillie in *A Diary of Private Prayer*

SELECTIONS FOR MEDITATION

✦ All the world is one great sacramental loaf. We are not—
nor will we ever be, God save us—solitary intelligences spin-
ning in the dark void of space. He crowds upon us from Sheol
to the sea; he jostles our thoughts along the pathways in our
brains. He hides in the bushes, jumping out in flames to star-
tle us into seeing. He sequesters himself in stables and swad-
dling so as to take us unawares. He veils himself in flesh, the
same flesh that drips into fingers at the end of my arms and
sprouts into hair on my head.

Either the world is holy or it's not. Either the creator's work is a sign of himself or it's a sham. Where else can one draw the line between sacred and profane except around all the cosmos? For "profane" meant, originally, outside the temple, and all creation was, in the beginning, a temple for God's "very good." Whenever we eat, drink, breathe, see, take anything in by any means, we are commanded to remember the sacrifice. We try to hedge in the holy, to pour it into tiny, trivial cups, to make bread as pale and tasteless as possible, like fingernails. We are saying to God: Get away from me. Just so the desert Israelites implored Moses to keep God on the mountain and not bring him down among their tents. As though our immolation by the holy were not our only hope.

Still, we take the big black crayon in our hands and draw these little islands where we will let God live in the world. In the tiny cups and on the unfamiliar silver plates so cold you can see your breath on them. We cover him up with white linen napkins just as they did in the grave. We draw more lines around Bibles and sanctuaries, thus adding a few more islands to this archipelago of the holy, and there you have it. Little concentration camps for Christ. Our incremental piety bristles around the perimeters like barbed wire, hemming him in.

—From *And the Trees Clap Their Hands*
by Virginia Stem Owens

✦ God is in fact always passing into the everyday and often colorless fabric of the life of each one of us. This everyday experience may even be the sphere into which he prefers to introduce his grace. The slightest event in our lives and the least discernible movement of his grace point to the passing of his justice and mercy into our lives and to his desire to appeal to our faithfulness and to draw us toward him.

He passes in this way among us in order to fashion us into his form and likeness and to perfect us in his love. Sometimes he does this slowly and silently, acting like drops of water that take so many years to hollow out the rock, and with so much discretion that we are hardly aware of it. At other times, he acts so quickly that he takes us by surprise. . . .

. . . If we are to perceive the Lord's passing and be aware of its significance every time it happens, we must become very sensitive and intuitive and be quietly open to his presence and faithful to it. If we are really listening, we shall know that the one who is eternally young never passes in the same way more than once. He is inexhaustibly inventive.

The soul that is able to hear the slightest inflections of his voice also knows that its echoes, both in the most intimate part of man's being and in the things and events outside him, are very vague. The soul that is sensitive to the light of God's presence knows too that the light that illuminates the step that it is about to take—"your word is a lamp to my feet and a light on my path" (Ps. 119:105)—is not the same as the light that will illuminate the next step. But the soul always recognizes the voice and the light of the one who is always passing, because he is the eternal present and eternal love.

—From *The Presence of God* by Elisabeth-Paule Labat

✦ The soul may ask God for anything, and never fail. You may ask God for his presence, or for wisdom, and receive each at his hands. Or you may ask God, in the words of the shopkeeper's little gag sign, that he not go away mad, but just go away. Once, in Israel, an extended family of nomads did just that. They heard God's speech and found it too loud. The wilderness generation was at Sinai; it witnessed there the thick darkness where God was: "and all the people saw the thunderings, and the lightnings, and the noise of the trumpet, and the mountain smoking." It scared them witless. Then they asked Moses to beg God, please, never speak to them directly again. "Let not God speak with us, lest we die." Moses took the message. And God, pitying their self-consciousness, agreed. He agreed not to speak to the people anymore. And he added to Moses, "Go say to them, Get into your tents again."

It is difficult to undo our own damage, and to recall to our

presence that which we have asked to leave. It is hard to dese-
crate a grove and change your mind. The very holy mountains
are keeping mum. We doused the burning bush and cannot
rekindle it; we are lighting matches in vain under every green
tree.

What have we been doing all these centuries but trying to
call God back to the mountain, or, failing that, raise a peep out
of anything that isn't us? What is the difference between a
cathedral and a physics lab? Are they not both saying: Hello!
We spy on whales and on interstellar radio objects; we starve
ourselves and pray till we're blue.

—From *Teaching a Stone to Talk* by Annie Dillard

✦ I can never say, "God is there and I am here," as if I were
separated from my Source. For God is the core of my being
and the core of all beings. He is closer to me than I am to
myself.

—From *Christian Mysticism Today* by William Johnston

✦ Adam sinned and, in his panic, frantically tried to do the
impossible: he tried to hide from the Presence of God. David
also must have had wild thoughts of trying to escape from the
Presence, for he wrote, "Whither shall I go from thy spirit? or
whither shall I flee from thy presence?" Then he proceeded
through one of his most beautiful psalms to celebrate the
glory of the divine imminence. "If I ascend up into heaven,
thou art there: If I make my bed in hell, behold, thou art
there. If I take the wings of the morning, and dwell in the
uttermost parts of the sea; even there shall thy hand lead me,
and thy right hand shall hold me." And he knew that God's
being and God's seeing are the same, that the seeing Presence
had been with him even before he was born, watching the
mystery of unfolding life.

. . . If God is present at every point in space, if we cannot
go where He is not, cannot even conceive of a place where
He is not, why then has not that Presence become the one
universally celebrated act of the world? The patriarch Jacob,
"in waste howling wilderness," gave the answer to that ques-

tion. He saw a vision of God and cried out in wonder, "Surely the Lord is in this place; and I knew it not." Jacob had never been for one small division of a moment outside the circle of that all-pervading Presence. But he knew it not. That was his trouble, and it is ours. Men do not know if God is here. What a difference it would make if they knew.

—From *The Pursuit of God* by A. W. Tozer

✦ Everything is gestation and then bringing forth. To let each impression and each germ of a feeling come to completion wholly in itself, in the dark, in the inexpressible, the unconscious, beyond the reach of one's own intelligence, and await with deep humility and patience the birth-hour of a new clarity: that alone is living the artist's life: in understanding as in creating.

There is here no measuring with time, no year matters, and ten years are nothing. Being an artist means, not reckoning and counting, but ripening like the tree which does not force its sap and stands confident in the storms of spring without the fear that after them may come no summer. It does come. But it comes only to the patient, who are there as though eternity lay before them, so unconcernedly still and wide, I learn it daily, learn it with pain to which I am grateful: patience is everything!

—From *Letters to a Young Poet* by Rainer Maria Rilke

✦ God does not, by the instant gift of His Spirit, make us always feel right, desire good, love purity, aspire after Him and His Will. Therefore either He will not, or He cannot. If He will not, it must be because it would not be well to do so. If He cannot, then He would not if He could; else a better condition than God's is conceivable to the mind of God. . . . The truth is this: He wants to make us in His own image, choosing the good, refusing the evil. How should He effect this if He were always moving us from within, as He does at divine intervals, toward the beauty of holiness? . . . For God made our individuality as well as, and a greater marvel than, our dependence; made our apartness from Himself, that freedom should bind us divinely dearer to Himself, with a new and inscrutable marvel of love; for the Godhead is still at the root, is the making root of our individuality, and the freer the man, the stronger the bond that binds him to Him who made his freedom.

—From *An Anthology of George MacDonald.*
Edited by C. S. Lewis

✦ At various times, in the past and present, the sad old saw is revived that God is dead, gone, unnoticeable. And this always strikes a partly confirming chord, for God is not a shown phenomenon. On the surface he sometimes does seem to be missing. We sense a similar absence within ourselves, a lack of something, an insufficiency. Yet it is this very lack that spurs our self-surpassing reach toward infinity, toward an unobstrusive God whose seeming dormancy becomes in us a feature of his activity. Our thoughts stretch to the universe; yet compared to it, we are as nothing. We are radically, constitutionally limited. That is our pathos, our ingrained predicament, the longing from which we flee alternately into work, diversion, or boredom. Our greatness is, not something that belongs to us, but something to which we belong.

Yet, externally, it is hidden. The nature in which we move is itself a vast mystery, an ever-extending puzzle. "All things cover up some mystery," says the scientist-philosopher Pascal. "All things are the veils which cover God." If that is the case, and everything masks God, then everything also speaks of him, and his outwardly seeming absence becomes a constant countersign of his presence. We do, indeed, walk in semi-darkness and, in realizing it, are also aware of light and our need for it.

—From *The Untamed God* by George Cornell

✦ One of the experiences of prayer is that it seems that nothing happens. But when you stay with it and look back over a long period of prayer, you suddenly realize that something has happened. What is most close, most intimate, most present, often cannot be experienced directly but only with a certain distance. When I think that I am only distracted, just wasting my time, something is happening too immediate for knowing, understanding, and experiencing. Only in retrospect do I realize that something very important has taken place. Isn't this true of all the really important events of life? When I am together with someone I love very much, we seldom talk about our relationship. The relationship, in fact, is too central to be a subject of talk. But later after we have separated and write letters, we realize how much it all meant to us, and we even write about it.

—From *The Genesee Diary* by Henri J. Nouwen

SECTION THREE
patterns for living inwardly

Over and over again in the writings and journals of ardent spiritual pilgrims there is the admonition to use short prayers. Jesus himself warned against praying with many words and when asked by his disciples to be taught to pray he gave them a remarkably brief prayer to use as a model prayer.

This short section is devoted to showing you how to use some patterns from the Bible for formulating your prayers. The Lord's Prayer, the Beatitudes and the Parables from the teachings of Jesus are filled with meanings and truths. When they are prayed slowly, phrase by phrase, even word by word, they will bring concentration and centeredness to you. They will often lead you into so-called critical moments in prayer; moments when you are called into some new awareness of his goodness or of some attitude or quality of your own life that is hindering your progress.

There are also readings that will lead you into new understanding of the Lord's Supper and its rich meanings for you. Praying in the many moods that this simple, sacramental meal radiates will cause your soul to both rejoice in the life that it brings and celebrate the hope that it gives. And it will surely bring you to somber confession for your own deeds and misdeeds that would crucify him afresh.

The final week is spent in using The Jesus Prayer as a short, focusing petition that can serve to open you up to God.

The lesson to be learned during these days of your prayer pilgrimage is that it is better to pray a few well-intentioned, deeply felt, and God-directed words than it is to fill the air with many words that do not and cannot carry your deep heartcry with them. Select a phrase or two that expresses where you are on your journey or where you would hope to be and patiently breathe it heavenward with all the concentration and loving attentiveness your heart can muster. The Father, "who sees you in secret, will reward you openly."

30. The Lord's Prayer

Lord Jesus! reveal me to the Father. Let His name, His infinite Father-love, the love with which He loved Thee, according to Your prayer, be in me. Then shall I say aright, "My Father?" Then shall I apprehend Your teaching, and the first spontaneous breathing of my heart will be: "My Father, Your Name, Your Kingdom, Your Will." Amen.

Andrew Murray in *With Christ in the School of Prayer*

PSALM 65

DAILY SCRIPTURE

Monday	Matthew 26:40–41
Tuesday	John 16:23–24
Wednesday	Luke 11:1–14
Thursday	Matthew 6:6–15
Friday	Luke 18:1–8
Saturday	John 17
Sunday	John 12:23–28

SELECTIONS FOR MEDITATION

PERSONAL MEDITATION

PRAYER

The only lesson that the disciples asked Jesus to teach them was how to pray. And recorded in the Lord's Prayer is the model which Jesus incorporated to teach them how to have sweet communion with the Father. Let it shape your prayer life, and be the model of communion for you.

HYMN   "The Lord's Prayer"

> Our Father, which art in heaven,
> Hallowed be Thy name.
> Thy kingdom come,
> Thy will be done on earth
> as it is in heaven.
> Give us this day
> our daily bread,
> and forgive us our debts
> as we forgive our debtors.
> And lead us not into temptation,
> but deliver us from evil,
> for Thine is the Kingdom,
> and the Power,
> and the Glory,
> Forever.
> Amen.

BENEDICTION

Father, what can I say in this hour but to cry out as these
disciples cried out, Lord, teach me how to pray. Teach me my
need. Tear away this veil from my eyes that makes me think I
have any adequacy in myself. . . . Give me rather, this conscious sense of dependence, this awareness that nothing I do
will be of any value apart from a dependence upon you. In
Jesus' name, Amen.

Ray C. Stedman in Jesus Teaches on Prayer

SELECTIONS FOR MEDITATION

✦ "Every just man," says Osuna, "needs the seven things for
which this prayer—or this scheme of prayer—asks." Taken
together they cover all the realities of our situation, at once
beset by nature and cherished by grace: establishing Christian
prayer as a relation between wholes, between man in his
completeness and God who is all.

And we note their order and proportion. First, four classes
entirely concerned with our relation to God; then three concerned with our human situation and needs. Four hinge on
the First Commandment, three hinge on the Second. Man's

twisted, thwarted and embittered nature, his state of sin, his sufferings, helplessness and need, do not stand in the foreground; but the splendor and beauty of God, demanding a self-oblivion so complete that it transforms suffering, and blots out even the memory of sin.

—From *Abba* by Evelyn Underhill

✦ "Our Father, which art in heaven." We are the children of God and therefore inheritors of heaven. Here is the source alike of our hope and our penitence; the standard which confounds us, the essence of religion, the whole of prayer. . . . It is a statement of fact, which takes us clean away from the world of religious problems and consolations, the world of self-interested worries and strivings, and discloses the infinite span and unfathomable depth of that supernatural world in which we really live. From our distorted life "unquieted with dreads, bound with cares, busied with vanities, vexed with temptations" the soul in its prayer reaches out to center its trust on the Eternal, the existent.

—From *Abba* by Evelyn Underhill

✦ Hallowed be Thy Name. . . . the four words of this petition can cover, criticize and re-interpret the whole of our personal life; cleansing it from egoism, orientating it towards reality and reminding us that our life and work are without significance, except insofar as they glorify that God to whom nothing is adequate though everything is dear. Our response to each experience which He puts in our path, from the greatest disclosure of beauty to the smallest appeal to love, from perfect happiness to utmost grief, will either hallow or not hallow His Name; and this is the only thing that matters about it.

—From *Abba* by Evelyn Underhill

✦ In the greatest of all prayers we are taught to pray, "Forgive us our trespasses, as we forgive those who trespass against us." This does not mean, of course, that there can be any exact balancing of God's forgiveness and ours. God does not do business by keeping a ledger, and what in his overflowing mercy he forgives in us is far beyond what in our limited righteousness we are able to forgive in others. What it probably means—and says in language so terse that any explanation is cumbersome—is that we cannot expect God's forgiveness until we open the way for it by trying to put away rancor toward others. We cannot hope to be forgiven until we "bring forth . . . fruit worthy of repentance" by our attitudes toward our fellow men.

—From *Prayer and the Common Life* by Georgia Harkness

✦ It is not part of the life of a natural man to pray. We hear it said that a man will suffer in his life if he does not pray; I question it. What will suffer is the life of the Son of God in him, which is nourished not by food, but by prayer. When a man is born from above, the life of the Son of God is born in him, and he can either starve that life or nourish it. Prayer is the way the life of God is nourished. Our ordinary views of prayer are not found in the New Testament. We look upon prayer as a means of getting things for ourselves; the Bible idea of prayer is that we may get to know God himself.

—From *My Utmost for His Highest* by Oswald Chambers

✦ According to Jesus, by far the most important thing about praying is to keep at it. The images he uses to explain this are all rather comic, as though he thought it was rather comic to have to explain it all. He says God is like a friend you go to borrow bread from at midnight. The friend tells you in effect to drop dead, but you go on knocking anyway until he finally gives you what you want so he can go back to bed again (Luke 11:5–8). Or God is like a crooked judge who refuses to hear the case of a certain poor widow, presumably because he knows there's nothing much in it for him. But she keeps on hounding him until finally he hears her case just to get her out of his hair (Luke 18:1–8). Even a stinker, Jesus says, won't give his own child a black eye when he asks for peanut butter and jelly, so how all the more will God when his children ask—(Matthew 7:9–11).

Be importunate, Jesus says—not, one assumes, because you have to beat a path to God's door before he will open it, but because until you beat a path maybe there's no way of getting to your door. "Ravish my heart," John Donne wrote. But God will not usually ravish. He will only court.

—From *Wishful Thinking* by Frederick Buechner

✦ "Our Father which art in heaven!" To appreciate this word of adoration aright, I must remember that none of the saints had in Scripture ever ventured to address God as their Father. The invocation places us at once in the center of the wonderful revelation the Son came to make of His Father as our Father too. . . . The words are the key to the whole prayer, to all prayer. It takes time, it takes life to study them; it will take eternity to understand them fully. The knowledge of God's Father-love is the first and simplest, but also the last and highest lesson in the school of prayer. It is in the personal relation to the living God, and the personal conscious fellowship of love with Himself, that prayer begins. It is in the knowledge of God's Fatherliness, revealed by the Holy Spirit, that the power of prayer will be found to root and grow.

—From *With Christ in the School of Prayer*
by Andrew Murray

✦ While we ordinarily first bring our own needs to God in prayer, and then think of what belongs to God and His interests, the Master reverses the order. First Thy name, Thy kingdom, Thy will; then, give us, forgive us, lead us, deliver us. The lesson is of more importance than we think. In true worship the Father must be first, must be all. The sooner I learn to forget myself in the desire that He may be glorified, the richer will the blessing be that prayer will bring to myself. No one ever loses by what he sacrifices for the Father.

—From *With Christ in the School of Prayer*
by Andrew Murray

✦ When first the child has yielded himself to the Father in the care for His Name, His Kingdom, and His Will, he has full liberty to ask for his daily bread. A master cares for the food of his servant, a general of his soldiers, a father of his child. And will not the Father in heaven care for the child who has in prayer given himself up to His interests? We may indeed in full confidence say: Father, I live for Thy honor and Thy work; I know thou carest for me. Consecration to God and His will gives wonderful liberty in prayer for temporal things: the whole earthly life is given to the Father's loving care.

—From *With Christ in the School of Prayer*
by Andrew Murray

✦ Our daily bread, the pardon of our sins, and then our being kept from all sin and the power of the evil one, in these three petitions all our personal need is comprehended. The prayer for bread and pardon must be accompanied by the surrender to live in all things in holy obedience to the Father's will, and the believing prayer in everything to be kept by the power of the indwelling Spirit from the power of the evil one.

—From *With Christ in the School of Prayer*
by Andrew Murray

✦ The name of God in the Bible is the expression of His Being, especially insofar as he has revealed Himself to man. So the first supplicaton is that God should be sanctified not only in the one praying, but in all creation. The petition is that God should work so inwardly upon the one who prays, and upon all others, that they shall recognise Him in His self-revelation and serve Him as the Holy One—that they should render to Him, the divine Father, all honor and adoration and should love and obey Him with their whole heart.

—From *Commentary on the Gospel of Luke*
by Norval Geldenhuys

✦ The prayer is that the Father's divine sovereignty should more and more fully attain its rightful place in the heart and life of fallen mankind, who otherwise are bound under the sway of powers of darkness; that instead of living in sin and rebellion against God men should be brought to live their whole life more and more under the control of God's sovereign rule.

—From *Commentary on the Gospel of Luke*
by Norval Geldenhuys

✦ "And bring us not into temptation." He who sincerely seeks and entreats forgiveness of sins, longs to be able to sin no more. So he prays, conscious of his own weakness, that God may guide his life away from circumstances in which he is exposed to evil temptations. God himself does not tempt (James 1:13), but nevertheless. He allows the faithful to be tempted in order to test and to purify us. According to James 1:2, when, under the guiding hand of God, a man finds himself in circumstances where temptations assail him, he should regard it as a cause for rejoicing, since he knows that Christ gives the victory and that everything of this kind contributes to the steadfast believer's purification and spiritual uplift. But nevertheless it is also necessary, and it is indeed the Lord's commandment, that we should pray that we may as far as possible be spared these temptations, for there is always the danger that we shall not live sufficiently in His power and that we shall accordingly be liable to be overcome by temptations. Therefore we must pray that we be led as seldom as possible into circumstances fraught with temptation. But when God nevertheless allows us to be led into such circumstances, we must rejoice in the Lord who gives us the victory and causes everything to contribute towards the good of those that love Him (Rom. 8:28).

—From *Commentary on the Gospel of Luke*
by Norval Geldenhuys

31. The Lord's Supper

INVOCATION

Father, it is a humbling thing to be died for. On this day let me remember that Jesus Christ, your Son, did exactly that for me. And he went to his death knowing full well how often I would forget his love. Let no pride keep me from kneeling at the foot of that Cross. In the name of Jesus my Savior I pray. Amen.

The Prayers of Peter Marshall

PSALM 22

DAILY SCRIPTURE

Monday	Mark 8:1–21
Tuesday	Matthew 26:17–30
Wednesday	John 6:25–58
Thursday	1 Corinthians 11:17–34
Friday	Philippians 2:1–11
Saturday	Matthew 27:32–56
Sunday	Luke 22:14–22

SELECTIONS FOR MEDITATIONS

PERSONAL MEDITATION

PRAYER

Your focus in prayer this week could be on the coming of God into the affairs of men in the sacraments. In the waters of baptism, in the bread and the wine of communion, in the laying on of hands in ordination. And in believing that all he touches is sacramental.

HYMN   "When I Survey the Wondrous Cross"

When I survey the wondrous cross
On which the Prince of Glory died,

My richest gain I count but loss,
And pour contempt on all my pride.

Forbid it, Lord, that I should boast,
Save in the cross of Christ, my God.
All the vain things that charmed me most,
I sacrifice them to Thy blood.
. . . . .
Were the whole realm of nature mine,
That were a present far too small.
Love so amazing, so divine,
Demands my soul, my life, my all.

Isaac Watts

BENEDICTION

Father, let the mystery of your love, as portrayed in the bread
and the wine, melt the coldness of my heart and soften the
stubbornness of my will. Let it make me wholly yours. Amen.

SELECTIONS FOR MEDITATION

✦ One of the greatest hindrances to internal peace which
the Christian encounters is the common habit of dividing our
lives into two areas, the sacred and the secular.

. . . Our trouble springs from the fact that we who follow
Christ inhabit at once two worlds, the spiritual and the natural.

This tends to divide our total life into two departments.
We come unconsciously to recognize two sets of actions. The
first are performed with a feeling of satisfaction and a firm
assurance that they are pleasing to God. These are the sacred
acts and they are usually thought to be prayer, Bible reading,
hymn singing, church attendance and such other acts as
spring directly from faith. They may be known by the fact that
they have no direct relation to this world, and would have no
meaning whatever except as faith shows us another world,
"an house not made with hands, eternal in the heavens."

Over against these sacred acts are the secular ones. They
include all of the ordinary activities of life which we share
with the sons and daughters of Adam: eating, sleeping, working, looking after the needs of the body and performing our

dull and prosaic duties here on earth. These we often do reluctantly and with many misgivings, often apologizing to God for what we consider a waste of time and strength. The upshot of this is that we are uneasy most of the time. We go about our common tasks with a feeling of deep frustration, telling ourselves pensively that there's a better day coming when we shall slough off this earthly shell and be bothered no more with the affairs of this world.

. . . Let us think of a Christian believer in whose life the twin wonders of repentance and the new birth have been wrought. He is now living according to the will of God as he understands it from the written Word. Of such a one it may be said that every act of his life is or can be as truly sacred as prayer or baptism or the Lord's Supper. To say this is not to bring all acts down to one level; it is rather to lift every act up into a living kingdom and turn the whole life into a sacrament.

—From *The Pursuit of God* by A. W. Tozer

✦ And suddenly, as I looked at the same cross, he changed to an appearance of joy. The change in his appearance changed mine, and I was as glad and joyful as I could possibly be. And then cheerfully our Lord suggested to my mind: Where is there any instant of your pain or of your grief? And I was very joyful.

Then our Lord put a question to me: Are you well satisfied that I suffered for you? Yes, good Lord, I said; all my thanks to you, good Lord, blessed may you be! If you are satisfied, our Lord said, I am satisfied. It is a joy and a bliss and an endless delight to me that ever I suffered my Passion for you, for if I could suffer more, I would.

. . . For Jesus has great joy in all the deeds which he has done for our salvation. . . . We are his bliss, we are his reward, we are his honor, we are his crown.

What I am describing now is so great a joy to Jesus that he counts as nothing his labor and his bitter sufferings and his cruel and shameful death. And in these words: If I could suffer more, I would suffer more, I saw truly that if he could die as often as once for every man who is to be saved, as he did once for all men, love would never let him rest till he had done it.

—From *Julian of Norwich: Showings*

◆ A sacrament is when something holy happens. It is transparent time, time which you can see through to something deep inside time.

Generally speaking, Protestants have two official sacraments (the Lord's Supper, Baptism) and Roman Catholics these two plus five others (Confirmation, Penance, Extreme Unction, Ordination, and Matrimony). In other words, at such milestone moments as seeing a baby baptized or being baptized yourself, confessing your sins, getting married, dying, you are apt to catch a glimpse of the almost unbearable preciousness and mystery of life.

Needless to say, church isn't the only place where the holy happens. Sacramental moments can occur at any moment, any place, and to anybody. Watching something get born. Making love. A high-school graduation. Somebody coming to see you when you're sick. A meal with people you love. Looking into a stranger's eyes and finding out he's not a stranger.

If we weren't blind as bats, we might see that life itself is sacramental. —From *Wishful Thinking* by Frederick Buechner

◆ It (faith) derives its vitality not from Christ healing as a superhuman, divine miracle-worker, but on the contrary from the fact that he brings help through his wounds and through what from the human point of view is his impotent suffering. "When my heart is most fearful, help me out of my fears, through thy fear and pain," says a hymn by Paul Gerhardt. This mysticism of the passion has discovered a truth about Jesus Christ which ought not to be suppressed by being understood in a superficial way. It can be summed up by saying that suffering is overcome by suffering, and wounds are healed by wounds. For the suffering in suffering is the lack of love, and the wounds in wounds are the abandonment, and the powerlessness in pain is unbelief. And therefore the suffering of abandonment is overcome by the suffering of love, which is not afraid of what is sick and ugly, but accepts it and takes it to itself in order to heal it. Through his own abandonment by God, the crucified Christ brings God to those who are abandoned by God. Through his suffering he brings salvation to those who suffer. Through his death he brings eternal life to those who are dying. And therefore the tempted, rejected, suffering and dying Christ came to be the center of religion of the oppressed and piety of the lost.

—From *The Crucified God* by Jurgen Moltmann

◆ This sacrament is the sacrament of memory. It is a simple fact that in the New Testament the only definite instruction regarding the sacrament of the Lord's Supper is: "Do this in remembrance of me."

. . . the memory turns into an experience and an encounter.

It is in this way that I would think of the real presence of Jesus Christ in the sacrament. The Risen Lord is universally present. He is not present in the sacrament any more than He is present anywhere else. As Brother Lawrence said, he felt as near to his Lord when he was washing the greasy dishes in the monastery kitchen as ever he did at the blessed sacrament. But what happens is that at the sacrament everything is done and designed to make us aware of that presence. He is not specially present, but we are made specially aware of his presence.

There is a power of places. It is long since my father and mother died, and there are times when I forget them, and even when I think of them the days seem very far away when they were here. But, if I go and stand beside a certain grave in a little highland cemetery, I can feel that, if I stretch out my hand, I will touch them. The sacrament of the Lord's Supper is not so much the place where we realize the reality of the real presence of our Lord. The presence is not specially located in the bread and the wine, nor in the Church. It is a presence which is present always, everywhere. But the sacrament is the place where memory, realization, appropriation end in encounter, because we are compelled to become aware of him there.

—From *The Lord's Supper* by William Barclay

✦ . . . the common, daily, necessary business of eating is just that—common, daily, and necessary—but that it is also a picture of the thing that lies at the root of all life; namely, the principle of exchange. My Life For Yours. We enact that principle whenever we assemble and sit down at the table. We may be sitting down to cornflakes, pizza, or Beluga caviar, but whatever it is, life has been laid down for us. We are receiving life by chewing and swallowing the life of something else. We have to do it to stay alive. We have to do it daily. As long as we live, we will be doing it. Nothing could be more ordinary and functional. But there it is—the biggest mystery of all, right there before us, three times a day. We are enacting the rite. We are participating in the holy mystery.

The idea that ordinariness should be thus fraught with heaven, and that a thing like mere eating should open out onto vistas that we thought were the province of religious mystery—it is all too heady. Not that we are transported every time we sit down to our cornflakes, . . . But the thing which from time to time we are given to see when our vision is roused—that eating is a mysterious thing. . . .—it is there all along, cloaked in the demure mantle of ordinariness. It is only now and again that we are vouchsafed a clear vision of it. In the ordinary run of things, we live with it, and affirm it if we ever think of it, and draw our life from it. . . . This food really is exchanged life; but it is only in the eucharist vision that this becomes apparent.

What is this "eucharist vision" that is supposed to be at work over our cereal? Is it not simply the setting into focus of what we see in a blur all the time anyway; namely, that we have no life except that we owe to the laying down of some other life, and hence that thanksgiving is the appropriate response?

—From *Hallowed Be This House* by Thomas Howard

✦ "Tell me about me." To prove that an accent on this notion is not just a way of catering to modern selfishness, it is necessary to look at the original records. What did the Host at this meal have in mind in offering himself through it and along with it? The first words of Jesus to be transmitted in writing are quoted in Paul's First Letter to the Corinthians. Before we hear anything else from Jesus' lips, we hear him saying, "This is my body which is for you." The initial act of Jesus is to overcome the distance between Jerusalem and our town, to cut across the years from his own time to ours. He clears away all the debris and clutter of secondary themes and says, "for you." That reaching out to us meets two profound demands of the heart. It shows that the speaker, who was himself near a sentence of death, knew that you do not want to be run through a catechism, that you wish to be grasped and loved as a dying person. And it also meets the demands each reader makes on an author or each listener poses to a speaker; it knows that the hearers of the word of God given through Paul are saying, "Tell me about me."

—From *The Lord's Supper* by Martin E. Marty

32. The Beatitudes

INVOCATION

My Father, for the truth which Jesus channeled to me concerning your Kingdom, I express my moving thanks. Be in me increasingly that your Kingdom, your rule, may guide my decisions, inspire my will, and determine my actions. Amen.

—From *Deep Is the Hunger* by Howard Thurman

PSALM 67

DAILY SCRIPTURE

Monday	Matthew 5:1–12
Tuesday	Luke 6:20–23
Wednesday	Matthew 7:28–29
Thursday	Luke 4:14–21
Friday	2 John 9
Saturday	Mark 13:28–31
Sunday	John 6:66–69

SELECTIONS FOR MEDITATION

PERSONAL MEDITATION

PRAYER

Ask God to show you the importance of these foundational truths which Jesus has taught us. Pray that he will reveal to you the kernel of truth that is buried beneath each Beatitude and also, that he would show you best how to live that truth.

HYMN   "Sitting at the Feet of Jesus"

Sitting at the feet of Jesus,
Oh, what words I hear Him say!
Happy place! so near, so precious!
May it find me thru each day. . . .
Asa Hull

BENEDICTION

Bless the Lord, O my soul. All that is within me bless his holy name. Amen.

SELECTIONS FOR MEDITATION

✦ "Blessed are you."

No stranger words ever startled the ears of the poor, the humble, the meek, the mourning. What had been considered a curse is proclaimed a blessing! A living death is called "a more abundant life." Bad news becomes "Good News."

The beatitudes are Jesus' self-portrait, the most personal description we have of Him in the Gospels. They are the timeless image of Christ.

. . . We have often longed to know what Jesus actually looked like. What would a painting, a photograph have shown us? Would we today recognize Him if we saw Him? Although the mystery of the face of Jesus remains, each of us carries his own inner picture of Him. Consciously or unconsciously we are always looking for the Christ figure Who walks into each of our lives; each of us hopes for a secret or unexpected rendezvous. As an adopted child looks unceasingly for his real parents, or a parent for a missing child hoping for a meeting, a recognition—so we long for the Emmaus experience. "Now as they talked this over, Jesus came and walked by their side, but something prevented them from recognizing Him" (Luke 24:15).

We are all, in a sense, Zacchaeus, "anxious to see what kind of man Jesus was." Like him we listen to hear our name called as no one has ever spoken it before, to hear Him say, "Come down. Hurry, because I must stay at your house today." Yet it is in the Beatitudes that we truly recognize Him.

—From *Surprised by the Spirit* by Edward Farrell

✦ . . . the Beatitudes are foundational attitudes of the spiritual life and that they give form to it as a whole. They are responses to the human aspiration to experience the blessed life, or what St. Catherine of Genoa calls the "instinct for beatitude." They are invitations from a personal God to each of us as persons, calling us to the destiny of peace and joy. These eight attitudes involve all that we have been, all that we are, all that we shall become. They communicate a living expression of the divine direction of each human life.

The Beatitudes preserve the wisdom of the formation tradition, a wisdom we can rely upon in the ebb and flow of changing times. They provide a solid foundation on which to build our life of faith. When we live the Beatitudes in and with the Lord, we become liberated persons in the fullest sense. We follow the path of purgation until, with Jesus, we are filled with the peace of surrender to the Father and led by his Spirit to new depths of intimacy with the Indwelling Trinity. These ways of going to God offer us a truly holistic pattern of formation that involves our entire existence from birth to death and beyond.

—From *Blessings That Make Us Be*
by Susan Annette Muto

✦ Beware of placing Our Lord as a Teacher first. If Jesus Christ is a Teacher only, then all He can do is to tantalize me by erecting a standard I cannot attain. What is the use of presenting me with an ideal I cannot possibly come near? I am happier without knowing it. What is the good of telling me to be what I never can be—to be pure in heart, to do more than my duty, to be perfectly devoted to God? I must know Jesus Christ as Saviour before His teaching has any meaning for me other than that of an ideal which leads to despair. But when I am born again of the Spirit of God, I know that Jesus Christ did not come to teach only: He came to make me what He teaches I should be. The Redemption means that Jesus Christ can put into any man the disposition that ruled His own life, and all the standards God gives us are based on that disposition.

The teaching of the Sermon on the Mount produces despair in the natural man—the very thing Jesus means it to do. As long as we have a self-righteous, conceited notion that we can carry out Our Lord's teaching, God will allow us to go on until we break our ignorance over some obstacle, then we are willing to come to Him as paupers and receive from Him. "Blessed are the paupers in spirit," that is the first principle in the Kingdom of God. The bedrock in Jesus Christ's kingdom is poverty, not possession; not decisions for Jesus Christ, but a sense of absolute futility—I cannot begin to do it. Then Jesus says—Blessed are you. That is the entrance, and it does take us a long while to believe we are poor! The knowledge of our own poverty brings us to the moral frontier where Jesus Christ works.

—From *My Utmost for His Highest* by Oswald Chambers

✦ The New Testament notices things which from our standards do not seem to count. "Blessed are the poor in spirit," literally—Blessed are the paupers—an exceedingly commonplace thing! The preaching of today is apt to emphasize strength of will, beauty of character—the things that are easily noticed. The phrase we hear so often, Decide for Christ, is an emphasis on something Our Lord never trusted. He never asks us to decide for Him, but to yield to Him—a very different thing. At the basis of Jesus Christ's Kingdom is the unaffected loveliness of the commonplace. The thing I am blessed in is my poverty. If I know I have no strength of will, no nobility of disposition, then Jesus says—Blessed are you, because it is through this poverty that I enter His Kingdom. I cannot enter His Kingdom as a good man or woman, I can only enter it as a complete pauper.

—From *My Utmost for His Highest* by Oswald Chambers

✦ The beatitudes set forth the balanced and variegated character of Christian people. These are not eight separate and distinct groups of disciples, some of who are meek, while others are merciful and yet others are called upon to endure persecution. They are rather eight qualities of the same group who at one and the same time are meek and merciful, poor in spirit and pure in heart, mourning and hungry, peacemakers and persecuted.

Further, the group exhibiting these marks is not an elitist

set, a small spiritual aristocracy remote from the common run of Christians. On the contrary, the beatitudes are Christ's own specification of what every Christian ought to be. All these qualities are to characterize all his followers. Just as the nine-fold fruit of the Spirit which Paul lists is to ripen in every Christian character, so the eight beatitudes which Christ speaks of describe his ideal for every citizen of God's kingdom. Unlike the gifts of the Spirit which he distributes to different members of Christ's body in order to equip them for different types of service, the same Spirit is concerned to work all these Christian graces in us all. There is no escape from our responsibility to covet them all.

—From *The Message of the Sermon on the Mount*
by John R. W. Stott

✦ The Beatitudes are not so much ethics of obedience as ethics of grace. They imply God as a gracious giver and man as a humble receiver. They do not mean: you must do these things in order to deserve and win the divine approval. Rather do they say: God gives his blessedness to those who claim no merit for themselves but, knowing their own heart's needs, are content to rest wholly on the mercy of God.

—From *A Pattern for Life* by Archibald Hunter

✦ A true man, says the objector, should believe in virtue for virtue's sake. All talk of reward, here or hereafter, savours of the quid pro quo morality—the "contract" idea of religion—which disfigured Judaism at its worst and from which Christians have not always kept themselves free. How shall we answer?

We all like the suggestion of the hymn:
Whatever, Lord, we lend to Thee
Repaid a thousand-fold will be.
Should we not rather agree:
My God, I love Thee; not because
I hope for heaven thereby,
Not yet for fear that loving not
I might forever die?

Yet that does not mean that we should wholly reject the idea of reward. Indeed, in a universe directed to moral ends good action and character must issue in some kind of satisfaction; and in the highest ethical systems it is arguable that there must be satisfactions. The real questions are: What is to be the nature of the rewards? And how far are they held out as inducements—as bribes?

... C. S. Lewis says ... the proper rewards are not simply tacked on to the activity for which they are given, but are the activity itself in consummation. So it is with the Christian doctrine of reward. The rewards offered by Jesus to the righteous are simply the inevitable issue of goodness in a world ruled over by a good God. Those who have attained the Beatific Vision know that it is no mere bribe but simply fit consummation of their earthly communication with God.

—From *A Pattern for Life* by Archibald Hunter

You, dear friends, are the children of God.
There is no language or human medium
    that can communicate the beauty and significance
    of that blessed relationship.
It is altogether beyond the comprehension
    of earthbound creatures.
Yet it is this that God makes possible
    for you through Jesus Christ.
It means that you need no priest to stand
    between you and God.
Nor do you need sacrificial altars
    upon which to offer your gifts to Him
    or stately temples in which to worship Him.
As a little child boldly approaches his father
    in love and need, so God is your Father,
    and you may confidently come to Him,
    worshipfully, penitentially, joyfully,
    daring to air your doubts, your fears,
    your problems and needs,
    knowing that He hears,
    that He rejoices in the faith of His children,
    and that He responds to their urgent requests.
You must, however, be open to God and your fellow beings.

As you claim His divine forgiveness,
   so you are to relate in forgiving love
   to those about you.
As you relate your needs to Him,
   you must submit to His will for you.
As you seek His gifts, you are to share such gifts
   with your brothers and sisters.
As you look to Him for guidance, you are expected
   to walk in the paths He lays out for you.

When you worship or pray or sing His praises,
   be aware that this is done to relate to God—
   not to impress your peers.
Your Father knows your needs far better than you do;
   yet He desires that you communicate with Him,
   rely on Him, trust Him, abide in Him.
He rejoices in the love of His children;
   He urges you as His children to continually regard Him
   as your loving Father.

—From *Jesus/Now* by Leslie F. Brandt

33. The Parables

INVOCATION

O Eternal Christ, understandable to even me, I thank you for putting the latchstring so low I can reach it. I can reach the Highest, for you are the Highest become lowly, reachable. And so I come, for in you I "see"—see everything I need. I thank you. Amen.

E. Stanley Jones in *The Way*

PSALM 103

DAILY SCRIPTURE

Monday	Mark 4:1–34
Tuesday	Matthew 13:10–17
Wednesday	2 Samuel 12:1–25
Thursday	Romans 10:1–21
Friday	John 16:1–16
Saturday	Proverbs 6:20–23
Sunday	Isaiah 48:14–22

SELECTIONS FOR MEDITATION

PERSONAL MEDITATION

PRAYER

Jesus often explained the deep things about his Father with stories from everyday life. Ask him this week to speak to you from all the events and people of your daily living.

HYMN   "Wonderful Words of Life"

> Sing them over again to me,
> Wonderful words of life!
> Let me more of their beauty see,
> Wonderful words of life!

Words of life and beauty,
Teach me faith and duty:
Beautiful words, wonderful words,
Wonderful words of life. . . .

P. P. Bliss

BENEDICTION

O gracious Christ, you have so lavishly given yourself to every part of all that surrounds me. Let me hear you, see you, know you. Cleanse me of the sin of inattention. Amen.

SELECTIONS FOR MEDITATION

✦ Jesus used parables to teach spiritual truths. The condition of each hearer determines whether that aim is realized or not. But Jesus used the parables to throw light on the reign of God, on the demands of God, on the response of men to the demands of God, and the like. . . . Those who were helped by the parables were those who really saw, who really heard. They were far different from those who went through the motions of seeing but did not see, who went through the motions of hearing but did not hear.

—From *Interpreting the Bible* by A. Berkeley Mickelsen

✦ Every parable of Jesus was meant to evoke a response and to strike for a verdict. "What do you think?" he sometimes begins, and where the words are not found, the question is implied. There follows, as a rule, a true-to-life story or the description of a familiar happening; and the hearer is invited to transfer the judgment formed on the happening or story to the urgent issues of the Kingdom of God, which is the theme of all his parables. "He who has ears to hear," he sometimes concludes, "let him hear." Which must mean: "This is more than just a pleasant story. Go and work it out for yourselves."

—From *Interpreting the Parables* by A. M. Hunter

✦ Jesus Himself was very reticent about spreading abroad the reports of the external results of His inner prayer life. How often we read after something especially striking had happened, "He cautioned them that they should tell no man!" His reason for this, it seems to me, was His deep inner intuition that all people are not at the same time at the same level of spiritual unfoldment. The kind of treatment necessary for the growing grain is not, for instance, what is needed for the ripened corn. The food for the grown-up may be too strong for the little child. Most of the people about Him were in the childhood of spiritual evolution, not ready to see through the outer husk to the inner spirit. Therefore He must dole out very carefully the outer miracles or clothe them in forms that would be more easily assimilative to their souls.

The form that He used most frequently to convey spiritual truths to the unripened mind was the parable. By this method He could keep the inner experience concealed from those whose hearts were hardened and unprepared like untilled soil is hardened and unprepared for the planting. Yet at the same time the parable shell was adapted for holding all the essence of truth hermetically sealed, so to speak, and as safely preserved as a grain of corn preserves within itself the germ of new life, ready for instant immolation and growth the moment the soil opens to receive it.

When requests come to me to tell some of the miracles of answered prayer that have fallen within my own experience, I naturally turn to this vehicle which was so frequently used, and so blessed in its use, by Jesus the Christ. The twelve "parable miracles" that follow may be read by those who so desire as so many pretty little fairy stories to gladden the heart and brighten an idle hour. To others they may be accepted for just what they are—true accounts of actual happenings, in which the events have been minimized and understated rather than overstated. But for all who read them they are intended as seeds to be planted as rapidly as the soil is made ready to receive them. It is trusted that from this simple planting may come forth a harvest of grain either now or in the days to come—grain that may furnish food for the very bread of life, bread that may be assimilated unto oneself and become the bone of one's bone and flesh of one's flesh— bringing additional strength to some who may need it, some who may be facing long days and nights of weary travel along life's hard pathway.

—From *I Will Lift Up Mine Eyes* by Glenn Clark

◆ Because the word that God speaks to us is always an incarnate word—a word spelled out to us not alphabetically, in syllables, but enigmatically, in events, even in books we read and the movies we see—the chances are we will never get it just right. We are so used to hearing what we want to hear and remaining deaf to what it would be well for us to hear that it is hard to break the habit. But if we keep our hearts and minds open as well as our ears, if we listen with patience and hope, if we remember at all deeply and honestly, then I think we come to recognize, beyond all doubt, that, however faintly we may hear him, he is indeed speaking to us, and that, however little we may understand of it, his word to each of us is both recoverable and precious beyond telling.

—From *Now and Then* by Frederick Buechner

◆ Jesus had a way of putting things that time does not wear out. He might have discussed neighborliness in the abstract, like a lawyer analyzing in terms of current practice. Had he done so, we probably should never have heard of it. Instead, he personified neighborliness in the good Samaritan, making him stand out in vivid contrast with the unneighborly priest and Levite, so that not only did his contemporaries grasp his meaning, but we do also. Personal incarnations have a perennial continuance in the understanding of the race. Abstract condemnations of economic greed have been both frequent and transient, but the rich man who "feasted sumptuously every day," while "a poor man named Lazarus, full of sores," begged at his gate has not been transient; nor that other rich man who said to his soul, "Soul, you have ample goods laid up for many years; take your ease, eat, drink, be merry." Such incarnations walk the streets of New York and London as plainly as they walked the streets of Jerusalem.

—From *The Man from Nazareth*
by Harry Emerson Fosdick

✦ Texts do their disclosing best when they are capable of upsetting the reader's world. That is why it is limiting to think of them as merely being relevant to our worlds as we already think of them. Texts that are full of reversals and that most surprise admit an approach that impels one to look for the world that was in front of them. For that reason, many scholars like to restudy and revisit the parables of Jesus. They are upsetting, reversing, and surprising. In them, the smallest becomes largest, the last becomes first, the outsider turns insider, the humblest is exalted at the expense of the proud, the remote gets seated at the head table. This, the reader says, is not how things naturally are. Fathers of prodigal sons keep score on their wanderings, even if in the end they yield to the emotions that welcome their sons home. The parable discloses because it is different from our contemporary experience.

—From *A Cry of Absence* by Martin E. Marty

✦ One of the differences between great art and mediocre art is that with great art you can never get all that is there. A comic strip can be enjoyed and discarded with the Sunday newspaper, but the Mona Lisa can be hung on the wall and enjoyed for a lifetime. You can never get all that is there. A television soap opera can be quickly comprehended and soon forgotten, but a Shakespearean drama can be seen again and again, with each new viewing communicating fresh ideas and perspectives. You can never get all that is there. The parables of Jesus are like great art. They express a profound simplicity. The familiar stories yield new vistas of thought each time they are explored. But you can never get all that is there.

The parable of the prodigal son is one of the best-known stories of all time. Read it again, and see what you missed the last time.

—From *Parables for Christian Living* by Douglas Beyer

✦ ... the parables have an arresting quality which has etched them deep in memory. They are based on things seen, and they awake immediate and vivid images which are seen again in the mind. As John Bunyan knew, the citadel of Man-

Soul is stormed more easily through eye-gate than through ear-gate; and it is because they enter through the visual imagination that the parables have penetrated so surely into the thought and conscience of so many folk. Into the thought and also into the conscience, be it noted, for the parables provoke far more than curiosity. They not only arrest attention; they arouse something deep within. It was said of Jesus that the common people heard him gladly; and no wonder, for the extraordinary quality of his teachings, and especially of his parables, was that they said what ordinary men and women could take hold of. When Jesus spoke, it was not as though some unfamiliar idea were coming from outside, but rather as though an instinctive recognition were being awakened in the listeners' own selves. "That is the way life really works," they felt. "That is how truth is." The parables did not bring alien information; rather they focused and called into action what people already half knew was so, and now suddenly could fully see.

—From *The Interpreter's Bible, Volume 7.*
Edited by G. A Buttrick

✦ "Hmmm, Dodye Feig's grandson," the Rebbe repeated as if to himself. His eyes were resting upon me and I wondered whom he saw. And why he turned sad all of a sudden. Then I realized that unlike him I have changed in more than one way; I was no longer his disciple.

"Rebbe," I said, "I have been working hard to acquire a name for myself. Yet, to you I am still attached to my grandfather's." It was a poor attempt to break the tension; it failed. Now he seemed somewhat angry: "So, that's what you have been doing all these years," he remarked. He nodded his head and added: "What a pity."

. . . "Tell me what you are doing," the Rebbe said in a soft voice. I told him I was writing. "Is that all?" he asked in disbelief. I said, yes that's all. His expression was so reproachful that I had to elaborate and explain that some writings could sometimes, in moments of grace, attain the quality of deeds. He did not seem to understand.

I was afraid of that. If I had waited so many years before I came to see him—although I knew where he could be found—it was because I did not want to acknowledge the distance between us. I was afraid both of its existence and its absence. All the words that for twenty years I have been trying to put together, were they mine or his? I did not have the answer but, somehow, I was afraid that he did.

"What are you writing?" the Rebbe asked. "Stories," I said. He wanted to know what kind of stories: true stories. "About people you knew?" Yes, about things that happened or could have happened. "But they did not?" No, not all of them did. In fact, some were invented from almost the beginning to the end. The Rebbe leaned forward as if to measure me up and said with more sorrow than anger: "That means you are writing lies!" I did not answer immediately. The scolded child within me had nothing to say in his defense. Yet, I had to justify myself: "Things are not that simple, Rebbe. Some events do take place but are not true; others are—although they never occurred."

—From the Introduction to *Legends of Our Time*
by Elie Wiesel

34. The Jesus Prayer

INVOCATION

Dear Lord Jesus, may my prayers this day be bounded by my deepest needs on one side and by your greatness on the other. And may their expression be in simple longings and words that would lift my soul into your presence. Amen.

PSALM 31

DAILY SCRIPTURE

Monday	Luke 18:35–43
Tuesday	Colossians 1:15–23
Wednesday	Ephesians 1:1–14
Thursday	Philippians 2:1–11
Friday	Romans 6:1–23
Saturday	2 Corinthians 5:17–21
Sunday	Matthew 8:1–17

SELECTIONS FOR MEDITATION

PERSONAL MEDITATION

PRAYER

Sometimes words themselves get in the way of our praying. Try using a few simple phrases—such as those in the Jesus Prayer to focus your attention upon God.

HYMN   "Dear Lord and Father of Mankind"

Dear Lord and Father of mankind,
Forgive our feverish ways!
Reclothe us in our rightful mind;
In purer lives Thy service find,
In deeper rev'rence praise.

In simple trust, like theirs who heard,
Beside the Syrian sea,
The gracious calling of the Lord.
Let us, like them, without a word,
Rise up and follow Thee. . . .
                                    John G. Whittier

BENEDICTION

Lord Jesus Christ, Son of God, have mercy on me. Amen.
                                    The Jesus Prayer

SELECTIONS FOR MEDITATION

✦ One of the simplest of all Christian prayers, this consists in a single brief sentence, "Lord Jesus Christ, Son of God, have mercy on me." Ten words in English, in other languages it is even shorter—in Greek and Russian, no more than seven words. Yet around those few words many Orthodox over the centuries have built their spiritual life, and through this one prayer they have entered into the deepest mysteries of Christian knowledge.

—From *The Art of Prayer* by Igumen Chariton of Valamo

✦ Three things in the Jesus Prayer call for special comment, and help to account for its extraordinary wide appeal. First, the Jesus Prayer brings together, in one short sentence, two essential "moments" of Christian devotion: adoration and compunction. Adoration is expressed in the opening clause, "Lord Jesus Christ, Son of God"; compunction, in the prayer for mercy that follows. The glory of God and the sin of man—both are vividly present in the Prayer; it is an act of thanksgiving for the salvation that Jesus brings, and an expression of sorrow for the weakness of our response. The Prayer is both penitential and full of joy and loving confidence.

In the second place, it is an intensely Christological prayer—a prayer addressed to Jesus, concentrated upon the Person of the Incarnate Lord, emphasizing at once both His life on earth—"Jesus Christ"—and His divinity—"Son of God."

... In the third place, the Invocation of the Name is a prayer of the utmost simplicity. It is a way of praying that anyone can adopt: no special knowledge is required, and no elaborate preparation. As a recent writer puts it, all we must do is "simply begin": "Before beginning to pronounce the Name of Jesus, establish peace and recollection within yourself and ask for the inspiration and guidance of the Holy Ghost. . . . Then simply begin."

—From *The Art of Prayer* by Igumen Chariton of Valamo

◆ What I have in mind now is something which is specifically used by the Orthodox. It is what we call the "Jesus prayer," a prayer which is centered on the name of Jesus. "Lord Jesus Christ, Son of God, have mercy on me a sinner." This prayer is used by monks and nuns but also it is used by our lay people. It is the prayer of stability, because it is the prayer that is not discursive—we do not move from one thought to the other—it is a prayer that places us face to face with God through a profession of faith concerning Him, and it defines a situation concerning us. It is the profession of faith which, according to the mind of most Orthodox ascetics and mystics, is a summing up of the whole Gospel. We profess the Lordship of Christ, His sovereign right upon us, the fact that He is our Lord and our God, and this implies that all our life is within His will and that we commit ourselves to His will and to no other way. That is the name of "Jesus" in which we confess the reality of the Incarnation and all that the Incarnation stands for. Christ in whom we see the Incarnate Word of God in the line of the Old and the New Testament, the anointed of Yahweh. Then the perfect profession of faith, of what He is—the Son of God. This is not only a profession of faith in Jesus Christ, but it also opens up the Trinitarian way because He is the Son of the Father and no one can recognize in the prophet of Galilee the Incarnate Son of God unless the Holy Spirit teaches him to see, to understand and to commit himself. So here we have the fourth profession of faith that allows us to stand face to face with God in truth, and profess in spirit. And then, "have mercy on us." "Have mercy" is the

English rendering of the word "eleison." When you say the Kyrie Eleison, you are using Greek words which mean "Lord, have mercy."

—From *Beginning to Pray* by Anthony Bloom

✦ As I noticed that he was always in prayer and versed in the inward prayer of the heart, and as he spoke Russian perfectly, I questioned him on this matter. He readily told me a great deal about it and I listened with care. I even wrote down many things that he said. Thus, for example, he taught me about the excellence and greatness of the Jesus Prayer in this way. "Even the very form of the Jesus Prayer," he said, "shows what a great prayer it is. It is made up of two parts. In the first, i.e., 'Lord Jesus Christ, Son of God,' it leads our thoughts to the life of Jesus Christ, or, as the holy Fathers put it, it is the whole Gospel in brief. In the second part, 'Have mercy on me, a sinner,' it faces us with the story of our own helplessness and sinfulness. And it is to be noted that the desire and petition of a poor, sinful, humble soul could not be put into words more wise, more clear cut, more exact than these—'have mercy on me.' No other form of words would be as satisfying and full as this. . . . It is a cry for mercy—that is, for grace—which will show itself in the gift of strength from God, to enable us to resist temptation and overcome our sinful inclinations. It is like a penniless debtor asking his kindly creditor not only to forgive him the debt but also to pity his extreme poverty and to give him alms—that is what these profound words 'have mercy on me' express."

—From *The Way of a Pilgrim* and *The Pilgrim Continues His Way.* Author Unknown

✦ A short utterance like the Jesus Prayer—"Lord Jesus Christ, Son of God, have mercy on me, a sinner" —when repeated over and over, becomes part of the warp and woof of our being, altering our lives in ways we didn't think possible. The Way of a Pilgrim shows us how this form of meditation can change us and as a result, alter both our circumstances and those of others. The beautiful thing about this particular type of meditation is that it can be practiced while we are typing a letter, cooking a meal, or driving the car. It can be as integral to us as breathing. Time assumes a new depth and importance as we examine our lives in the light of such a prayer, for our priorities reorder themselves according to our commitment to a truly devotional life.

—From *Transcend* by Morton T. Kelsey

✦ When these prayers are in words, as they very seldom are, they are only in very few words; in fact, the fewer the better. Indeed, if it is but a little word of one syllable it seems to me to be better than a word of two syllables or more. This is in accordance with the work of the spirit, for a spiritual worker should always be at the highest and ultimate point of the spirit.

You can see that this is so by an example drawn from the course of nature. When a man or a woman is overcome by fear in any sudden emergency such as fire, a person dying, or anything of that kind, he is impelled immediately to cry out from the intensity of his feeling calling for help to come at once. Yes, and how does he do this? Certainly it is not in many words; and it is not even in one word of two syllables. The reason is that it would take him too long should he try to explain the nature of his need. He therefore bursts out all at once with a great spirit and cries a little word of one syllable, such as the word "fire" or the word "help."

And just as this little word "fire" stirs and pierces the ears of the hearers much more quickly, so does a little word of one syllable do the same when it is not only spoken or thought but secretly intended in the depth of the spirit. This depth is height, for spiritually all is one, height and depth, length and breadth. It pierces the ears of the Almighty God more than does any psalter thoughtlessly mumbled in one's teeth. This is the reason it is written that short prayer pierces heaven.

—From *The Cloud of Unknowing*
translated by Ira Progoff

✦ Over the past few years my most steady prayer of solidarity has been based on the "Jesus Prayer": "Lord Jesus Christ, Son of God, have mercy on me, a sinner." This ancient, simple prayer is based on Paul's exhortation to pray constantly (1 Thess. 5:17) and on the Gospel cries of "Lord, have mercy." It was shaped by the early Desert Fathers and eventually became a classic form of prayer practiced widely to this day, especially among Eastern Orthodox Christians.

Historically the prayer has been flexible in its form except for the constant of the name Jesus ("Never say or do anything except in the name of the Lord Jesus"—Col. 3:17; "Everyone who calls upon the name of the Lord will be saved"—Rom. 10:13). In some historic uses it is done in rhythm with breathing, such as "Lord Jesus Christ" on the in-breath, and "have mercy on me" with the out-breath. I have found this coalescence with breathing very natural.

—From *Living Simply Through the Day*
by Tilden H. Edwards

✦ For many years after my conversion I never used any readymade forms except the Lord's Prayer. In fact, I tried to pray without words at all—not to verbalize the mental acts. Even in praying for others I believe I tended to avoid their names and substituted mental images of them. I still think the prayer without words is the best—if one can really achieve it. But I now see that in trying to make it my daily bread I was counting on a greater mental and spiritual strength than I really have. To pray successfully without words one needs to be "at the top of one's form." Otherwise the mental acts become merely imaginative or emotional acts—and a fabricated emotion is a miserable affair. When the golden moments come, when God enables one really to pray without words, who but a fool would reject the gift? But He does not give it—anyway not to me—day in, day out. My mistake was what Pascal, if I remember rightly, calls "Error of Stoicism"; thinking we can do always what we can do sometimes. . . .

For me words are . . . secondary. They are only an anchor. Or, shall I say, they are the movements of a conductor's baton: not the music. They serve to canalize the worship, or penitence, or petition, which might without them—such are our minds—spread into wide and shallow puddles.

. . . At present—for one's practice changes and, I think, ought to change—I find it best to make "my own words" the staple but introduce a modicum of the ready-made. . . .

Perhaps I shan't find it so easy to persuade you that the ready-made modicum has . . . its use: for me, I mean—I'm not suggesting rules for anyone else in the world.

First, it keeps me in touch with "sound doctrine." Left to oneself, one could easily slide away from "the faith once given" into a phantom called "my religion."

Secondly, it reminds me "what things I ought to ask" (perhaps especially when I am praying for other people). The crisis of the present moment, like the nearest telegraph post, will always loom largest. Isn't there a danger that our great, permanent, objective necessities—often more important—may get crowded out?

Finally, they provide an element of the ceremonial.

—From *The Joyful Christian* by C. S. Lewis

SECTION FOUR
inward graces of the centered life

One of the statements most often made concerning prayer is that it "changes things." But it is also true that the first thing that prayer changes is the one who prays. It is readily observable that we become like those with whom we associate. If this is true with earthly friends and companions, how much more it is true of the "inner man." Time spent faithfully and devotedly in "the presence" will most surely result in our becoming more and more Christlike in both spirit and in action.

The process is like watching the growth of a child. If one is with them each day it will be hard to see them growing. It is only as we measure them against a mark on the doorpost or try to fit them into last spring's clothes that we realize the extent of their growth. And even though the process may be imperceptible to us at a given moment we will begin to note by reading back through our journal or by sensing our responses and attitudes in everyday matters and relationships that he is changing us and endowing us with the fruits of his spirit.

Eight attributes of Christ have been chosen for study and prayer in this section. We should recognize these qualities of Christlikeness and seek to encourage and foster them in our heart and life. The first fruits of our prayers will be deep within our own hearts.

Now we will be beginning to understand one of the great paradoxes of prayer. Tasting these fruits of the spirit within us will cause us to feel that our spiritual appetite is both satisfied and intensified. We will sense both the "hunger" and the being "filled" which the Beatitude describes. We will begin to see that our constancy in prayer has laid the foundation upon which we can build. But more and more it will be this paradox—"hunger and filling"—that calls us to continual prayer.

Reuben Job, a lifelong model of faithfulness to the inner journey, spoke of this patterning of consistent, personal prayer time. He concluded that if a person would make it a regular practice for a period of at least thirty days he would never abandon it. His reasoning was that the changes in one's heart and life would be so dramatic and substantial that the thought of living the old way again would become unthinkable.

35. Humility

INVOCATION

O Christ, your blessed faith in me sends me to my knees. I am humbled at your confidence in me. Now help me to be in some measure worthy of your faith. Amen.

E. Stanley Jones in *Mastery*

PSALM 24

DAILY SCRIPTURE

Monday	Jeremiah 10:23–35
Tuesday	Romans 1:1–17
Wednesday	Isaiah 6:1–8
Thursday	Matthew 23:1–12
Friday	Acts 10:1–48
Saturday	Matthew 3:1–17
Sunday	Galatians 6:11–18

SELECTIONS FOR MEDITATION

PERSONAL MEDITATION

PRAYER

Pray this week that God will free you of all thoughts of precedence. Rejoice in the thought that he has made you an equal brother or sister in Christ. Be careful of titles and positions that would cause you to think you are either above or below others. Strive to make all those you meet also sense their special standing.

HYMN   "O Love That Wilt Not Let Me Go"

> O Love that wilt not let me go,
> I rest my weary soul in Thee
> I give Thee back the life I owe,

That in Thine ocean depths its flow
May richer, fuller be.

O Light that fol'west all my way,
I yield my flickering torch to Thee;
My heart restores its borrowed ray,
That in Thy sunshine's blaze its day
May brighter, fuller be.

O Joy that seekest me through pain,
I cannot close my heart to Thee;
I trace the rainbow through the rain,
And feel the promise is not vain
That morn shall tearless be.

O Cross that liftest up my head,
I dare not ask to fly from Thee;
I lay in dust life's glory dead,
And from the ground there blossoms red
Life that shall endless be.

George Matheson

BENEDICTION

O Father, I thank you that I can stand before you neither above or below any person. Help me to take that privilege and give it to every other person. Amen.

SELECTIONS FOR MEDITATION

✦ Humility opens our inner ears. It enables us to acknowledge the truth of who we are and who God is. Only the humble can understand the deep resonance of God's voice in the whole of creation. Humility withstands any arrogant tendency to reduce the word to our purposes. When we live in humble presence, God may reveal to us while we read insights that transcend human expectations.

—From *Pathways of Spiritual Living*
by Susan Annette Muto

✦ Humility is a virtue, not a neurosis.
It sets us free to act virtuously, to serve God and to know Him. Therefore true humility can never inhibit any really vir-

tuous action, nor can it prevent us from fulfilling ourselves by doing the will of God.

Humility sets us free to do what is really good, by showing us our illusions and withdrawing your will from what was only an apparent good.

A humility that freezes our being and frustrates all healthy activity is not humility at all, but a disguised form of pride. It dries up the roots of the spiritual life and makes it impossible for us to give ourselves to God.

—From *Thoughts in Solitude* by Thomas Merton

✦ Lord, Thou knowest better than I know myself that I am growing older, and will some day be old.

Keep me from getting talkative, and particularly from the fatal habit of thinking I must say something on every subject and on every occasion.

Release me from craving to try to straighten out everybody's affairs.

Keep my mind free from the recital of endless details—give me wings to get to the point.

I ask for grace enough to listen to the tales of others' pains. Help me to endure them with patience.

But seal my lips on my own aches and pains—they are increasing and my love of rehearsing them is becoming sweeter as the years go by.

Teach me the glorious lesson that occasionally it is possible that I may be mistaken.

Keep me reasonably sweet; I do not want to be a saint—some of them are so hard to live with—but a sour old woman is one of the crowning works of the devil.

Make me thoughtful, but not moody; helpful, but not bossy. With my vast store of wisdom, it seems a pity not to use it all—but Thou knowest, Lord, that I want a few friends at the end.

—From *Little Book of Prayers* by a Mother Superior who wishes to be anonymous

✦ The first barrier to meekness arises whenever we claim as

our own what is really a gift of God. To live in meekness, we must try to remember that all we are, have, and can do is a gift. It is an act of arrogance to place ourselves at the center of being and doing. Only God belongs there.

Arrogance is the opposite of humility. It compels us to treat our limits not as unique openings through which God can reveal his goodness but as diseases to be cured. We find it almost impossible to be self-effacing, as if we must maintain a know-it-all posture that demands a final answer to mystery. Basically, we perceive any sign of tenderness as a threat to our claim to be fully capable of caring for ourselves.

This arrogant aloofness leads to a second obstacle to lowliness, and that is the tendency to dominate others. We feel compelled to be "top dog." It would demean our proud self-image were we to walk hand in hand with others. Instead, we want to force upon them our aims and opinions. If this means becoming loud and demanding, so what? We refuse to compromise our point or to let others have the last word.

. . . The third obstacle to living meekly stems from the tendency to see only what is wrong in a situation and never to affirm the good. This trait breeds a joylessness that lacks beatitude. We become literally killjoys, murdering that spirit of lightheartedness that signifies union with God. Without joy, we can never experience carefree playing before the face of the Father. If we do not know how to play, we may be unable to pray. We exclude displeasure and are prone to pick fights. Others perceive a hostile streak in us. We are prone to insult people. We lack patience. What flows from our mouths is not blessing but barbs of bitterness.

—From *Blessings That Makes Us Be*
by Susan Annette Muto

✦ . . . the way to power lies through the realization of helplessness; that the way to victory lies through the admission of defeat; that the way to goodness lies through the confession and the acknowledgment of sin. Herein is an essential truth which runs through all life. If a man is ill, the first necessity is that he should admit and recognize that he is ill, and that then he should seek for a cure in the right place. The way to knowledge begins with the admission of ignorance. The one man who can never learn is the man who thinks that he knows everything already.

. . . the way to independence lies through dependence, and the way to freedom lies through surrender. If ever a man is to be independent of the chances and the changes of life, that independence must come from his complete dependence on God. If ever a man is to know true freedom, that freedom must come through complete surrender to God.

. . . the way to bliss which the world can neither give nor take away lies through the recognition of our own need, and the conviction that the need can be met, when we commit to God in perfect trust.

—From *The Beatitudes and the Lord's Prayer for Everyman*
by William Barclay

✦ Such a person discovers that such abandonment loses nothing that is worth keeping but finds God with a quick vividness that is breath-taking and thrilling. When he prays, there are no more self-begotten plans and purposes intruding themselves between him and God. Nor is consciousness busied with dreams and demands rising out of a subtle egoism that assumes that it knows best. He wants God as a thirsty man wants water or a hungry man, bread. He wants God's will done as a sick man wants the will of the physician whom he trusts. He wants God's kingdom to come as a crusader wants, more than life itself, the triumph of his cause. So with his whole consciousness eagerly committing itself to God, he soon enters into a vivid awareness of the God who is always at hand, waiting to deal with human willingness, and to give himself when human willingness has been cleansed and made ready by disciplines and by grace.

So humility is not weakness but strength, for it receives the strength of God. It is not folly, but wisdom, for it is open to the ever available wisdom of God. It is not nothingness but fullness, for into the vacuum created by the demolition of human pride and self-sufficiency, pours the fullness of God.

"Blessed are the poor in spirit, for theirs is the kingdom of heaven." "He that humbleth himself shall be exalted." "Humble yourself therefore under the mighty hand of God that he may lift you up."

—From *Discipline and Discovery* by Albert E. Day

✦ Right prayer is a time of great, genuine humility. "Blessed are the poor in spirit." "Blessed are they that mourn." "Blessed are the meek." In the presence of God one is vividly aware that he is not what he should be, has not what he needs in order to become a real man, knows not what he must know about himself and life. He feels like a pauper as far as true wealth is concerned. He has no boast to make—rather does he bewail his state of soul. He is not morbid about it. But he is real. There is no pretense, no face-saving. How can there be? He is dealing with God now—and God knows all about him. His own concern is to see in himself what God sees. He does perceive in part—and so is very humble. He wants a fuller perception—and so is very teachable. No matter how good he is, he knows that he is not good enough. No matter how bad he is, he knows there is mercy. God is so much wiser, holier, more loving than he is that it is foolish to try to make a case for himself. His folly is as evident to God as a wrong answer on an examination paper. His sins are as apparent to God as an inkstain upon a wall. His unlovingness is as visible to God as a broken bone in an X ray photograph. "All things are naked and open to the eye of Him with whom we have to do." All he can do is to fling himself upon God's mercy. His need is his only defense and his only argument.

Let not conscience make you linger,
Nor of fitness fondly dream;
All the fitness He requireth
Is to feel your need of Him.

That old gospel song, in simplest words, epitomizes the real situation in true prayer.

—From *An Autobiography of Prayer* by Albert E. Day

✦ When we are self-conscious, we cannot be wholly aware;

we must throw ourselves out first. This throwing ourselves away is the act of creativity. So, when we wholly concentrate, like a child in play, or an artist at work, then we share in the act of creating. We not only escape time, we also escape our self-conscious selves.

The Greeks had a word for ultimate self-consciousness which I find illuminating: *hubris:* pride: pride in the sense of putting oneself in the center of the universe. The strange and terrible thing is that this kind of total self-consciousness invariably ends in self-annihilation. The great tragedians have always understood this, from Sophocles to Shakespeare. We witness it in history in such people as Tiberius, Eva Peron, Hitler.

I was timid about putting forth most of these thoughts, but this kind of timidity is itself a form of pride. The moment that humility becomes self-consciousness, it becomes hubris. One cannot be humble and aware of oneself at the same time. Therefore, the art of creating—painting a picture, singing a song, writing a story—is a humble act? This was a new thought to me. Humility is throwing oneself away in complete concentration on something or someone else.

—From *A Circle of Quiet* by Madeleine L'Engle

36. Obedience

INVOCATION

O Jesus! who has taught us that not all those who say Lord, Lord, shall enter into the kingdom of heaven, but only such as do the will of your Father, whose lives correspond with their belief, grant us a truly Christian spirit, a Christian heart, and guide us in the paths of a Christian life. Grant that I may become detached from all things and in all things seek you alone. Grant that I may direct all my knowledge, my whole capacity, all my happiness, and all my exertions, to please you, to love you, and to obtain your love for time and eternity. Amen.

Thomas à Kempis in *The Imitation of Christ*

PSALM 25

DAILY SCRIPTURE

Monday	Matthew 8:18–22
Tuesday	Luke 1:26–28
Wednesday	Deuteronomy 26:16–19
Thursday	Matthew 10:32–42
Friday	1 Samuel 15:12–15
Saturday	Matthew 19:16–30
Sunday	Acts 15:17–29

SELECTIONS FOR MEDITATION

PERSONAL MEDITATION

PRAYER

The real difference between Christians who are growing and ones who are not is the matter of obedience. Pray for strength to be obedient.

HYMN   "Trust and Obey"

> When we walk with the Lord
> In the light of His Word,
> What a glory He sheds on our way!
> While we do His good will,
> He abides with us still,
> And with all who will trust and obey.
>
> Not a shadow can rise,
> Not a cloud in the skies,
> But His smile quickly drives it away.
> Not a doubt or a fear,
> Not a sigh or a tear
> Can abide while we trust and obey.
>
> Not a burden we bear.
> Not a sorrow we share
> But our toil He doth richly repay.
> Not a grief or a loss.
> Not a frown or a cross
> But is blest if we trust and obey.
>
> But we never can prove
> The delights of His love
> Until all on the altar we lay:
> For the favor He shows
> And the joy He bestows
> Are for them who will trust and obey.
>
> Then in fellowship sweet
> We will sit at His feet.
> Or we'll walk by His side in the way.
> What He says we will do
> Where He sends we will go;
> Never fear, only trust and obey.
>
> Trust and obey,
> For there's no other way
> To be happy in Jesus
> But to trust and obey.

John Sammis

BENEDICTION

Speak, Lord, for your servant hears. Grant me ears to hear, eyes to see, a will to obey, a heart to love; then declare what you will, reveal what you will, command what you will, demand what you will. Amen.

Christina Rosetti in *Little Book of Prayers*

SELECTIONS FOR MEDITATION

✦ The great danger facing all of us—let me say it again, for one feels it tremendously—is not that we shall make an absolute failure of life, nor that we shall fall into outright viciousness, nor that we shall be terribly unhappy, nor that we shall feel that life has no meaning at all—not these things. The danger is that we may fail to perceive life's greatest meaning, fall short of its highest good, miss its deepest and most abiding happiness, be unable to render the most needed service, be unconscious of life ablaze with the light of the Presence of God—and be content to have it so—that is the danger. That some day we may wake up and find that always we have been busy with the husks and trappings of life—and have really missed life itself. For life without God, to one who has known the richness and joy of life with Him, is unthinkable, impossible. That is what one prays one's friends may be spared—satisfaction with a life that falls short of the best, that has in it no tingle and thrill which comes from a friendship with the Father.

—Phillips Brooks

✦ Prayer is, after all, a very dangerous business. For all the benefits it offers of growing closer to God, it carries with it one great element of risk: the possibility of change. In prayer we open ourselves to the chance that God will do something with us that we had not intended. We yield to possibilities of intense perception, of seeing through human masks and the density of "things" to the very center of reality. This possibility excites us, but at the same time there is a fluttering in the stomach that goes with any dangerous adventure. We foresee a confrontation with the unknown, being hurt, being frightened, being chased down.

Don't we know for a fact that people who begin by "just praying"—with no particular aim in mind—wind up trudging off to missionary lands, entering monasteries, taking part in demonstrations, dedicating themselves to the poor and the sick? To avoid this, sometimes we excuse ourselves from prayer by doing good works on a carefully controlled schedule. We volunteer for school committees, to be readers in church or youth counselors, doing good works in hopes that this will distract the Lord from asking us anything more difficult. By doing something specific and limited "for God," something we judge to be enough and more than enough, we skirt the possibility that God—in prayer—may ask us what he wants to ask, may suggest what we should do.

"Father, into your hands I entrust my spirit." Isn't that one of the most disturbing sentences in the Scriptures? We know God asks us hard things. We know he did not spare his own Son. We know Jesus prayed, not now and then, but all the time. Isn't this what holds us back—the knowledge of God's omnipotence, his unguessability, his power, his right to ask an All of us, a perfect gift of self, a perfect act of full surrender?

—From *Clinging—The Experience of Prayer*
by Emilie Griffin

✦ You are, I hope, starting to read this book because you want to see the fruit of the Spirit—love, joy, peace, patience, kindness, goodness, faithfulness, gentleness, self-control—in your life. Good! But how much do you want it? Take a piece of paper and a pencil. At the top of the paper write out the question once put by the Lord Jesus to a person in need. "What do you want me to do for you?" (Mark 10:51). Then, set down three things you want more than anything else in the world. Provided you are not suffering from what R. L. Stevenson called "the malady of not wanting," you may be able to identify your primary desires and long-term objectives. Now look at your three chief desires. Do you want to have, to do, or to be? Do they refer to possessions, achievements or character? When the question "What would you like me to give you?" was put to young Solomon, he asked for a quality of character. "Give me the wisdom I need" (I Kings 3:5, 9 GNB). I hope that one at least of your three desires has to do with character. For the grand purpose of God is that we should "become like his Son" (Romans 8:29 GNB). No Christian could possibly have a greater ambition. So, happy is the person who can truthfully give this answer to the question put by Jesus, "What I want you to do for me, Lord, is to make me a loving, joyful, peaceable, patient, kind, good, faithful, gentle, disciplined Christian."

—From *Fruits of the Spirit* by Stephen F. Winward

✦ . . . to define prayer is no simple matter. The best definition I have found is in the words of the Westminster Shorter Catechism, "Prayer is an offering up of our desires unto God, for things agreeable to His will."

This statement puts the emphasis where it rightly belongs—on God and his will. However sincere the desire, however devout the form of the words, a petition is not prayer unless God and the doing of his will are the center of it.

—From *Prayer and the Common Life*
by Georgia Harkness

✦ A famous example is the story of the monk who was told to plant a dry stick in the sand and to water it daily.
So distant was the spring from his
cell that he had to leave in the evening
to fetch the water and he only returned
in the following morning. For three
years he patiently fulfilled his
abba's command. At the end of this
period, the stick suddenly put forth
leaves and bore fruit. The abba
picked the fruit, took it to the
church, and invited the monks to
eat, saying, "Come and taste the
fruit of obedience."
Obedience implies a willingness to be a voluntary adult son or daughter in the intuition that such a relationship will help us relinquish those desires and ways that keep us ourselves from being mature spiritual mothers and fathers.

—From *Spiritual Friend* by Tilden H. Edwards

✦ Begin where you are. Obey now. Use what little obedience you are capable of, even if it be like a grain of mustard seed. Begin where you are. Live this present moment, this present hour as you now sit in your seats, in utter submission and openness toward Him. Listen outwardly to these words, but within, behind the scenes, in the deeper levels of your lives where you are all alone with God the Loving Eternal One, keep up a silent prayer, "Open Thou my life. Guide my thoughts where I dare not let them go. Be Thou darest. Thy will be done." Walk on the streets and chat with your friends. But every moment behind the scenes be in prayer, offering yourselves in continuous obedience. I find this internal continuous prayer life absolutely essential. It can be carried on day and night, in the thick of business, in home and school. Such a prayer of submission can be so simple. It is well to use a single sentence, repeated over and over and over again, such as this: "Be Thou my will. Be Thou my will."

—From *A Testament of Devotion* by Thomas R. Kelly

✦ To him who obeys, and thus opens the door of his heart to receive the eternal gift, God gives the Spirit of His Son, the Spirit of Himself, to be in him, and lead him to the understanding of all truth. . . . The true disciple shall thus always know what he ought to do, though not necessarily what another ought to do.

—From *An Anthology of George MacDonald.*
Edited by C. S. Lewis

✦ Arrange what claim lies against you; compulsion waits behind it. Do at once what you must do one day. As there is no escape from payment, escape at least the prison that will enforce it. Do not drive justice to extremities. Duty is imperative; it must be done. It is useless to think to escape the eternal law of things: yield of yourself, nor compel God to compel you.

—From *An Anthology of George MacDonald.*
Edited by C. S. Lewis

◆ The golden rule of understanding spiritually is not intellect, but obedience. If a man wants scientific knowledge, intellectual curiosity is his guide; but if he wants insights into what Jesus Christ teaches, he can only get it by obedience. If things are dark to me, then I may be sure there is something I will not do. Intellectual darkness comes through ignorance; spiritual darkness comes because of something I do not intend to obey.

No man ever receives a word from God without instantly being put to the test by it. We disobey and then wonder why we don't go on spiritually. "If when you come to the altar," said Jesus, "there you remember your brother hath ought against you . . . don't say another word to Me, but first go and put that thing right." The teaching of Jesus hits us where we live. We cannot stand as humbugs before Him for one second. He educates us down to the scruple. The Spirit of God unearths the spirit of self-vindication; He makes us sensitive to things we never thought of before.

When Jesus brings a thing home by His word, don't shirk it. If you do, you will become a religious humbug. Watch the things you shrug your shoulders over, and you will know why you do not go on spiritually. First go—at the risk of being thought fanatical you must obey what God tells you.

—From *My Utmost for His Highest* by Oswald Chambers

◆ "Ye call me Master and Lord"—but is He? Master and Lord have little place in our vocabulary, we prefer the words Saviour, Sanctifier, Healer. The only word to describe mastership in experience is love and we know very little about love as God reveals it. This is proved by the way we use the word obey. In the Bible obedience is based on the relationship of equals, that of a son with his father. Our Lord was not God's servant, He was His Son. "Though He were a Son, yet learned He obedience. . . ." If our idea is that we are being mastered, it is a proof that we have no master; if that is our attitude to Jesus, we are far away from the relationship He wants. He wants us in the relationship in which He is easily Master without our conscious knowledge of it, all we know is that we are His to obey.

—From *My Utmost for His Highest* by Oswald Chambers

◆ We must not be satisfied with exteriorly submitting to obedience and in things that are easy, but we must obey with our whole heart and in things the most difficult. For the greater the difficulty, the greater also is the merit of obedience. Can we refuse to submit to man for God's sake when God, for love of us, submits to man, even to His very executioners?

Jesus Christ was willingly obedient during His whole life and even unto the death of the cross, and am I unwilling to spend my life in the exercise of obedience and to make it my cross and my merit? Independence belongs to God, who has made man dependent on others that his subordination may be to him the means of his sanctification. I will therefore form myself upon the model of my submissive, dependent, and obedient Saviour, and dispose of nothing in myself, not even of my own will.

—From *Imitation of Christ* by Thomas à Kempis

37. Simplicity

INVOCATION

Strengthen me, O God, by the grace of your Holy Spirit; grant me to be strengthened with might in the inner man, and to put away from my heart all useless anxiety and distress, and let me never be drawn aside by various longings after anything whatever, whether it be worthless or precious; but may I regard all things as passing away, and myself as passing away with them. Amen.

Thomas à Kempis in *Little Book of Prayers*

PSALM 23

DAILY SCRIPTURE

Monday	Luke 18:18–25
Tuesday	Matthew 6:25–34
Wednesday	1 Thessalonians 5:12–28
Thursday	Luke 9:18–27
Friday	3 John
Saturday	Matthew 18:1–4
Sunday	Luke 12:22–34

SELECTIONS FOR MEDITATION

PERSONAL MEDITATION

PRAYER

Ask God this week to begin to simplify your life beginning with your desires and your appetites. Ask him to begin to take his rightful place within your heart so that you may see your way among the conflicting claims of the society in which we live.

HYMN   "Close to Thee"

> Thou, my everlasting portion,
> More than friend or life to me,
> All along my pilgrim journey,
> Saviour, let me walk with Thee.
>
> Not for ease or worldly pleasure,
> Nor for fame my prayer shall be;
> Gladly will I toil and suffer,
> Only let me walk with Thee. . . .
> Fanny J. Crosby

BENEDICTION

Grant me, O Lord, to know what I ought to know, to love what I ought to love, to praise what delights You most, to value what is precious in Your sight, to hate what is offensive to You. Amen.

Thomas à Kempis in *Little Book of Prayers*

SELECTIONS FOR MEDITATION

✦ He was a direct, simple, naked soul dressed only in the seamless garment of his Christianity.

By grace of that garment, his flesh was as if it were not. When I said, for example, "It is not warm this morning," he would answer mechanically, "No, it is not warm"; but he did not feel the cold. "Cold" to him was merely a word; and if he stopped up the door, or livened up the lamp, it was for my sake he did it. He had nothing to do with "those things," and this struggle was not his struggle: he was somewhere else, living another life, fighting with other weapons. He was right and I was wrong in those moments when I rebelled against his existence, and insisted rashly that he "could not live like this." I was stupid not to see, then, that he truly had no need of anything. He lived, he sustained himself, by prayer. Had he been dependent only upon human strength he would have lived in despair, been driven mad. But he called upon other forces, and they preserved him. Incredible as it will seem to the incredulous, when the blizzard was too intense to be borne, he prayed, and the wind dropped. When, one day, he was about to die of hunger—he and the single Eskimo who accompanied him—he prayed; and that night there were two seals in their net. It was childish of me to attempt to win him back to reality: he could not live with reality.

I, the "scientist," was non-existent beside this peasant mystic. He towered over me. My resources were as nothing compared to his, which were inexhaustible. His mystical vestment was shelter enough against hunger, against cold, against every assault of the physical world from which he lived apart. Once again I had been taught that the spirit was immune and irresistible, and matter corruptible and weak. There is something more than cannon in war, and something more than grub and shelter in the existence of this conqueror of the Arctic.

—From *Kabloona* by Gontran de Poncins

✦ Consider that wonderful world of life in which you are placed, and observe that its great rhythms of birth, growth and death—all the things that really matter—are not in your control. That unhurried process will go forward in its stately beauty, little affected by your anxious fuss. Find out, then, where your treasure really is. Discern substance from accident. Don't confuse your meals with your life, and your clothes with your body. Don't lose your head over what perishes. Nearly everything does perish: so face the facts, don't rush after the transient and unreal. Maintain your soul in tranquil dependence on God; don't worry; don't mistake what you possess for what you are. Accumulating things is useless. Both mental and material avarice are merely silly in view of the dread facts of life and death. The White Knight would have done better had he left his luggage at home. The simpler your house, the easier it will be to run. The fewer the things and the people you "simply must have," the nearer you will be to the ideal of happiness—"as having nothing, to possess all."
—From *The House of the Soul and Concerning the Inner Life* by Evelyn Underhill

✦ The life of discipleship can only be maintained as long as nothing is allowed to come between Christ and ourselves— neither the law, nor personal piety, nor even the world. The disciple always looks only to his master, never to Christ and the law, Christ and religion, Christ and the world. He avoids all such notions like the plague. Only by following Christ alone can he preserve a single eye. His eye rests wholly on the light that comes from Christ, and has no darkness or ambiguity in it. As the eye must be single, clear and pure in order to keep light in the body, as hand and foot can receive light from no other source save the eye, as the foot stumbles and the hand misses its mark when the eye is dim, as the whole body is in darkness when the eye is blind; so the follower of Christ is in the light only so long as he looks simply to Christ and at nothing else in the world. Thus the heart of the disciple must be set upon Christ alone. If the eye sees an object which is not there, the whole body is deceived. If the heart is devoted to the mirage of the world, to the creature instead of the Creator, the disciple is lost.

—From *The Cost of Discipleship* by Dietrich Bonhoeffer

✦ Seldom or never do we hear anything about simplicity as an essential discipline of the spiritual life.

Most of us have only a vague idea of the meaning of the word.

Perhaps we had better begin with a definition. Simplicity means "absence of artificial ornamentation, pretentious styles, or luxury." It is "artlessness, lack of cunning or duplicity."

Where there is simplicity, words can be taken at their face value. There are no hidden or double meanings. One says what one means and means what one says. There is no "joker" concealed in the language to nullify its obvious intent. Simplicity does not mean "easy to understand." Paul was not always easy to understand. Nor was Jesus. Men are still wrestling with their great utterances. But both Jesus and Paul are characterized by simplicity. Their intention was not to confuse or deceive but to clarify and illumine.

Where there is simplicity there is no artificiality. One does not try to appear younger, or wiser, or richer than one is—or more saintly! Moffatt's translation of 1 Corinthians 13:4 hits it exactly, when it says: "Love makes no parade, gives itself no airs."

—From *Discipline and Discovery* by Albert E. Day

✦ Every morning, when I left for work, I would take something in my hand and walk off with it, for deposit in the big municipal wire trash basket at the corner of Third, on the theory that the physical act of disposal was the real key to the problem. My wife, a strategist, knew better and began quietly mobilizing the forces that would eventually put our goods to rout. A man could walk away for a thousand mornings carrying something with him to the corner and there would still be a home full of stuff. It is not possible to keep abreast of the normal tides of acquisition. A home is like a reservoir equipped with a check valve: the valve permits influx but prevents outflow. Acquisition goes on day and night— smoothly, subtly, imperceptibly. I have no sharp taste for acquiring things, but it is not necessary to desire things in order to acquire them. Goods and chattels seek a man out; they find him even though his guard is up. Books and oddities arrive in the mail. Gifts arrive on anniversaries and fete days. Veterans send ballpoint pens. Banks send memo books. If you happen to be a writer, readers send whatever may be cluttering up their own lives; I had a man once send me a chip of wood that showed the marks of a beaver's teeth. Someone dies, and a little trickle of indestructible keepsakes appears, to swell the flood. This steady influx is not counterbalanced by any comparable outgo. Under ordinary circumstances, the only stuff that leaves a home is paper trash and garbage; everything else stays on and digs in.

—From *Essays of E. B. White*

✦ Our Lord referred to this tyranny of things when he said to his disciples, "If any man will come after me, let him deny himself, and take up his cross, and follow me. For whosoever will save his life shall lose it: and whosoever shall lose his life for my sake shall find it."

Breaking this truth into fragments for our better understanding, it would seem that there is within each of us an enemy which we tolerate at our peril. Jesus called it "life" and "self," or as we would say, the self-life. Its chief characteristic is its possessiveness: the words "gain" and "profit" suggest this. To allow this enemy to live is in the end to lose everything. To repudiate it and give up all for Christ's sake is to lose nothing at last, but to preserve everything unto life eternal. And possibly also a hint is given here as to the only effective way to destroy this foe: it is by the Cross. "Let him take up his cross and follow me."

The way to deeper knowledge of God is through the lonely valleys of soul poverty and abnegation of all things. The blessed ones who possess the Kingdom are they who have repudiated every external thing and have rooted from their hearts all sense of possessing. These are the "poor in spirit." They have reached an inward state paralleling the outward circumstances of the common beggar in the streets of Jerusalem; that is what the word "poor" as Christ used it actually means. These blessed poor are no longer slaves to the tyranny of things. They have broken the yoke of the oppressor; and this they have done not by fighting but by surrendering. Though free from all sense of possessing, they yet possess all things. "Theirs is the kingdom of heaven."

Let me exhort you to take this seriously. It is not to be understood as mere Bible teaching to be stored away in the mind along with an inert mass of other doctrines. It is a marker on the road to greener pastures, a path chiseled against the steep sides of the mount of God. We dare not try to by-pass it if we would follow on in this holy pursuit. We must ascend a step at a time. If we refuse one step we bring our progress to an end.

—From *The Pursuit of God* by A. W. Tozer

✦ There is nothing more certain to resist the wiles of the flesh than simplicity; it effectively evades every trick without recognizing them or even being conscious of doing so. Divine action can make simple souls take exactly the right steps to surprise those who wish to surprise them, and even to profit by their attempts to do so. They are buoyed up by humiliation, every vexation becomes a blessing, and, by leaving their adversaries alone, they derive such a lasting and satisfactory benefit that all they need to think about is being on God's side and doing work inspired by his will, whose instruments their enemies are. Souls have but to look serenely on at what God is doing and humbly follow it, successfully led by the heavenly insight of the Holy Spirit, which invariably influences circumstances and directs them so aptly without their knowing that whatever opposes them is always destroyed.

The unique and infallible power of divine action always influences the simple in the right way, inwardly directing them to react wisely to everything. They welcome all that comes their way, everything that happens to them, everything they experience excepting sin. Sometimes this happens consciously; but sometimes simple souls are moved by mysterious impulses, unconsciously to say, do or ignore things, often for quite natural reasons, in which they see no mystery; things which seem like pure chance, necessity or convenience and seem even to have no significance either to themselves or to others. And yet divine action, in the form of intelligence, wisdom and advice of their friends, uses them all for the benefit of these souls, ingeniously foiling the plans of those who scheme to harm them. To deal with the pure heart is to deal with God.

—From *The Sacrament of the Present Moment*
by Jean-Pierre de Caussade.
Translated by Kitty Muggeridge

38. The Mind of Christ

INVOCATION

You, O Christ, who were tempted in all points like as I am, yet without sin, make me strong to overcome the desire to be wise and to be reputed wise by others as ignorant as myself. I turn from my wisdom as well as from my folly and flee to You, the wisdom of God and the power of God. Amen.

A. W. Tozer in *The Knowledge of the Holy*

PSALM 72

DAILY SCRIPTURE

Monday	1 Corinthians 2:6–16
Tuesday	Philippians 2:1–11
Wednesday	Hebrews 5:11—6:3
Thursday	Isaiah 11:1–5
Friday	1 Peter 4:1–6
Saturday	Romans 8:5–11
Sunday	Matthew 13:10–17

SELECTIONS FOR MEDITATION

PERSONAL MEDITATION

PRAYER

Saint Paul tells us that one must even attempt to emulate the mind of Christ. This is an enormous proposition. And yet it is true. Christ had a clarity of purpose which guided his words and deeds; without which our actions are just that, our actions.

HYMN "I Want to Be Like Jesus"

> I have one deep, supreme desire.
> That I may be like Jesus.

To this I fervently aspire,
That I may be like Jesus. . . .
                    Thomas Chisholm

BENEDICTION

O Christ, I want the Spirit within me to duplicate nothing—nothing except You. For I want no manifestation that doesn't manifest You—manifest You in Your sanctity and Your sanity. For You are life. Amen.

                    E. Stanley Jones in *The Way to Power and Poise*

SELECTIONS FOR MEDITATION

✦ "Having therefore these promises." I claim the fulfillment of God's promises, and rightly, but that is only the human side; the divine side is that through the promises I recognize God's claim on me. For instance, am I realizing that my body is the temple of the Holy Ghost, or have I a habit of body that plainly will not bear the light of God on it? By sanctification the Son of God is formed in me, then I have to transform my natural life into a spiritual life by obedience to Him. God educates us down to the scruple. When He begins to check, do not confer with flesh and blood, cleanse yourself at once. Keep yourself cleansed in your daily walk.

I have to cleanse myself from all filthiness of the flesh and spirit until both are in accord with the nature of God. Is the mind of my spirit in perfect agreement with the life of the Son of God in me, or am I insubordinate in intellect? Am I forming the mind of Christ, Who never spoke from His right to Himself, but maintained an inner watchfulness whereby He continually submitted His spirit to His Father? I have the responsibility of keeping my spirit in agreement with His Spirit, and by degrees Jesus lifts me up to where He lived—in perfect consecration to His Father's will, paying no attention to any other thing.

—From *My Utmost for His Highest* by Oswald Chambers

✦ If we are not heedful of the way the Spirit of God works in us, we will become spiritual hypocrites. We see where other folks are failing, and we turn our discernment into the gibe of criticism instead of into intercession on their behalf. The revelation is made to us not through the acuteness of our minds, but by the direct penetration of the Spirit of God, and if we are not heedful of the source of the revelation, we will become criticizing centers and forget that God says—". . . he shall ask, and He shall give his life for them that sin not unto death." Take care lest you play the hypocrite by spending all your time trying to get others right before you worship God yourself.

—From *My Utmost for His Highest* by Oswald Chambers

✦ When Paul received his sight, he received spiritually an insight into the Person of Jesus Christ, and the whole of his subsequent life and preaching was nothing but Jesus Christ— "I determined not to know anything among you, save Jesus Christ, and Him crucified." No attraction was ever allowed to hold the mind and soul of Paul save the face of Jesus Christ.

We have to learn to maintain an unimpaired state of character up to the last notch revealed in the vision of Jesus Christ.

The abiding characteristic of a spiritual man is the interpretation of the Lord Jesus Christ to himself, and the interpretation to others of the purposes of God. The one concentrated passion of the life is Jesus Christ. Whenever you meet this note in a man, you feel he is a man after God's own heart.

Never allow anything to deflect you from insight into Jesus Christ. It is the test of whether you are spiritual or not. To be unspiritual means that other things have a growing fascination for you.

—From *My Utmost for His Highest* by Oswald Chambers

✦ When we discern that people are not going on spiritually and allow the discernment to turn to criticism, we block our way to God. God never gives us discernment in order that we may criticize, but that we may intercede.

—From *My Utmost for His Highest* by Oswald Chambers

✦ The Spirit is the pledge of the abiding presence of Jesus, and of our fellowship with him. He imparts true knowledge of his being and of his will. He teaches us and reminds us of all that Christ said on earth. He guides us into all truth so that we are not without knowledge of Christ and the gifts which God has given us in him. The gift which the Holy Spirit creates in us is not uncertainty, but assurance and discernment. Thus we are enabled to walk in the Spirit and to walk in assurance.

—From *The Cost of Discipleship* by Dietrich Bonhoeffer

✦ . . . "solid food is for fullgrown men, even those who by reason of use have their senses exercised to discern good and evil." (Hebrews 5:14) That is to say, the more advanced doctrines are adapted to the more mature Christians, whose spiritual faculties have been so developed that they are able to discriminate between teaching that is wholesome and teaching that is harmful. Such Christians can appreciate and appropriate the more profound truths concerning Christ which the author is planning to disclose.

These references to spiritual infancy are not to be understood as disparaging the reality of a new birth or the blessedness of spiritual childhood. All persons begin the Christian life as mere "babes in Christ." There is a radiant beauty about each newborn soul. What the author does deprecate is arrested development. An infant is lovable, but if as the years pass the child remains a helpless babe, the case is pitiful and pathetic. Thus it is sad to see men and women, who for years have been professed Christians, to whom the deeper spiritual realities have no meaning, no power, no appeal.

. . . What the writer does intend to emphasize is the fact that use is a law of growth. The faculty which is never exercised grows weak. The talent which is unemployed is lost. Thus the simplest knowledge of Christ may be so appropriated, so appreciated, so comprehended, as to prepare one for the reception of more advanced teaching. On the other hand, the neglect or disregard of Christian truth may result in such a loss of discernment, such an atrophy of the faculties, as to induce a second childhood, a pitiable spiritual infancy.

—From *The Epistle to the Hebrews* by Charles R. Erdman

✦ One who participates in the life of the Spirit in the Christian fellowship examines all things, is free to investigate all things pertaining to God. Paul proposed that there should be no censorship nor obstruction to the systematic search for truth. This implies that the spiritual person is capable of evaluating properly the good and evil he confronts, of estimating what things are worthwhile and what things are not. For Paul this included: matters not covered by clear Christian precedent (I Cor. 7:40); virtues and attitudes of life in relation to one another that do not conform to the prudence or customs of the world and that do not arise spontaneously from natural human impulses and desires (Gal. 5:18, 22–25); wisdom to make judgment by virtue of divine reconciliation (I Cor. 6:3–6); and the new mode of exercising powers and gifts for the benefit and progress of the whole Christian community (I Cor. 12).

—From *I Corinthians, Commentary*
by William F. Orr and James Arthur Walther

✦ "For every one that useth milk is unskillful in the word of righteousness: for he is a babe" (Heb. 5:13). The writer uses the inverse form in order to emphasize the fact that one who has advanced no further than a milk diet is still a babe. As such he is "unskillful" or "inexperienced," and at best can speak only of childish things (I Cor. 13:11). To this state the Hebrew Christians had brought themselves. Using their spiritual senses less and less, their development had become so arrested as to make them unable to discriminate between the good and evil. They were therefore unprepared for the great truths. . . .

—From *The Epistle to the Hebrews* by H. Orton Wiley

✦ In reading the Gospels, I am taken by how often Jesus used the phrase "Abba, Father." These words seem to distill his life of prayer, as companionship. Consequently, I have begun the discipline of "Abba evocation" as the ground for companion prayer. One repeats over and over again the name "Abba, Father." It is analogous to the way one learns to type—repeating until it becomes second nature, never forgotten, so that even after a long absence one can nevertheless type immediately, but not without errors. To render indelible the name is to encounter the plague of forgetting.

    —From *The Province Beyond the River* by W. Paul Jones

✦ You must adapt Your word to my smallness, so that it can enter into the tiny dwelling of my finiteness—the only dwelling in which I can live—without destroying it. Then I shall be able to understand; such a word I can take in without that agonizing bewilderment of mind and that cold fear clutching my heart. If You should speak such an "abbreviated" word, which would not say everything but only something simple which I could grasp, then I could breathe freely again.

    O Infinite God, You have actually willed to speak such a word to me! You have restrained the ocean of Your Infinity from flooding in over the poor little wall which protects my tiny life's-acre from Your vastness. Not the waters of Your great sea, but only the dew of Your Gentleness is to spread itself over my poor little plot of earth. You have come to me in a human word. For You, the Infinite, are the God of Our Lord Jesus Christ.

    —From *Encounters with Silence* by Karl Rahner

✦ Christ Jesus . . . made himself nothing.

    He made himself nothing, emptied himself—the great kenosis. He made himself no reputation, no image.

    I can recall my father shaking his head and repeating over and over to himself, "If I only knew what this meant. There is something powerful here. If I only understood it." Maybe that is why this Scripture has glued itself to my mind and equally disturbs me. Reputation is so important to me. I want to be seen with the right people, remembered in the right light, advertised with my name spelled right, live in the right neighborhood, drive the right kind of car, wear the right kind of clothing. But Jesus made himself of no reputation!

    —From *The Jesus Style* by Gayle D. Erwin

✦ If a friend does something which puzzles us, we might ask

what it was that he "had in mind" in doing it. It is in this sense that Paul uses the word mind in Philippians 2:5. What was it that seemed important to Jesus? What principles did he cherish? What objectives? On what footing were his choices made?

The revelation of the mind of Christ is presented here as the story of a great change. It befits with one who was in the form of God (verse 6), that is, one who possessed inwardly and displayed outwardly the very nature of God himself.

As is plain, verse 6 is speaking of the Lord Jesus Christ before his incarnation. . . . What a change is expressed in verse 8 when he who was in the form of God became obedient unto death! Wesley put it justly when he wrote:

"'Tis mystery all! The Immortal dies!"

Mystery indeed, but at the same time the testimony of the Bible. How it could happen we cannot know, that it did happen we are assured.

There is great stress on the fact that this change came about by voluntary decision and in this we begin to enter into the "mind of Christ." Verse 7 says he emptied himself, and verse 8, he humbled himself. In each case the reflexive expression points to personal decision and action.

—From *The Message of Philippians* by Alec Motyer

39. Generosity

INVOCATION

Father, you give to me with a lavish hand, you do not withhold from me of your great grace and mercy. Let me live and serve you also with a generous heart. In the name of your Son, who gave his all. Amen.

PSALM 77

DAILY SCRIPTURE

Monday	Exodus 35:4–29
Tuesday	2 Corinthians 8:1–15
Wednesday	Mark 12:41–44
Thursday	Philippians 4:10–23
Friday	1 Timothy 6:6–21
Saturday	2 Corinthians 9:6–15
Sunday	Luke 7:36–50

SELECTIONS FOR MEDITATION

PERSONAL MEDITATION

PRAYER

Our prayers should be freeing us from our self-centeredness and opening us up to others. Pray for specific direction to ways of generosity to others, for releasing, for sharing.

HYMN   "Something for Thee"

Saviour, Thy dying love,
Thou gavest me;
Nor should I aught withhold,
Dear Lord, from Thee.
In love my soul would bow,
My heart fulfill its vow,
Some off'ring bring Thee now,
Something for Thee.

At the blest mercy seat,
Pleading to Thee,
My feeble faith looks up,
Jesus to Thee.
Help me the cross to bear,
Thy wondrous love declare,
Some song to raise or prayer,
Something for Thee. . . .
                    S. D. Phelps

BENEDICTION

Dear Father, you who have given so much to me, give one thing more, a generous heart. Amen.

SELECTIONS FOR MEDITATION

◆ When the founding members, young and poor, were forming themselves into a properly incorporated community of faith, they struggled for a discipline of membership that would help them and future members to deal concretely with at least some aspects of the handling of money. In its first writing the discipline read, "We commit ourselves to giving 10 percent of our gross income to the work of the Church."

Their proposed constitution and disciplines were submitted to Reinhold Niebuhr, an eminent theologian of the last generation, who had agreed to read them and comment. His only suggestion concerned the discipline on money. "I would suggest," Niebuhr said, "that you commit yourselves not to tithing but to proportionate giving, with tithing as an economic floor beneath which you will not go unless there are some compelling reasons." The discipline was rewritten and stands today in each of the six new faith communities:

We covenant with Christ and one another to give proportionately beginning with a tithe of our incomes.

None of us has to be an accountant to know what 10 percent of a gross income is, but each of us has to be a person on his knees before God if we are to understand our commitment to proportionate giving. Proportionate to what? Proportionate to the accumulated wealth of one's family? Proportionate to one's income and the demands upon it, which vary from family to family? Proportionate to one's sense of security and the degree of anxiety with which one lives? Proportionate to the keenness of our awareness of those who suffer? Proportionate to our sense of justice and of God's ownership of all wealth? Proportionate to our sense of stewardship for those who follow after us? And so on, and so forth. The answer, of course, is in proportion to all of these things.

—From *Letters to Scattered Pilgrims*
by Elizabeth O'Connor

✦ Going to town one day to sell some small articles, Abba Agathon met a cripple on the roadside, paralysed in his legs, who asked him where he was going. Abba Agathon replied, "To town, to sell some things." The other said, "Do me the favor of carrying me there." So he carried him to the town. The cripple said to him, "Put me down where you sell your wares." He did so. When he had sold an article, the cripple asked, "What did you sell it for?" and he told him the price. The other said, "Buy me a cake," and he bought it. When Abba Agathon had sold all his wares, wanted to go, he said to him, "Are you going back?" and he replied, "Yes." Then he said, "Do me the favor of carrying me back to the place where you found me." Once more picking him up, he carried him back to that place. Then the cripple said, "Agathon, you are filled with divine blessings, in heaven and on earth." Raising his eyes, Agathon saw no man; it was an angel of the Lord, come to try him.

—From *The Desert Christian.*
Translated by Benedicta Ward

✦ I wonder if we realize the significance of generosity in the struggle to free the consciousness for fellowship of God. Generosity is not merely a trait which pleases God. It is a practice which releases us from bondage to the ego, and also to things.

The ego is strongly possessive. Its possessiveness is revealed in all its relationships. Psychologists used to talk about the instinct for acquisition. Instincts are not so much in caste as they used to be. But acquisitiveness remains, whether as instinct or behavior pattern or inherited tendency or what have you.

Left to itself, the ego is persistent in acquiring and in keeping. Sharing is not one of its passions.

. . . No, giving is not a trait of the ego. Owning is! "Mine" is its dearest adjective. "Keep" is its most beloved verb!

The ego is possessive. Its possessiveness in property manifests itself as stinginess, miserliness, greed. Its possessiveness of people makes jealous friends, husbands, wives, parents.

Most persons who are possessive never recognize the fact. So complete is the domination of the ego that it is unconscious. It just seems natural. It is natural in the sense that it is characteristic of our perverted egocentric nature. It is not natural in the sense that it is characteristic of the nature God intended us to have and we may have by his grace.

Because of this possessiveness of the ego, the practice of generosity is very significant. It is a denial, a repudiation of the ego. Faithfully practiced, generosity weakens the ego's authority. Every departure from the pattern the ego sets makes the next variation easier. We are made that way.

Consciousness is a mystery but we at least know this much—consciousness is flexible. It easily falls into patterns, which we call habits. But it is capable of a wide variety of patterns. It can be habitually willful or obedient, artful or simple, proud or humble, extravagant or frugal, miserly or generous, egocentric or we-centric, or God-centric. The task of changing the patterns is in part ours. It may be done by a fixed purpose and by consistent practice and by that prayer which exposes the finite consciousness to the Infinite, Universal Consciousness, God!

There is no place where the lives of saintly people bear a clearer witness. They have all undertaken the disciplines of generosity.

—From *Discipline and Discovery* by Albert E. Day

✦ The mysteries have not changed, at least as far as Christians are concerned. The mystery which was supposed to be at work in the life of Israel (as opposed to what was cele-brated among the Hittites and the Amorites, say) and which was made present to them in the rite in the Tabernacle, was the mystery upon which all life proceeds and which will never be outgrown since it is there at the root of all things. It is the mystery of My Life for Yours. It is expressed in the words "I owe my life to you, and I lay down my life for you."

No one has ever drawn a single breath on any other basis. No child has ever received life to begin with without a "laying down" of life by the two people to whom he owes his con-ception, and by the laying down of his mother's life for months in bearing and nourishing him. And somebody had to lay down his life for the child year after year in caring for him and training him and providing for him. And no one has ever sat down to the smallest pittance of food that he did not owe to somebody's life having been laid down, if it was only a prawn or a lettuce leaf; to say nothing of the work (a form of laid-down life) somebody had to do to plant and cultivate and pick and market the leaf, or catch the prawn. No one has ever learned a single thing that he did not owe to somebody's hav-ing taught him or helped him one way or another. Morning, noon, and night, we owe it all to others. My Life for Yours. I owe my life to you, and I lay mine down for you.

It was this, true for Israel as it is for every people whether they acknowledge it or not, that was kept present to their imagination by the rite going on in their midst. Their ordinary life was hallowed by this perpetual acknowledgment that it was God to whom they finally owed everything since it was from him that it had all come to begin with.

—From *Hallowed Be This House* by Thomas Howard

✦ During the Great Depression a man, woman, and five chil-dren moved wearily along a country road in the springtime and stopped at a farmer's house. They had walked across Oklahoma, Arkansas and Louisiana. They had no food, no money and only the clothes they were wearing and the few things they could carry.

"We know how to work the land," they told a Mississippi

farmer, "but we have no land to work. We lost all that we owned."

"I will let you use a share of my land," the man replied.

"We have no shelter."

"See that creek? If you follow it to the back side of the clearing you will find a small house."

"We will need furniture."

"There are beds there. A table and chairs and a few other pieces. Use them as if they were your own."

"We have no team. No tools to plow and cultivate the fields. No fertilizer. Not even seeds for planting."

"All that will be provided," the farmer told them. "I will buy you clothes and shoes and straw hats to shield you from the sun. And food enough to get you through the season."

Throughout the summer their needs were met, and when autumn came and it was time for the land to rest the harvest was bountiful. There was cotton to sell, corn for bread, dried fruits and beans for winter.

They came again to the farmer's house. "We are moving on," they said. "Before we go we have come to ask you if we owe you anything."

"You owe me everything," the farmer said. "The land, seeds, food, teams and tools. I owned it all. You brought nothing with you and you lived well at my expense. Everything you have now you owe to me."

The dispirited sharecroppers turned to walk away. "But wait," the owner called. "You were strangers from a distant land and I took you in. I love you now. All of you. All that you have is yours to keep. I forgive the debt. You are free to go if you like. But you are also free to stay."

—From *God on Earth* by Will Campbell

✦ Jesus obviously expected his disciples to be generous givers. His words condemn the "selfish stinginess of many," as Ryle put it.

Generosity is not enough, however. Our Lord is concerned throughout this Sermon with motivation, with the hidden thoughts of the heart. In his exposition of the sixth and seventh commandments he indicated that both murder and adultery can be committed in our heart, unwarranted anger being a kind of heart-murder and lustful looks a kind of heart-adultery. In the matter of giving he has the same concern about secret thoughts. The question is not so much what the hand is doing (passing over some cash or a check) but what the heart is thinking while the hand is doing it. There are three possibilities. Either we are seeking the praise of men, or we preserve our anonymity but are quietly congratulating ourselves, or we are desirous of the approval of our divine Father alone.

—From *The Message of the Sermon on the Mount*
by John R. W. Stott

40. Truthfulness

INVOCATION

O Savior, You do not only save me, You save truth—save it from being a proposition and made it into a Person. You did say, "I am the truth," and lo, Truth is lovable and livable and not a dry-as-dust proposition. I am at Your feet, Gracious Truth. Amen.

E. Stanley Jones in *The Word Became Flesh*

PSALM 52

DAILY SCRIPTURE

Monday	Proverbs 12:19
Tuesday	Deuteronomy 32:1–4
Wednesday	Matthew 7:1–6
Thursday	Luke 16:1–13
Friday	2 Corinthians 4:1–6
Saturday	Romans 9:1
Sunday	Luke 18:15–17

SELECTIONS FOR MEDITATION

PERSONAL MEDITATION

PRAYER

It is a characteristic of human nature to be semitransparent with other people. And we reveal only what we want to reveal. And we don't really do much better before God either. What good is there to be gained by being dishonest with God? How do we ever expect to be transformed into His image if we continually cover those things we don't want God to know about? Ask God to help you be truthful both to Him and to others.

HYMN   "Open My Eyes, That I May See"

> Open my eyes, that I may see
> Glimpses of truth Thou hast for me;
> Place in my hands the wonderful key
> That shall unclasp and set me free. . . .
>   Clara H. Scott

BENEDICTION

Continue to have mercy upon me, to stir me from the doldrums of sin, to deliver me from my selfish involvements, to forgive me my sins and failures, to shore up the weak places in my life. Help me to feel something of Your loving acceptance and to reflect to others the joy of being Your son and servant. Amen.

Leslie Brandt in *Psalms/Now*

SELECTIONS FOR MEDITATION

✦ Take all your present perplexities then to Jesus. Tell Him you only want to know and obey His voice, and ask Him to make it plain to you. Promise Him that you will obey, whatever it may be. Believe implicitly that He is guiding you, according to His word. Surrender all the doubtful things until you have a clearer light. Look and listen for His dear voice continually, and the moment you are sure of it yield an immediate obedience. Trust Him to make you forget the impression if it is not His will, and if it continues, and is in harmony with all His other voices, do not be afraid to obey.

—From *The Christian's Secret of a Happy Life*
By Hannah Whitall Smith

✦ When Jesus says that he has come to bear witness to the truth, Pilate asks, "What is truth?" (John 18:38) Contrary to the traditional view that his question is cynical, it is possible that he asks it with a lump in his throat. Instead of Truth, Pilate has only expedience. His decision to throw Jesus to the wolves is expedient. Pilate views man as alone in the universe with nothing but his own courage and ingenuity to see him through. It is enough to choke up anybody.

Pilate asks What is truth? And for years there have been politicians, scientists, theologians, philosophers, poets, and so on to tell him. The sound they make is like the sound of empty pails falling down the cellar stairs.

Jesus doesn't answer Pilate's question. He just stands there. "Stands," and stands "there."

—From *Wishful Thinking* by Frederick Buechner

✦ It is interesting that most of our relationships with other people are contacts, as one billiard ball contacts another billiard ball. We become like oranges in a box; we mingle with others externally, but do not commune with others in a common task: "News of the hour, on the hour" keeps us buried in the trivialities of external stimuli, lulling us into the belief that we are in contact with reality. The inner life is never given a moment to see ourselves as we really are.

—From *The Wit and Wisdom of Bishop Fulton J. Sheen*

✦ A spiritually minded man will never come to you with the demand—"Believe this and that;" but with the demand that you square your life with the standards of Jesus. We are not asked to believe the Bible, but to believe the One Whom the Bible reveals (cf. John 5:39–40). We are called to present liberty of conscience, not liberty of view. If we are free with the liberty of Christ, others will be brought into that same liberty—the liberty of realizing the dominance of Jesus Christ.

Always keep your life measured by the standards of Jesus. Bow your neck to His yoke alone, and to no other yoke whatever; and be careful to see that you never bind a yoke on others that is not placed by Jesus Christ. It takes God a long time to get us out of the way of thinking that unless everyone sees as we do, they must be wrong. That is never God's view. There is only one liberty, the liberty of Jesus at work in our conscience enabling us to do what is right.

—From *My Utmost for His Highest* by Oswald Chambers

✦ "Let your speech be Yea, yea, and Nay, nay." This is not to say that the disciples are no longer answerable to the omniscient God for every word they utter, it means that every word they utter is spoken in his presence, and not only those words which are accompanied by an oath. Hence they are forbidden to swear at all. Since they always speak the whole truth and nothing but the truth, there is no need for an oath, which would only throw doubt on the veracity of all their other statements. That is why the oath is "of the evil one." But a disciple must be a light even in his words.

—From *The Cost of Discipleship* by Dietrich Bonhoeffer

✦ In this questioning of truthfulness, what matters first and last is that a man's whole being should be exposed, his whole evil laid bare in the sight of God. But sinful men do not like this sort of truthfulness, and they resist it with all their might. That is why they persecute it and crucify it. It is only because we follow Jesus that we can be genuinely truthful, for then he reveals to us our sin upon the Cross. The Cross is God's truth about us, and therefore it is the only power which can make us truthful. When we know the Cross we are no longer afraid of the truth. We need no more oaths to confirm the truth of our utterances, for we live in the perfect truth of God.

There is no truth toward Jesus without truth toward man. Untruthfulness destroys fellowship, but truth cuts false fellowship to pieces and establishes genuine brotherhood. We cannot follow Christ unless we live in revealed truth before God and man.

—From *The Cost of Discipleship* by Dietrich Bonhoeffer

✦ Somewhere I heard a story about Michelangelo's pushing a huge piece of rock down a street. A curious neighbor sitting lazily on the porch of his house called to him and inquired why he labored so over an old piece of stone. Michelangelo is reported to have answered, "Because there is an angel in that rock that wants to come out."

This story comes to mind when I think about the gifts or talents given to each of us. Every person has the task of releasing angels by shaping and transfiguring the raw materials that lie about him so that they become houses and machinery and pictures and bridges. How we do this—how we "build the earth," to use Teilhard de Chardin's phrase—is determined by the discovery and the use of our gifts.

Because our gifts carry us out into the world and make us participants in life, the uncovering of them is one of the most important tasks confronting any one of us. When we talk about being true to ourselves—being the persons we are intended to be—we are talking about gifts. We cannot be ourselves unless we are true to our gifts. When we talk about vocation, whether we are artists or engineers, we are talking about gifts. In a discussion about commitment, we are on the same subject for the place of our concrete involvement is determined by our gifts. Serious reflection on almost any aspect of our lives leads into a consideration of gifts.

—From *The Eighth Day of Creation*
by Elizabeth O'Connor

◆ R. has just told me that Bernard (a priest and a friend, a wonderful, remarkable, generous man of action who gave his all) has died, defeated by depression.

. . . I am going to the funeral. I had hesitated—why go? For him? I can pray for him right here. For his family, friends, myself? Perhaps. However I know that I will be going to very little more than a show. I can already hear the sudden concert of unanimous praise and the miraculous disappearance of all criticism and reservation. Like all sensitive beings, Bernard wanted a bit of approval, a little encouragement. But he would never have believed the amount of praise that's going to be heaped on him now. The tragic thing is that just a fraction of it could have perhaps saved him. Despite all, I'm going to the interment. I haven't got the courage not to go.

—From *With Open Heart* by Michael Quoist

◆ It is impossible to make a general statement
that covers every exception, and yet
conversation so often consists of each
person pointing out the obvious exceptions
to the other person's statements.

I can't legitimately disagree with what you
say about yourself, only with what you
say about what is not yourself. The most
I can answer to what you say about
yourself is that I'm different.

The statements that communicate most
clearly are about me, you, now, here;
and all final authorities are present.

A generalization is an assertion that what
is true for me is also true for not-me.
I notice that I often talk in generalities to
produce the illusion that my "truth" is
shared. In this way I pick up a little
support (sameness) for my individualness
and don't feel so alone.

Sometimes when I generalize I am saying,
"Let's pretend I am God," and of course
the other person argues that point endlessly.
But I notice that if the other person
takes a stand for himself and states
his thoughts as his thoughts, I pay more
attention to what he is saying and look
deeper in myself.

If you tell me the way you see it rather
than the way it "is," then this helps me
to more fully discover the way I see it.
　　　　　—From *Notes to Myself* by Hugh Prather

✦ Then the Germans invaded our little town and the
nostalgic singing of the pupils and their teachers was interrupted. To hear it once more, I would give all I possess, all
that has been promised me.

From time to time I sit down again with a tractate of the
Talmud. And a paralyzing fear comes over me: it is not that I
have forgotten the words, I would still know how to translate
them, even to comment on them. But to speak them does not

suffice: they must be sung and I no longer know how. Suddenly my body stiffens, my glance falters, I am afraid to turn around: behind me my masters are gathered, their breath burning, they are waiting, as they did long ago at examination time, for me to read aloud and demonstrate to the past generations that their song never dies. My masters are waiting and I am ashamed to make them wait. . . .

And so for the tenth time I read the same passage in the same book, and my masters, by their silence, indicate their disapproval; I have lost the key they entrusted to me.

Today other books hold me in their grip and I try to learn from other storytellers how to pierce the meaning of an experience and transform it into legend. But most of them talk too much. Their song is lost in words, like rivers in the sand.

It was the "Selishter Rebbe" who told me one day: "Be careful with words, they're dangerous. Be wary of them. They begat either demons or angels. It's up to you to give life to one or the other. Be careful, I tell you, nothing is as dangerous as giving free rein to words."

At times I feel him standing behind me, rigid and severe. He reads over my shoulder what I am trying to say; he looks and judges whether his disciple enriches man's world or impoverishes it, whether he calls forth angels, or on the contrary kneels before demons of innumerable names.

—From *Legends of Our Time* by Elie Wiesel

41. Purity

Gracious Father, cleanse me from all unrighteousness. Create within me a clean heart, and renew a right spirit within me is my prayer this day. Amen.

PSALM 51

DAILY SCRIPTURE

Monday	Luke 11:37–41
Tuesday	Ephesians 4:17—5:14
Wednesday	John 8:2–11
Thursday	Mark 7:1–8
Friday	2 Timothy 2:14–26
Saturday	Hebrews 9:11–28
Sunday	Romans 7:7—8:17

SELECTIONS FOR MEDITATION

PERSONAL MEDITATION

PRAYER

If you are to become pure you will have to ask God to begin his work very deep in your heart. For he must start with your desires, your motives, your purposes, your hopes, your ambitions, all these things that control your actions. Tell him you are ready for him to come and do his cleansing work.

HYMN   "Whiter Than Snow"

> Lord Jesus, I long to be perfectly whole;
> I want Thee forever to live in my soul.
> Break down every idol, cast out every foe.
> Now wash me and I will be whiter than snow.

Lord Jesus, look down from Thy throne in the skies,
And help me to make a complete sacrifice.
I give up myself, and whatever I know.
Now wash me and I shall be whiter than snow.

Lord Jesus, for this I most humbly entreat.
I wait, blessed Lord, at Thy crucified feet.
By faith, for my cleansing I see Thy blood flow,
Now wash me and I shall be whiter than snow.

Whiter than snow, yes whiter than snow.
Now wash me and I shall be whiter than snow.

James Nicholson

BENEDICTION

Dear Lord, let me come to love cleanness better than anything that would continue to soil my soul. Let me open my
heart and will to your healing, cleansing power. Amen.

SELECTIONS FOR MEDITATION

✦ The saintly and simple Cure d'Ars was once asked the secret of his abnormal success in converting souls. He replied
that it was done by being very indulgent to others and very
hard on himself; a recipe which retains all its virtue still. And
this power of being outwardly genial and inwardly austere,
which is the real Christian temper, depends entirely on the
use we make of the time set apart for personal religion. It is
always achieved if courageously and faithfully sought; and
there are no heights of love and holiness to which it cannot
lead, no limits to the power which it can exercise over the
souls of men.
—From *The House of the Soul and Concerning the Inner Life*
by Evelyn Underhill

✦ If there is one instance in the Rule when the loving and
benign Father of Monte Cassino speaks with vehemence, it is
when he condemns the vice of murmuring. As we perceive
the good of obedience, we can see why he does. If the heart

of obedience is a quest to be a complete "yes" to God in love, murmuring is diametrically opposed to this. Obedience with murmuring is a charade. It is obedience motivated by some intention not worthy of the human person. It is to miss the whole point of obedience.

—From *A Place Apart* by M. Basil Pennington

◆ Purity means freedom from anything foreign to the essential character of a thing.

Pure water is water in which there is nothing but H_2O.

Pure poetry is poetry that has nothing in it that is alien to the nature of poetry—no doggerel, no lumbering prose, no acrid didacticism.

Pure science is science that has no extraneous or irrelevant interest, but is concerned only with objective reality.

A pure person is one in whom is nothing alien to the character which was God's intention for him.

That intention was a finite being, in quality like God himself.

Who then can hope to be pure? Did you ever know anybody in whom there was absolutely nothing in the least contrary to God? Probably not. Yet here at least is our goal. Jesus did not deal in relatives but in absolutes. He summoned us to the very perfections of God. To aim at anything less is to have a lower aim for ourselves than Christ had for us. To argue about whether such purity is attainable is scarcely the business of most of us who have never made it our serious consecration, let alone our possession.

"Blessed are the pure in heart for they shall see God." Instead of throwing up our hands in despair or throwing away our hunger for God in reversion to some lesser idol, seek it. Seek it for ten years, for twenty years, for thirty. Then come back and tell me what you think. Men have been searching for values of vastly less significance for a longer period. Some of them died searching. Are we to refuse the challenge of the quest? On this I would venture my eternal salvation—if you will make the purity of God your indefatigable quest, the God of purity will give himself to you in such fullness, that your questions will be transcended in the splendor of the experience which has overtaken you.

— From *Discipline and Discovery* by Albert E. Day

✦ Let us remind ourselves that the purity we seek can never be our own achievement. There is a strange paradox here— only the pure in heart shall see God; only those who see God shall be pure in heart.

No disciplines, none proposed here nor elsewhere, can make us pure.

But, it is equally true, without self-discipline there can be no divine deliverance.

. . . For the attainment of that lower purity, from the indulgence of the flesh:

—Read no books and see no pictures which inflame desire. If the book you have innocently purchased is doing that, lay it aside, if a picture is the offender, get up and leave the place.

—Indulge in no stories nor listen to any that have an unclean sex-reference. Turn away from the company where these are the vogue.

—Avoid anything which lowers your inhibitions. How does the use of alcoholic beverages appear in the light of such a test?

—Set a watch at the door of your eyes. Lusting often begins with looking.

—Guard your imagination. In a contest between the will and imagination, the imagination usually wins. Your will to purity is unlikely to be able to cope with an imagination full of impure imagery. "Whatsoever things are pure"—let these fill your imagination.

—Do not run into temptation. Some associations are very corrupting.

—Restrain your indulgent curiosity. That is especially important for youth. "The fruit of the tree of knowledge of good and evil" has cost more than one youth his Eden.

—Let your thoughts dwell on what to do and be rather than on what to avoid or shun.

—Especially keep your mind occupied with Christ and the pattern he has given you.

— From *Discipline and Discovery* by Albert E. Day

✦ The strongest prayer, one well-nigh almighty in what it can effect, and the most exalted work a man can do proceed from a pure heart. The more pure it is, the more powerful, and the more exalted, useful, laudable, and perfect is its prayer and work. A pure heart is capable of anything.

What is a pure heart?

A pure heart is one that is unencumbered, unworried, uncommitted, and which does not want its own way about anything but which, rather, is submerged in the loving will of God, having denied self. Let a job be ever so inconsiderable, it will be raised in effectiveness and dimension by a pure heart.

We ought so to pray that every member and faculty, eyes, ears, mouth, heart, and the senses shall be directed to this end and never cease prayer until we attain unity with him to whom our prayers and attention are directed, namely, God.

—From *Meister Eckhart.* Translated by Raymond Blakney

✦ I may be exaggerating slightly,
    but I perceive that some of these words
        like sanctification and holiness and redemption,
           which at one time were profoundly relevant,
               which were precious and beautiful

                                  life-words,
        have, for many people, lost their luster
          and much of their beauty and

                            magnetism.
                  Do I make myself clear?
Some of these precious words—these life-words—
    at one time had juice in them;
        they had stuff in them;
           they connoted things;
             they denoted things;
               they were glorious words;
                  they were magnetic words.
But, for many, they have lost something:
    the juice has dried up;
        and they have become technical terms,
        and maybe shibboleths.

. . . At the same time, I see something else
   going on in the world where I live.
      While some of the old terms have

                           lost their luster,
                        I perceive there is
                     a growing, deep-heart
                        hunger to be holy!
                  I believe that with all my soul!
Maybe this is the hunger to which
   all other hungers are related.
      Maybe this fundamental hunger to be holy
         is that God-shaped vacuum

                        in the heart of every person.
                           And, oddly enough,
                     though that hunger persists,
                        it is seldom expressed.
I don't know if we can find
   new terms,
   new language,
   new lingo
      that would help us.
      but I know that there is within us
      a hunger to be holy.
And I know that the heart-hunger
   of our Lord for His Church
      is that the people of God
       be sanctified and
   made meet for the Master's use.
                  —From *Let's Listen to Jesus* by Reuben Welch

✦ When it stands before You and Your infallible Truthfulness,
doesn't my soul look just like a market place where the sec-
ondhand dealers from all corners of the globe have assembled
to sell the shabby riches of this world? Isn't it just like a noisy
bazaar, where I and the rest of mankind display our cheap
trinkets to the restless, milling crowds?

Many years ago, when I was a schoolboy distinguished by
the name of "philosopher," I learned that the soul is somehow

everything. O God, how the meaning of that lofty-sounding phrase has changed! How different it sounds to me now, when my soul has become a huge warehouse where day after day the trucks unload their crates without any plan or discrimination, to be piled helter-skelter in every available corner and cranny, until it is crammed full from top to bottom with the trite, the commonplace, the insignificant, the routine.

. . . Maybe at that last reckoning, at the time of the great disillusionment that will take the place of the great illusion of my tritely spent earthly life, maybe then, O God, if you have been merciful to me, the genuine yield of my ingenuine life will be only a few blessed moments, made luminous and living by Your grace. Maybe then I shall see the few precious instants when the grace of Your Love has succeeded in stealing into an obscure corner of my life, in between the countless bales of second-hand goods that fill up my everyday routine.

—From *Encounters with Silence* by Karl Rahner

42. Charity

INVOCATION

Almighty God, my Father, I call upon You and request of You
that Your love may be found in me Your servant. I know not
how to love as I ought; but You who are Love can reveal it
unto me. Show me the way to Love. Amen.

PSALM 82

DAILY SCRIPTURE

Monday	1 Corinthians 13:1–13
Tuesday	Matthew 5:38–48
Wednesday	1 John 3:11–18
Thursday	John 13:1–17
Friday	Romans 5:1–8
Saturday	1 John 4:7–19
Sunday	Luke 6:37–42

SELECTIONS FOR MEDITATION

PERSONAL MEDITATION

PRAYER

Love comes in many ways and many forms. God will teach us
how to truly love others if that is our desire. Is it?

HYMN   "He Loves Me"

> Alas! and did my Saviour bleed?
> And did my Sov'reign die?
> Would He devote that sacred head
> For such a worm as I?

> Was it for crimes that I have done
> He groaned upon a tree?
> Amazing pity! grace unknown!
> And love beyond degree!

Well might the sun in darkness hide,
And shut His glories in.
When Christ, the mighty Maker, died
For man, the creature's, sin.

But drops of grief can ne'er repay
The debt of love I owe.
Here, Lord, I give myself away;
'Tis all that I can do.

He loves me; He loves me;
He loves me, this I know.
He gave himself to die for me
Because He loves me so!

Isaac Watts

BENEDICTION

I am sure that there is in me nothing that could attract the love of One as holy and as just as You are. Yet You have declared Your unchanging love for me in Christ Jesus. If nothing in me can win Your love, nothing in the universe can prevent You from loving me. Your love is uncaused and undeserved. You are Yourself the reason for the love wherewith I am loved. Help me to believe the intensity, the eternity of the love that has found me. Then love will cast out fear; and my troubled heart will be at peace, trusting not in what I am but in what You have declared Yourself to be. Amen.

A. W. Tozer in *The Knowledge of the Holy*

SELECTIONS FOR MEDITATION

✦ Jesus taught that God is the Father of life, of all Mankind; that the character of the relationship by which men are bound one to another does not derive primarily from one man's feeling for another, but from a man's interpretation of the will of God for him in his relationship to another. To Jesus, each human being is of infinite worth to God and before God; there is one God, and to that One God every human being in the world is related. A man's significance is precisely in that fact. Therefore, in dealings with other human beings I must act from within that presupposition. How terrible that is! It means that social classifications, within which my life and

your life exist, have no validity. A Republican and a Democrat, a Socialist and a Communist, a Methodist and a Baptist, a Buddhist and a Hindu, a poor man and a rich man, a male human being and a female human being, an ignorant person and a learned person, a sick person and a well person—none of these classifications has meaning before God. Each one is a human being, not because of his social standing, not because of his relation to another human being, not according to his context, or to the character of his life—No! Every human being as a human being relates to God. That is the point!
—From *The Growing Edge* by Howard Thurman

✦ "No one ever wins a fight"—thoughtfully, and with eyes searching the depths of me, my grandmother repeated the words. I was something to behold. One eye was swollen, my jacket was ripped with all the buttons torn from their places, and there was a large tear in the right knee of my trousers. It was a hard and bitter fight. I had stood all I could, until at last I threw discretion to the winds and the fight was on. The fact that he was larger and older and had brothers did not matter. For four blocks we had fought and there was none to separate us. At last I began to gain in power; with one tremendous effort I got him to the ground and, as the saying went, "made him eat dirt." Then I had to come home to face my grandmother. "No one ever wins a fight," were her only words as she looked at me. "But I beat him," I said. "Yes, but look at you. You beat him, but you will learn someday that nobody ever wins a fight." Many years have come and gone since that afternoon in early summer. I have seen many fights, big and little. I have lived through two world wars. The wisdom of these telling words becomes clearer as the days unfold. There is something seductive about the quickening sense of power that comes when the fight is on. There is a bewitching something men call honor, in behalf of which they often do and become the dishonorable thing. It is all very strange. How often honor is sacrificed in defense of honor. Honor is often a strange mixture of many things—pride, fear, hate, shame, courage, truth, cowardice—many things. The mind takes many curious twistings and turnings as it runs the interference for one's survival. And yet the term survival alone is not quite what is meant. Men want to survive, yes, but on their own terms. And this is most often what is meant by honor. "No one ever wins a fight." This suggests that there is always some other way; or does it mean that man can always choose the weapons he shall use? Not to fight at all is to choose a weapon by which one fights. Perhaps the authentic moral stature of a man is determined by his choice of weapons which he uses in his fight against the adversary. Of all weapons, love is the most deadly and devastating, and few there be who dare trust their fate in its hands.

—From *Deep Is the Hunger* by Howard Thurman

✦ The invading Love of the Eternal Now must break in through us into this time—now.
—From *A Testament of Devotion* by Thomas R. Kelly

✦ Have you experienced this concern for the sparrow's fall? This is not just Jesus' experience. Nor is it His inference about God's tender love; it is the record of His experience in God. There is the tendering of the soul, toward everything in creation, from the sparrow's fall to the slave under the lash. The hardlined face of a money-bitten financier is as deeply touching to the tendered soul as are the burned-out eyes of miners' children, remote and unseen victims of his so-called success. There is a sense in which, in this terrible tenderness, we become one with God and bear in our quivering souls the sins and burdens, the benightedness and the tragedy of the creatures of the whole world, and suffer in their suffering, and die in their death.

—From *A Testament of Devotion* by Thomas R. Kelly

✦ A man must not choose his neighbor: he must take the neighbor that God sends him. . . . The neighbor is just the man who is next to you at the moment, the man with whom any business has brought you into contact.

—From *An Anthology of George MacDonald.*
Edited by C. S. Lewis

✦ The first stage is to believe that there is only one kind of love. The middle stage is to believe that there are many kinds of love and that the Greeks had a different word for each of them.

The last stage is to believe that there is only one kind of love.

The unabashed eros of lovers, the sympathetic philia of friends, agape giving itself freely no less for the murderer than for his victim (the King James version translates it as charity)—these are all manifestations of a single reality. To lose yourself in another's arms, or in another's company, or in suffering for all men who suffer, including the ones who inflict suffering upon you—to lose yourself in such ways is to find yourself. Is what it's all about. Is what love is.

—From *Wishful Thinking* by Frederick Buechner

✦ Of all powers, love is the most powerful and the most powerless. It is the most powerful because it alone can conquer that final and most impregnable stronghold which is the human heart. It is the most powerless because it can do nothing except by consent.

—From *Wishful Thinking* by Frederick Buechner

✦ The first thing Paul says about love is that it is patient: "Love is patient." (I Cor. 13:4). The dictionary definition of patience is: "The suffering of afflictions, pain, toil, calamity, provocation, or other evil, with a calm unruffled temper; endurance without murmuring or fretfulness." The root of patience is pati (suffer). The first emphasis, then, is that love can suffer, can take it. Since love is outgoing, and since by its very nature it insinuates itself into the sins and sufferings of loved ones, its very first capacity must be to be patient, to have a capacity to take suffering and sorrow patiently. The very first step takes us to the Cross at once, where, in a supreme way, Love showed its capacity to take on Itself everything that would fall upon the loved one. So if love can go to the Cross straight off, it can go anywhere. It meets the supreme test, and all the other tests have been met in this initial test.

—From *The Way to Power and Poise* by E. Stanley Jones

✦ It is strange that one as involved in the life of spirit as I should be is so turned off by "religious" things. Recently in going through a city I saw a sign: "Jesus Park." I cringed. The quest for spirit life must in many ways be a secret pilgrimage of inner transformation that makes all things new, but frees us not to be different from but to be involved with, in liberated ways. We do not become "religious"—we become free and thus faithful.

—From *The Province Beyond the River* by W. Paul Jones

✦ Every child's life gives forth hints and signs of the way that he is to go. The parent that knows how to meditate stores these hints and signs away and ponders over them. We are to treasure the intimations of the future that the life of every child gives to us so that, instead of unconsciously putting blocks in his way, we help him to fulfill his destiny. This is not an easy way to follow. Instead of telling our children what they should do and become, we must be humble before their wisdom, believing that in them and not in us is the secret that they need to discover.

Eric Hoffer tells a story about a Bavarian peasant woman who cared for him after his mother died and during the years that he was blind: "And this woman, this Martha took care of me. She was a big woman, with a small head. And this woman, this Martha, must have really loved me, because those eight years of blindness are in my mind as a happy time. I remember a lot of talk and laughter. I must have talked a great deal, because Martha used to say again and again, "You remember you said this, you remember you said that, . . ." She remembered everything I said, and all my life I've had the feeling that what I think and what I say are worth remembering. She gave me that. . . ."

—From *The Eighth Day of Creation*
by Elizabeth O'Connor

✦ Recently in a Midwestern university, there was an interesting sociological experiment with the students concerning sharing and giving. They asked that each student bring a dime.

They said, There are people starving in India. There is a plague and they really need help. If you feel that you'd like to give to that, put the dime in an envelope and write on it, "India." That's pretty far away, India. There are some people in a local ghetto, a family, that really need groceries to live now. If you want to help these people, it will be given to them anonymously. Put your dime in an envelope and put "poor family." Now, of course, we don't have a photocopier at the university and we need to get one for those of you who need to copy papers and manuscripts—and make it easily accessible. If you want to help buy a photocopier, put ten cents in the envelope and put "Copier." Eighty percent of that money went to a photocopy machine!

—From *Living, Loving, and Learning* by Leo Buscaglia

◆ There have been times when I have waited months, and even years, at someone's door.

You can't force your way into a house—it would be breaking and entering.

You must simply be there, like warm sunlight, so that seeing you through the window, the other will want to come out.

You must imitate God's unwavering patience with his children, whom he loves.

. . . But if the other hesitates too long to come out of his fortress, perhaps it is because my light is weak, so weak that it cannot illuminate the way.

—From *With Open Heart* by Michael Quoist

◆ Love is not premeditated, it is spontaneous, i.e., it bursts up in extraordinary ways. There is nothing of mathematical certainty in Paul's category of love. We cannot say—"Now I am going to think no evil; I am going to believe in all things." The characteristic of love is spontaneity. We do not set the statements of Jesus in front of us as a standard; but when His Spirit is having His way with us, we live according to His standard without knowing it, and on looking back we are amazed at the disinterestedness of a particular emotion, which is the evidence that the spontaneity of real love was there. In everything to do with the life of God in us, its nature is only discerned when it is past.

The springs of love are in God, not in us. It is absurd to look for the love of God in our hearts naturally, it is only there when it has been shed abroad in our hearts by the Holy Spirit.

If we try to prove to God how much we love Him, it is a sure sign that we do not love Him. The evidence of our love for Him is the absolute spontaneity of our love, it comes naturally. In looking back we cannot tell why we did certain things, we did them according to the spontaneous nature of His love in us. The life of God manifests itself in this spontaneous way because the springs of love are in the Holy Ghost. (Romans 5:5).

—From *My Utmost for His Highest* by Oswald Chambers

SECTION FIVE
outward fruits of the inner life

The inner life is not a life that is to be lived in some early morning tryst with God himself nor is it some late at night occurrence that takes place when the affairs of life have run their course, at least for one more day. Rather, it is to be lived in the midst of the sorrows and joys of life. It rises on two wings as an ancient saying reminds us—personal piety and community charity. Jesus taught us that the two great commandments were to love God and our neighbors. Elizabeth O'Connor describes this life in terms of "the inward journey" and "the outward journey." We cannot worship God unless we also are willing to do the will of God. Harvey and Lois Seifert remind us that the "two wings of soaring, liberated life are devotion and action."

This final section of the book will give you ten areas of outward expression of the life lived in God which can serve as measuring sticks for the authenticity of your prayer experience. Your newly intensified life in God has not removed you from the world and its needs and sorrows; indeed it should have made you more aware and more compassionate to those who are in need.

This effect of prayer is often described by true pilgrims by the word "transparency." Prayer, attention to God and your own inner person, will result in your seeing things, people, events, with a new clarity. They become open to you. You see them as they are. It brings an insight into existence itself.

This new vision will call you and lead you into areas of service, growth, liberty, commitment, priority, compassion and lifestyle. The life that is begun on the inside in private worship of God will soon burst forth into outwardness—toward others, toward their needs, toward their hurts.

Thus, the second witness to you of the validity of your prayers, can be seen in the ways you act and speak and live. Living from the center will gradually reorder and rearrange everything which lies on the circumference of your life.

43. Service

INVOCATION

Heavenly Father, as the day dawns and calls me to my labors I ask you to enable me to gladly do the work to which you beckon me. May I do it as a servant of Christ doing the will of God from my heart. Amen.

PSALM 90

DAILY SCRIPTURE

Monday	Luke 10:1–16
Tuesday	Matthew 5:13–16
Wednesday	1 Corinthians 12:12–31
Thursday	Luke 22:24–32
Friday	Matthew 6:1–4
Saturday	1 Corinthians 2:1–5
Sunday	Luke 1:76–80

SELECTIONS FOR MEDITATION

PERSONAL MEDITATION

PRAYER

Ask God to help you this week to see the tasks of your life not as opportunities for advancement or as stepping-stones to some future work. Rather may you see them as places where you have been called to serve and may you do them gladly.

HYMN   "O Master, Let Me Walk with Thee"

> O Master, let me walk with Thee
> In lowly paths of service free.
> Tell me Thy secret; help me bear
> The strain of toil, the fret of care.
>
> Help me the slow of heart to move
> By some clear, winning word of love.

Teach me the wayward feet to stay,
And guide them in the homeward way.

Teach me Thy patience! still with Thee
In closer, dearer company,
In work that keeps faith sweet and strong,
In trust that triumphs over wrong.

In hope that sends a shining ray
Far down the future's broadening way,
In peace that only Thou canst give,
With Thee, O Master, let me live.

W. Gladden

BENEDICTION

God give me work
Till my life shall end
And life
Till my work is done. Amen.

Yorkshire Tombstone

SELECTIONS FOR MEDITATION

✦ Rabbi Abraham Heschel said at the Liturgical Conference in Milwaukee that what we needed, what the world needed, was prayer.

And now I pick up Thomas Merton's last book, *Contemplative Prayer,* which I am starting to read, and the foreword by our good Quaker friend Douglas Steere brought back to my memory a strange incident in my life. He quotes William Blake: "We are put on earth for a little space that we may learn to bear the beams of love." And he goes on to say that to escape these beams, to protect ourselves from these beams, even devout men hasten to devise protective clothing. We do not want to be irradiated by love.

Suddenly I remembered coming home from a meeting in Brooklyn many years ago, sitting in an uncomfortable bus seat facing a few poor people. One of them, a downcast, ragged man, suddenly epitomized for me the desolation, the hopelessness of the destitute, and I began to weep. I had been struck by one of those "beams of love," wounded by it in a most particular way. It was my own condition that I was weeping about—my own hardness of heart, my own sinfulness. I recognized this as a moment of truth, an experience of what the New Catechism calls our "tremendous, universal, inevitable and yet inexcusable incapacity to love." I had not read that line when I had that experience, but that is what I felt. I think that ever since then I have prayed sincerely those scriptural verses, "Take away my heart of stone and give me a heart of flesh." I had been using this prayer as one of the three acts of faith, hope, and charity. "I believe, help Thou my unbelief." "In Thee I have hoped, let me never be confounded." "Take away my heart of stone and give me a heart of flesh," so that I may learn how to truly love my brother because in him, in his meanest guise, I am encountering Christ.

— From *By Little and By Little—The Selected Writings of Dorothy Day.* Edited by Robert Ellsberg

✦ It is as if within you there was a little log cabin in which you and Christ were very close; in this attitude you go about your business. . . . It means that within yourselves you have made a room, a secluded space. You have built it by prayer— the Jesus Prayer or whatever prayer you have found profitable. You should be more aware of God than anyone else, because you are carrying within you this utterly quiet and silent chamber. Because you are more aware of God, because you have been called to listen in your inner silence, you can bring God to the street, the party, the meeting, in a very special and powerful way. The power is God's but you have contributed yourself. God has asked you and chosen you to be the carrier of that silent place within yourself.

In a manner of speaking, nothing has changed in your daily schedule. So you attend all the meetings as before, knowing in deep faith and its accompanying darkness that you are bringing Christ, the Christ who prayed to his Father all night, alone on the mountain. You bring the Christ who stole away from the crowds to pray. You are now carrying him back to the crowds. So you should be "with" the crowds.

— From *Poustinia—Christian Spirituality of the East for Western Man* by Catherine de Hueck Doherty

✦ What then is it that we do receive in ministry? Is it the hidden insights and skills of those to whom we want to bear witness? Maybe so . . . but that can never be the true source of our own growth. Seeing how a person slowly becomes aware of his or her own capacities might make us happy for awhile, but that is not enough for a grateful life. A grateful life is a life in which we come to see that the Lord himself is the gift. The mystery of ministry is that the Lord is to be found where we minister. That is what Jesus tells us when he says: "Insofar as you did this to one of the least of these brothers of mine, you did it to me" (Matt. 25:40). Our care for people thus becomes the way to meet the Lord. The more we give, help, support, guide, counsel, and visit, the more we receive, not just similar gifts, but the Lord himself. To go to the poor is to go to the Lord. Living this truth in our daily life makes it possible to care for people without conditions, without hesitation, without suspicion, or without the need for immediate rewards. With this sacred knowledge, we can avoid becoming burned out.

—From *Gracias!* by Henri J. Nouwen

✦ You have your work. It will be more meaningful for you, whatever it may be, if you take all the opportunities it affords to serve and give joy to others; if you reverence the things you work with and are conscious that your working with them gives them an opportunity to express themselves at a higher level through your activity and love; if you share some of the fruit of your labor with those less fortunate; if you do all for the love and glory of the heavenly Father, knowing then that your work is part of the transformation of the whole creation, including especially yourself.

—From *A Place Apart* by M. Basil Pennington

✦ It is a particularization of my responsibility also, in a world too vast and a lifetime too short for me to carry all responsibilities. My cosmic love, or the Divine Lover loving within me, cannot accomplish its full intent, which is universal saviourhood, within the limits of three score years and ten. But the Loving Presence does not burden us equally with all things, but considerately puts upon each of us just a few central tasks, as emphatic responsibilities. For each of these special undertakings are our share in the joyous burdens of love.

Thus the state of having a concern has a foreground and a backgound. In the foreground is the special task, uniquely illuminated, toward which we feel a special yearning and care. This is the concern as we usually talk about it or present it to the Monthly Meeting. But in the background is a second level, or layer, of universal concern for all the multitude of good things that need doing. Toward them all we feel kindly, but we are dismissed from active service in most of them. And we have an easy mind in the presence of desperately real needs which are not our direct responsibility. We cannot die on every cross, nor are we expected to.

—From *A Testament of Devotion* by Thomas R. Kelly

◆ The disciples spread the lunch and told Jesus it was time to eat. But He tells them He has already eaten. They looked around for a McDonald's bag or some evidence of some lunch. Not that I think He would throw trash on the ground.

"Maybe somebody else brought Him some food," they wondered.

And He explained, "I had lunch with my Father."

We call it work. He said it was meat and drink to Him.

In the church there always seemed to be the need for devising some new plan with a catchy title and slogan to once again enroll the saints in the Father's work. It's even better if someone writes a song for the kickoff rally. It is usually about as easy to sing as "The Star-Spangled Banner."

Once in our fellowship we had a denomination-wide program to help us find those in the community who needed Christ. We were all trained. Leaders came from headquarters to teach us in district gatherings and then in zone meetings and finally in each local church. We were armed with the forms and cards and door-opening questions.

"Do you know a boy or girl in this neighborhood who does not go to Sunday School?"

We called it Visitation Evangelism, but He would have called it lunch. We sometimes call it Thursday Night Visitation, but He calls it dinner. We may call it Soul-winning, but He says it is fried chicken and green beans and sliced tomatoes and a tall glass of iced tea. Jesus came to do the work of the Father and He liked it as well as He did eating.

—From *In Quest of the Shared Life* by Bob Benson

✦ We have fallen into the temptation of separating ministry from spirituality, service from prayer. Our demon says: "We are too busy to pray; we have too many needs to attend to, too many people to respond to, too many wounds to heal. Prayer is a luxury, something to do during a free hour, a day away from work or on a retreat. The few who are exclusively concerned with prayer—such as Trappists, Poor Clares, and some isolated hermits—are not really involved in ministry. They are set free for single-minded contemplation and leave Christian service to others." But to think this way is harmful; harmful for ministers as well as for contemplatives. Service and prayer can never be separated; . . .

—From *The Living Reminder* by Henri J. Nouwen

✦ Forward! Thy orders are given in secret. May I always hear them—and obey.

Forward! Whatever distance I have covered, it does not give me the right to halt.

Forward! It is the attention given to the last steps, before the summit which decides the value of all that went before.

—From *Markings* by Dag Hammarskjöld

✦ I do not suppose that Arthur consciously gave me the last year of his life, nor that he chose to teach me. Yet, by his mere being; by forcing me to take that life, real, unsweetened, barenaked, hurting and critical; by demanding that I serve him altogether unrewarded; by wringing from me first mere gestures of loving and then the love itself—but a sacrificial love, a Christlike love, being love for one so indisputably unlovable—he did prepare me for my ministry.

My tears were my diplomas, his death my benediction, and failure my ordination. For the Lord did not say, "Blessed are you if you know" or "teach" or "preach these things." He said, rather, "Blessed are you if you do these things."

When, on the night in which he was betrayed, Jesus had washed his disciples' feet, he sat and said, "If I then, your Lord and Teacher, have washed your feet, you also ought to wash one another's feet. For I have given you an example, that you also should do as I have done to you. Truly, truly, I say unto you, a servant is not greater than his master; nor is he who is sent greater than he who sent him. If you know these things," said Jesus, "blessed are you if you do them."

Again and again the Lord expanded on this theme: "Drink to the stinking is drink to Me!" One might have learned by reading it. . . .

But it is a theme made real in experience alone, by doing it.

And the first flush of that experience is, generally, a sense of failure; for this sort of ministry severely diminishes the minister, makes him insignificant, makes him the merest servant, the least in the transaction. To feel so small is to feel somehow failing, weak, unable.

But there, right there, begins true servanthood: the disciple who has, despite himself, denied himself.

And then, for perhaps the first time, one is loving not out of his own bowels, merit, ability, superiority, but out of Christ: for he has discovered himself to be nothing and Christ everything.

In the terrible, terrible doing of ministry is the minister born. And, curiously, the best teachers of that nascent minister are sometimes the neediest people, foul to touch, unworthy, ungiving, unlovely, yet haughty in demanding—and then miraculously receiving—love. These poor, forever with us, are our riches.

—From *Ragman and Other Cries of Faith*
by Walter Wangerin, Jr.

44. Growth

INVOCATION

Show me Your glory, I pray to You, that so I may know You indeed. Begin in mercy a new work of love within me. Say to my soul, "Rise up, my love, my fair one, and come away." Then give me grace to rise and follow you up from this misty lowland where I have wandered so long. In Jesus' Name, Amen.

A. W. Tozer in *The Pursuit of God*

PSALM 37

DAILY SCRIPTURE

Monday	Philippians 3:12–21
Tuesday	1 John 2:3–17
Wednesday	Ephesians 4:1–16
Thursday	Luke 6:43–45
Friday	Philippians 1:1–11
Saturday	2 Peter 1:3–11
Sunday	Luke 19:11–29

SELECTIONS FOR MEDITATION

PERSONAL MEDITATION

PRAYER

God's desire to move us on to spiritual maturity is a stronger desire than we believe. If you will seek his face, then he will fashion you into the image of himself.

HYMN   "Higher Ground"

I'm pressing on the upward way.
New heights I'm gaining every day,

Still praying as I onward bound,
"Lord, plant my feet on higher ground.". . .
Johnson Oatman, Jr.

BENEDICTION

Grow, dear friends; but grow, I beseech you, in God's way, which is the only effectual way. See to it that you are planted in grace, and then let the divine Husbandman cultivate you in His own way and by His own means.
Hannah Whitall Smith in The Christian's Secret
of a Happy Life

SELECTIONS FOR MEDITATION

✦ Prayer is the way in which the soul is infused by the power of the Holy Spirit. If one continues to pray in confidence and strength despite all outer diversions and inner discouragements, there will be a gradual change in one's disposition. The effect is neither rapid nor magical—growth, whether physical or spiritual, takes time and is unobtrusive when viewed on a day-to-day basis—but one's life proceeds so one becomes dimly aware of an inner composure and tolerance to events that would previously have disturbed one's equilibrium. One reacts less abruptly to the insensitive intrusion of other people into one's thoughts and private life; one becomes less jealous when one hears of another's success in one's own chosen field; one responds with greater calm in the face of unpleasant circumstances that before would have shattered one emotionally to the extent of preventing one from working properly or being decently aware of other people in the neighborhood. St. Paul says to his disciples in Philippi: "I wish you all joy in the Lord. I will say it again: all joy be yours. Let your magnanimity be manifest to all" (Phil. 4:4–5). This magnanimity is the fruit of intensive prayer.
—From Living Alone: The Spiritual Dimension
by Martin Israel

✦ Here are very profound implications for our lives. For we

must know that we are not through growing, developing; that man is not finished; but that also there is inherent in life itself that which places limitations upon us.

Suppose a tree couldn't stop growing; suppose your feet couldn't stop growing. But just grew on and on and there were nothing you could do about it. It is like a figure in Zarathustra called the "cripple in reverse," the man who had the ear lobe that extended from his head down to the ground—an ear lobe growing and growing, which apparently couldn't stop. It is a wonderful thing that inherent in the life process are limitations, so that though new things start growing, old things also stop growing.

I am always reminded that the experience which may be mine at a particular moment may be an experience in which things are stopping. Or it may be an experience in which things are just beginning. It is important that I know which process is taking place. An intimate part of growing into life is the development of a sensitiveness, an apprehension of process in its totality, that I may be enabled to know the character of the event with which I am dealing. Then I will not act in the house of death unnaturally by not accepting it. All of this is to say that there is inherent in life and brooding over the life of man the creative mind and the spirit of the living God.

—From *The Growing Edge* by Howard Thurman

✦ Now if you are to convey that spiritual certitude, it is plain that you must yourselves be spiritually alive. And to be spiritually alive means to be growing and changing; not to settle down among a series of systematized beliefs and duties, but to endure and go on enduring the strains, conflicts and difficulties incident to development. "The soul," said Baron von Hugel, "is a Force or an Energy: and Holiness is the growth of that energy in love, in full Being, in creative, spiritual Personality." One chief object of personal religion is the promoting of that growth of the soul: the wise feeding and training of it. However busy we may be, however mature and efficient we may seem, that growth, if we are real Christians, must go on. Even the greatest spiritual teachers, such as St. Paul and St.

Augustine, could never afford to relax the tension of their own spiritual lives; they never seem to stand still, are never afraid of conflict and change. Their souls too were growing entities, with a potential capacity for love, adoration and creative service: in other words, for holiness, the achievement of the stature of Christ. A saint is simply a human being whose soul has thus grown up to its full stature, by full and generous response to its environment, God. He has achieved a deeper, bigger life than the rest of us, a more wonderful contact with the mysteries of the Universe; a life of infinite possibility, the term of which he never feels that he has reached.

—From *The House of the Soul and Concerning the Inner Life*
by Evelyn Underhill

✦ It seems to me that there are four main things which must have a place in any full and healthy religious life: and that a remembrance of this will help us to make our own inner lives balanced and sane. We require, first, the means of gaining and holding a right attitude; secondly, right spiritual food—real, nourishing food with a bite in it, not desiccated and pre-digested piety. "I am the food of the full grown," said the voice of God to St. Augustine: "Grow and feed on Me." Thirdly, we need an education which shall help growth; training our spiritual powers to an ever greater expansion and efficiency. Fourthly, we have or ought to have some definite spiritual work, and must see that we fit ourselves to do it.

Now each of these four needs is met by a different type of prayer. The right attitude of the soul to God is secured and supported by the prayer of pure adoration. The necessary food for growth is obtained through our spiritual reading and meditation, as well as by more direct forms of communion. Such meditation will also form an important stage in the education of the spiritual faculties; which are further trained in some degree by the use of such formal, affective, or recollec-. tive prayer as each one of us is able to employ. Finally, the work which can be done by the praying soul covers the whole field of intercession and redemptive self-oblation.

—From *The House of the Soul and Concerning the Inner Life*
by Evelyn Underhill

✦ There seem to be many different kinds of spiritual energy. . . . In Western traditions spiritual energies are usually discussed as virtues. However, the sense of the Latin word *virtus* as a potential, power, or energy has receded in favor of virtue as a quality of behaving and responding. Thus the virtue of modesty, instead of being viewed as an inner source of energy, is seen as a style of behavior or dress.

In Christian tradition many spiritual energies (or virtues) are presented as "gifts" or graces. Thus there are the many gifts of the Holy Spirit, discussed in Paul's First Letter to the Corinthians, Chapters 12–13, or the nine "fruits" of the Holy Spirit—love, joy, peace, patience, kindness, goodness, faithfulness, gentleness, and self-control—which Paul presented in Galatians 5:22–23.

When one views spiritual gifts as fonts of energy—much as we view the sun, wind, tides, waterfalls, petroleum, coal, or wood as sources of energy—it is clear they need to be recognized, used, adapted, processed, worked at, cooperated with, and developed in order to be fully effective.

Often in burnout it is not that the supply of spiritual fuel has run out; rather, it appears that we block ourselves from our sources of spiritual energy, we are unaware of their presence, or we try to force them into uses for which they were never intended and where they prove ineffective.

—From *Prayerways*
by Louis M. Savary and Patricia H. Berne

✦ Any man may attain self-control if he only will. He must not expect to gain it save by long continued payment of price, in small progressive expenditures of energy. Nature is a thorough believer in the installment plan in her relations with the individual. No man is so poor that he cannot begin to pay for what he wants; and every small, individual payment that he makes, Nature stores and accumulates for him as a reserve fund in his hour of need.

The patient man expends in bearing the little trials of his daily life Nature stores for him as a wondrous reserve in a crisis of life. With Nature, the mental, the physical or the moral energy he expends daily in right-doing is all stored for him and transmuted into strength. Nature never accepts a cash payment in full for anything—this would be an injustice to the poor and to the weak.

It is only the progressive installment plan Nature recognizes. No man can make a habit in a moment or break it in a moment. It is a matter of development, of growth. But at any moment man may begin to make or begin to break any habit. This view of the growth of character should be a mighty stimulus to the man who sincerely desires and determines to live nearer to the limit of his possibilities.

—From *The Kingship of Self-Control*
by William George Jordan

✦ Most of the difficulty in forming a special habit is that we will not discipline ourselves. Read carefully this quotation from Professor William James' brilliant *Textbook of Psychology,* and apply it to the matter of prayer.

"The great thing, then, in all education, is to make our nervous system our ally instead of our enemy. It is to fund and capitalize our acquisitions, and live at ease upon the interest of the fund. For this we must make automatic and habitual, as early as possible, as many useful actions as we can, and guard against the growing into ways that are likely to be disadvantageous to us, as we should guard against the plague. . . . The first (maxim) is that in the acquisition of a new habit, or the leaving off of an old one, we must take care to launch ourselves with as strong and decided an initiative as possible. . . . The second maxim is: Never suffer an exception to occur till the new habit is securely rooted in your life. . . . A third maxim may be added to the preceding pair: Seize the very first possible opportunity to act on every resolution you make, and on every emotional prompting you may experience in the direction of the habit you aspire to gain."

Let us apply that lesson right now to ourselves, and take our Lord's advice home until it becomes character. You say you cannot get up early in the morning; well a very good thing to do is to get up in order to prove that you cannot! This does not contradict at all what has already been said, viz., that we must not put earnestness in the place of God; it means that we have to understand that our bodily mechanism is made by God, and that when we are regenerated He does not give us another body, we have the same body, and therefore the way we use our wits in order to learn a secular thing is the way to learn any spiritual thing. "But thou, when thou prayest—" begin now.

—From *Christian Discipline, Vol. 2* by Oswald Chambers

✦ "But grow in grace, and in the knowledge of our Lord and Saviour Jesus Christ." Now this text exactly expresses what we believe to be God's will for us, and what we also believe He has made it possible for us to experience. We accept, in their very fullest meaning, all the commands and promises concerning our being no more children, and our growing up into Christ in all things, until we come unto a perfect man, unto the measure of the stature of the fulness of Christ. We rejoice that we need not continue always to be babes, needing milk, but that we may, by reason of use and development, become such as have need of strong meat, skillful in the word of righteousness, and able to discern both good and evil. And none would grieve more than we at the thought of any finality in the Christian life beyond which there could be no advance.

—From *The Christian's Secret of a Happy Life*
by Hannah Whitall Smith

45. Liberty

INVOCATION

Father, my life, in so many ways and at so many places, seems shackled and bound. Help me to find freedom and liberty in you this day. Amen.

PSALM 121

DAILY SCRIPTURE

Monday	1 Corinthians 8:9–13
Tuesday	Colossians 2:6–23
Wednesday	1 Peter 2:13–25
Thursday	Galatians 5:13–25
Friday	Romans 6:15–23
Saturday	2 Corinthians 3:12–18
Sunday	Isaiah 61:1–11

SELECTIONS FOR MEDITATION

PERSONAL MEDITATION

PRAYER

Believe that God desires your life to be lived in liberty and dignity. Ask him to free you from desires, worries, habits that tend to imprison you. In your prayers this week try to come to know that real control over your bondages and yourself is found in surrender to God.

HYMN   "And Can It Be That I Should Gain?"

>   And can it be that I should gain
>   An int'rest in the Saviour's blood?
>   Died He for me, who caused His pain?
>   For me, who Him to death pursued;

Amazing love, How can it be
That Thou, my Lord, shouldst die for me? . . .
Charles Wesley

BENEDICTION

Almighty God, give me rule over indolent desires. Save me from any waste of life. In some great devotion set me at liberty from myself and give me to see my life as a charge from you to keep and to understand. Amen.

Robert R. Wicks in *Daily Prayer Companion*

SELECTIONS FOR MEDITATION

✦ This is the Kingdom, the sense that we are free from possession, and this freedom establishes us in a relationship where everything is love—human love and love divine.

Now if we reason in these terms, we can transfer the same idea to what was said earlier. Yes, we are rich. Yet we should never be beguiled by what we possess into imagining that now we can demolish the old barns and build new ones in order to store more of our riches. Nothing can be stored—nothing except the kingdom of God itself. And so we can discard one thing after another in order to go ahead free—free of being rich. Have you never noticed that to be rich always means an impoverishment on another level? It is enough for you to say, "I have this watch, it is mine," and close your hand upon it, to be in possession of a watch and to have lost a hand. And if you close your mind on your riches, if you close your heart so that you can keep what is in it safe, never to lose it, then it becomes as small as the thing on which you have closed yourself in.

Now if that is true, the moment you reach rock bottom, the moment you are aware of your utter dispossession of all things, then you are on the fringe of the kingdom of God, you are nearly aware that God is love and that He is upholding you by His love. And at that point you can say two things simultaneously. You can pray out of your utter misery, dereliction and poverty, and you can rejoice that you are so rich with the love of God.

—From *Beginning to Pray* by Anthony Bloom

✦ Forgiveness is, then, a renewal, and for love to grow it must be renewed every day. This renewal is not one that seeks somehow to return to the past, however; rather it seeks to revitalize the present. To carry a grudge is to live in the past, to live with the bitterness of disappointment or of the expectation of a future that never was—are illusionary worlds. To live in them is to make encampments in deception. Forgiveness frees a person to live in the reality of the relationship's true present.

I know a child of nine who was on his way out the door to get his younger brother the Christmas present he had been saving for when he discovered that that very brother had just broken one of his own favorite toys. He flew into a rage.

"What were you doing with it?" he yelled. "You didn't even ask me if you could use it. And why weren't you more careful? Just for that you can never play with my toys again. And also, I've decided that I'm not going to buy you a Christmas present this year." He stomped out of the room.

A moment later he returned to the kitchen and slipped on his coat. "I'm going, Mom," he said in a voice that in no way suggested the anger of a moment before.

"Going where?" his mother asked.

"To buy the present."

His mother couldn't hide her look of surprise.

"Well, he is my brother, isn't he?"

—From *A Way in the World* by Ernest Boyer, Jr.

✦ Granted that the daily routine is monotonous, that the personal equipment is extremely limited, that all the options were frozen long ago, that there is nothing on the horizon that sounds the trumpet call to the great adventure or the high demand—granted all of this. But there is always available to the individual another alternative even where options are frozen. One can make an offering of the self to God. This is far different from offering one's special talents, as important as that may be. It is more than the offering of resources, however great or limited they may be. It is to offer one's self: to put at the disposal of Life one's life, not merely one's needs, one's demands, one's frustrations, one's unresolved problems. This is to say to Life, "Here I am, I put myself at your disposal to be where I am—all of me. To do, where I am, with all of me. To respond to life where I am without bargaining or bartering." This means more than being a dutiful son or satisfied worker in a monotonous job. It means putting one's self at the disposal of the hours, of the days, of the months, to feel of their quality, to sense their demands independent of what one demands, independent of what one thinks should come back in dividends. With this freedom of movement within one's own spirit provision is made for the meaningful activity and the significant undertaking—all of this without any apparent change in one's external circumstances.

—From *The Inward Journey* by Howard Thurman

✦ We must learn to realize that the love of God seeks us in every situation, and seeks our good. His inscrutable love seeks our awakening. True, since this awakening implies a kind of death to our exterior self, we will dread His coming in proportion as we are identified with this exterior self and attached to it. But when we understand the dialectic of life and death we will learn to take the risks implied by faith, to make the choices that deliver us from our routine self and open to us the door of a new being, a new reality.

The mind that is the prisoner of conventional ideas, and the will that is the captive of its own desire cannot accept the seeds of an unfamiliar truth and a supernatural desire. For how can I receive the seeds of freedom if I am in love with slavery and how can I cherish the desire of God if I am filled with another and an opposite desire? God cannot plant His liberty in me because I am a prisoner and I do not even desire to be free. I love my captivity and I imprison myself in the desire for the things that I hate, and I have hardened my heart against true love. I must learn therefore to let go of the familiar and the usual and consent to what is new and unknown to me. I must learn to "leave myself" in order to find myself by yielding to the love of God. If I were looking for God, every event and every moment would sow, in my will, grains of His life that would spring up one day in a tremendous harvest.

—From *New Seeds of Contemplation* by Thomas Merton

✦ The liberty of the God who would have his creatures free, is in contest with the slavery of the creature who would cut his own stem from his root that he might call it his own and love it; who rejoices in his own consciousness, instead of the life of that consciousness; who poises himself on the tottering wall of his own being, instead of the rock on which that being is built. Such a one regards his own dominion over himself— the rule of the greater by the less—as a freedom infinitely larger than the range of the universe of God's being. If he says, "At least I have it in my own way!" I answer, you do not know what is your way and what is not. You know nothing of whence your impulses, your desires, your tendencies, your likings come. They may spring now from some chance, as of nerves diseased; now from some roar of a wandering bodiless devil; now from some infant hate in your heart; now from the greed of lawlessness of some ancestor you would be ashamed of if you knew him; or, it may be, now from some far-piercing chord of a heavenly orchestra: the moment comes up into your consciousness, you call it your own way, and glory in it.

—From *An Anthology of George MacDonald.*
Edited by C. S. Lewis

✦ Hunger is my native place in the land of passions. Hunger for fellowship, hunger for righteousness—for a fellowship founded on righteousness, and a righteousness attained in fellowship.

Only life can satisfy the demands of life. And this hunger of mine can be satisfied for the simple reason that the nature of life is such that I can realize my individuality by becoming a bridge for others, a stone in the temple of righteousness.

Don't be afraid of yourself, live your individuality to the full—but for the good of others. Don't copy others in order to buy fellowship, or make convention your law instead of living the righteousness.

To become free and responsible. For this alone was man created, and he who fails to take the Way which could have been his shall be lost eternally.

—From *Markings* by Dag Hammarskjöld

◆ Maturity: among other things, a new lack of self-consciousness—the kind you can only attain when you have become entirely different to yourself through an absolute assent to your fate.

He who has placed himself in God's hand stands free vis-a-vis men: He is entirely at his ease with them, because he has granted them the right to judge.

—From *Markings* by Dag Hammarskjöld

◆ Assured of your salvation by the unique grace of our Lord Jesus Christ, you do not impose discipline on yourself for its own sake. Gaining mastery of yourself has no aim other than to render you more available. Let there be no useless asceticism; hold only to the works God commands. Carry the burdens of others, accept the petty injuries of each day, so as to share concretely in the sufferings of Christ: this is our first discipline.

You fear that a common rule may stifle your personality, whereas its purpose is to free you from useless shackles, so that you may better bear the responsibilities of the ministry and make better use of its boldness. Like every Christian, you must accept the tension between the total freedom given by the Holy Spirit and the impossibilities in which you find yourself due to your neighbor's and your own fallen nature.

You would narrow your understanding of the Gospel if, for fear of losing your life, you were to spare yourself. Unless a grain of wheat dies, you cannot hope to see your own self open out in the fulness of Christian life.

—From *The Rule of Taize* by Br. Roger

✦ The grace of God has two dimensions.

One dimension is the forgiveness of all our sins.

The other dimension is, "I will give you a new heart and put a new spirit within you; and I will remove the heart of stone from your flesh and give you a heart of flesh. And I will put My Spirit within you and cause you to walk in My statutes, and you will be careful to observe My ordinances" (Ezekiel 36:26–27).

We receive the Holy Spirit, and the fruit of the Spirit is love, joy, peace, longsuffering, gentleness, goodness, faith, meekness, self-control, and "against such things there is no law" (Galatians 5:22–23).

Therefore, one who has the new heart doesn't need any law because the Holy Spirit makes the law unnecessary. This is why Jesus said that all the law and the prophets are fulfilled in one word, love.

Paul explained, "For this, 'You shall not commit adultery, you shall not murder, you shall not steal, you shall not covet,' and if there is any other commandment, it is summed up in this saying, 'You shall love your neighbor as yourself.' Love does no wrong to a neighbor; love therefore is the fulfillment of the law" (Romans 13:9–10).

The fruit of the Spirit causes us to do what the law aimed at, plus a great deal more. This makes the law unnecessary.

—From *Living with Jesus Today* by Juan Carlos Ortiz

46. Commitment

INVOCATION

Write Your blessed name, O Lord, upon my heart, there to remain so engraven that no prosperity, no adversity, shall ever move me from Your love. Amen.

Thomas à Kempis in *Little Book of Prayers*

PSALM 101

DAILY SCRIPTURE

Monday	Mark 10:17–31
Tuesday	John 12:20–33
Wednesday	Psalm 31:1–5
Thursday	2 Timothy 1:3–12
Friday	Joshua 24:1–24
Saturday	John 6:41–67
Sunday	1 Kings 8:54–61

SELECTIONS FOR MEDITATION

PERSONAL MEDITATION

PRAYER

One of the results of a deeper prayerlife should be a greater commitment to the one who was and is so deeply committed to you. But sometimes we get cross-purposed and continue to be committed to our own interests. Make it a point to ask God to show you how he feels your commitment level to be.

HYMN "Have Thine Own Way, Lord"

Have Thine own way, Lord!
Have Thine own way!
Thou art the Potter;
I am the clay

Mould me and make me
After Thy will,
While I am waiting,
Yielded and still. . . .
          Adelaide A. Pollard

BENEDICTION

Lord, take my lips and speak through them; take my mind, and
think through it; take my heart, and set it on fire. Amen.
          W. H. Aitken in *Little Book of Prayers*

SELECTIONS FOR MEDITATION

✦ This abandonment is the very heart and essence of Christian prayer, and it has nothing in common with strategy and
second-guessing. It is the pray-to-win mentality turned inside
out, and yet it is not a pray-to-lose mentality. It is the prayer
that has moved beyond intending, directing, steering, second-
guessing God. It is the dancer moving completely in the
rhythm of the partner, prayer that is utterly freeing because it
is completely at one. Utterly beyond asking, beyond the anger
that rattles heaven's gate. Prayer that does not plead, wants
nothing for itself but what God wants, it is the will-not-to-will,
rooted in grace, that makes it possible to be abandoned, free,
and then (by some further miracle) able to act with a sem-
blance of coherence and freedom even when completely sur-
rendered to and possessed by the loving will of God.

And it is this abandonment that is meant when we are told
to drop our nets and follow him; to pause not to bury our
dead fathers or tell our wives we will be traveling for a while;
it is in this abandonment that we sell all.
          —From *Clinging—The Experience of Prayer*
          by Emilie Griffin

✦ Meister Eckhart wrote: "There are plenty to follow our
Lord half-way, but not the other half. They will give up possessions, friends and honors, but it touches them too closely to
disown themselves." It is just this astonishing life which is
willing to follow Him the other half, sincerely to disown itself,

this life which intends complete obedience, without any reservations, that I would propose to you in all humility, in all boldness, in all seriousness. I mean this literally, utterly, completely, and I mean it for you and for me—commit your lives in unreserved obedience to Him.

—From *A Testament of Devotion* by Thomas R. Kelly

✦ I almost missed all of that! The privilege of loving dirty-faced, unruly kids until I didn't notice those things as much as their hurts and hearts.

I almost missed it.

During my three years at that school, I prayed with all my production casts and crews before our performances—over one thousand different kids. Since many students were in numerous productions, I prayed with most of them several times. There was never one complaint.

I almost missed it.

I almost missed the opportunity for personal growth—all because I looked at my plan . . . and initially said no to a job I didn't think suited me.

Looking back on those three years, I have to wonder how much I crippled God's purpose for that time because I kept resisting his direction. Kept hanging onto my own perception of what was right for me.

But . . . whatever it wasn't . . . one thing it was . . . it was the beginning of a crucial lesson:

It's not a plan we create that determines our fulfillment.

It's what we let God do in the plan of His choosing.

—From *When the Pieces Don't Fit* by Glaphre Gilliland

✦ Hold, hold as you have never done before. Watch each word and mood, beware of scattering and spilling; do anything—fall flat on the floor and wait till your valiant soul lifts you to your feet. Be ashamed of quailing. No, no! It is easy to see this great fear gripping and squeezing men into dwarfs, but, oh, my children, do not get caught in the feeling of the sick. Now is the appointed time. Hold. Do things to remind you to stay where you belong, tie knots on your fingers, put things up, hang them about so that you may train your foolish heads to remember your Creator now, and so give life to your world. I tell you in no uncertain words that what you actually think now holds your world together. One wrong evil thought coming into your galaxies (of thoughts) could sweep everything you see into Timbuctoo. Your only safety is to be within the center of your kingdom, living from within out, not from without in. Be there all the time, no compromise.

—From *Letters of the Scattered Brotherhood.*
Edited by Mary Strong

✦ Much depends upon making up your mind. The nature of the human animal, as you well know, is subject to suggestion; the feeling-nature, when left to human devices, is un-protected, easily dismayed, elated, bored, irritated. The mind is moved by noises, cold, heat, stupidities, a letter, the dis-loyalty of a friend. But when the mind is made up, all these challenges can be divinely met; you are not defenseless. You are only defenseless when you are spiritually asleep. Bring into focus your godhood, your divine manhood by saying, "I make up my mind to be in the light of faith always, while I talk to people, while I walk, while I eat, Wherever I go, into every house. I will use it against all alarms, I will dwell in his eternal patience, in God's name I will be reborn!"

—From *Letters of the Scattered Brotherhood.*
Edited by Mary Strong

✦ In order, therefore, to enter into a realized experience of this interior life, the soul must be in a receptive attitude, fully recognizing the fact that it is to be God's gift in Jesus Christ, and that it cannot be gained by any efforts or works of our own. This will simplify the matter exceedingly, and the only thing left to be considered then will be to discover upon whom God bestows this gift, and how they are to receive it. And to this I would answer in short, that He bestows it only upon the fully consecrated soul, and that it is to be received by faith.

—From *The Christian's Secret of a Happy Life*
by Hannah Whitall Smith

✦ We, who have heard the call of our God to a life of entire consecration and perfect trust, must do differently from all this. We must come out from the world and be separate, and must not be conformed to it in our characters or in our lives. We must set our affections on heavenly things and not on earthly ones, and must seek first the kingdom of God and His righteousness, surrendering everything that would interfere with this. We must walk through the world as Christ walked. We must have the mind that was in Him. As pilgrims and strangers, we must abstain from lusts of the flesh that war against the soul. As good soldiers of Jesus Christ, we must disentangle ourselves from the affairs of this life as far as possible, that we may please Him who hath chosen us to be soldiers. We must abstain from all appearance of evil. We must be kind to one another, tender-hearted, forgiving one another, even as God, for Christ's sake, hath forgiven us. We must not resent injuries or unkindness, but must return good for evil, and turn the other cheek to the hand that smites us. We must take always the lowest place among our fellow-men; and seek not our own honor, but the honor of others. We must be gentle and meek and yielding, not standing up for our own rights but for the rights of others. We must do all that we do for the glory of God. And, to sum it all up, since He who hath called us is holy, so must we be holy in all manner of conversation; because it is written, "Be ye holy, for I am holy."

—From *The Christian's Secret of a Happy Life*
by Hannah Whitall Smith

✦ Oh, be generous in your self-surrender! Meet His measureless devotion for you, with a measureless devotion to Him. Be glad and eager to throw yourself headlong into His dear arms, and to hand over the reins of government to Him. Whatever there is of you, let Him have it all. Give up forever everything that is separate from Him. Consent to resign from this time forward all liberty of choice. Glory in the blessed nearness of union which makes this enthusiasm of devotedness not only possible but necessary.

—From *The Christian's Secret of a Happy Life*
by Hannah Whitall Smith

✦ The battle is lost or won in the secret places of the will before God, never first in the external world. The Spirit of God apprehends me and I am obliged to get alone with God and fight the battle out before Him. Until this is done, I lose every time. The battle may take one minute or a year, that will depend on me, not on God; but it must be wrestled out alone with before God, and I must resolutely go through the hell of renunciation before God. Nothing has any power over the man who has fought out the battle before God and won there.

If I say, "I will wait till I get into the circumstances and then put God to the test," I shall find I cannot. I must get the thing settled between myself and God in the secret places of my soul where no stranger intermeddles, and then I can go forth with the certainty that the battle is won. Lose it there, and calamity and disaster and upset are sure as God's decree. The reason that the battle is not won is because I try to win it in the external world first. Get alone with God, fight it out before Him, settle the matter there once and for all.

In dealing with other people, the line to take is to push them to an issue of will. That is the way abandonment begins. Every now and again, not often, but sometimes, God brings us to a point of climax. That is the Great Divide in the life; from that point we either go towards a more and more dilatory and useless type of Christian life, or we become more and more ablaze for the glory of God—My Utmost for His Highest.

—From *My Utmost for His Highest* by Oswald Chambers

✦ When we say "Hallowed be thy name," we are praying, "May the whole of my life be a source of delight to you and may it be an honor to the name which I bear, which is your name. Hallowed be your name." We find the same thing in that prayer of David's at the close of one of his great psalms: "Let the words of my mouth and the meditation of my heart be acceptable in thy sight, O Lord, my rock and my redeemer" (Ps. 19:14).

The trouble is that we so frequently know there are great areas of our lives that are not hallowed. There are certain monopolies which we have reserved to ourselves, privileged areas which we do not wish to surrender, where the name of our boss or the name of our girlfriend or some other dear one means more to us than the name of God.

But when we pray, "Hallowed be thy name," if there is any degree whatsoever of sincerity or openness, or honestness, we are really praying, "Lord, I open to you every closet; I am taking every skeleton out for you to examine. Hallowed be thy name." There cannot be any contact with God, any real touching of his power, any genuine experiencing of the glorious fragrance and wonder of God at work in human life until we truly pray "Hallowed be thy name."

—From *Jesus Teaches on Prayer* by Ray C. Stedman

47. Priority

INVOCATION

Lord, deliver me from the small loyalties of habit or tradition that would keep me from larger loyalties of the spirit. Let me so incline myself to you that your presence in my life determines both what I think and what I do. Through Jesus, who understood the deeper meaning of freedom. Amen.

John Killinger in *A Devotional Guide to the Gospels*

PSALM 33

DAILY SCRIPTURE

Monday	Deuteronomy 4:32–40
Tuesday	Philippians 3:1–14
Wednesday	Matthew 6:19–24
Thursday	Luke 17:1–10
Friday	John 21:15–25
Saturday	Matthew 7:17–28
Sunday	Matthew 13:44–46

SELECTIONS FOR MEDITATION

PERSONAL MEDITATION

PRAYER

In a life where one has just so much time and energy it is important that we are doing the first things first. Ask him this week to show you the real priorities of your life. Examine your life in prayer.

HYMN   "Take My Life, and Let It Be"

> Take my life and let it be
> Consecrated, Lord, to Thee;

Take my hands and let them move
At the impulse of Thy love. . . .
                    Francis R. Havergae

BENEDICTION

Grant, O Lord, that I may live in Your fear, die in Your favor,
rest in Your peace, rise in Your power, reign in Your glory.
                    Archbishop Laud in *Little Book of Prayers*

SELECTIONS FOR MEDITATION

✦ If we are well satisfied with our civilization, our culture,
our institutions, it would not be unreasonable to say that
Jesus is our great enemy. He is the alien, the fleeting ghost
moving in and out among the shadows of the private mind,
and of the collective mind. A wanderer. Where can he find a
place in which he can be at home? He challenges the very
grounds of the common assumptions upon whch we live, day
after day. He was no radical social reformer; nor was he a
radical political reformer. But he was a religious man who,
out of his inner experience of God, spoke judgment upon the
established order.

God was the source and the touchstone, the point of referral, for Jesus. We have heard this all our days and there is
nothing new in it until we see the difference such a point of
referral makes when applied in our lives.

. . . Turn and look at the pattern of life of the normal ordinarily resourceful human being. As I look at my life, I see a
wide variety of scattered loyalties, scattered and splintered
devotions. Some basis of order, of integration, does govern my
experience, but it is likely to be a secondary principle, rather
than a primary one. A man's principle of integration, around
which the details of his life move in constellations, may be his
work, his vocation. Or it may be something less significant,
his golf, his neurosis. Every human being has a series of little
centers of integration in his life that express themselves perhaps in simple habits, simple etiquettes with reference to
things that are of no basic or perhaps no ultimate con-

sequence. Have you ever seen someone whose whole life became disorganized for the day because the breakfast coffee was cold? That's what I mean.

Instead of all this absorption with detail, Jesus insists upon an absolute loyalty to God. The questions which he raises about our pattern of life are these: "Do you dare yield the 'nerve center' of your consent to what you believe is the will of God, as your basic principle of integration, rather than to some secondary something, important as that is to you—vocation, family, business, anxiety, money, position, class, race? Do you dare shift the center of focus of your being away from these significant loyalties, that have defined the character of your living, and embrace what, deep within you, you know to be the ultimate devotion of your life?" Your life is the lung through which your loyalties breathe. If you are not willing to yield complete loyalty to the will of God, if you prefer to give first place to your secondary loyalties, you may try to establish a way of relating yourself to Jesus that will not disturb the pattern of your living. On the other hand, if you do accept Jesus' way for you then there is introduced at once into your life a principle that at first reduces to complete chaos the whole network of your relations. That is what Jesus says. Do you wonder that he can find no place to be at home in our whole world? Do you wonder?

—From *The Growing Edge* by Howard Thurman

♦ We can live any way we want. People take vows of poverty, chastity, and obedience—even of silence—by choice. The thing is to stalk your calling in a certain skilled and supple way, to locate the most tender and live spot and plug it into that pulse. This is yielding, not fighting. A weasel doesn't "attack" anything; a weasel lives as he's meant to, yielding at every moment to the perfect freedom of single necessity.

I think it would be well, and proper, and obedient, and pure, to grasp your one necessity and not let it go, to dangle from it limp wherever it takes you. Then even death, where you're going no matter how you live, cannot you part.

—From *Teaching a Stone to Talk* by Annie Dillard

✦ If I ever achieved an alert and active concentration on this spiritual work within my soul, it would then not matter at all what I did in eating or drinking, in sleeping or in speaking, or in any of my outward activities. And certainly I can tell you that I would much rather attain freedom in these things in this way, by not needing to be concerned about them, than by concentrating a great deal of attention on them.

—From *The Cloud of Unknowing* translated by Ira Progoff

✦ Earthly goods are given to be used, not to be collected. In the wilderness God gave Israel the manna every day, and they had no need to worry about food and drink. Indeed, if they kept any of the manna over until the next day, it went bad. In the same way, the disciple must receive his portion from God every day. If he stores it up as a permanent possession, he spoils not only the gift, but himself as well, for he sets his heart on his accumulated wealth, and makes it a barrier between himself and God. Where our treasure is, there is our trust, our security, our consolation and our God. Hoarding is idolatry.

But where are we to draw the line between legitimate use and lawful accumulation? Let us reverse the word of Jesus and our question is answered: "Where thy heart is, there shall thy treasure be also." Our treasure may of course be small and inconspicuous, but its size is immaterial; it all depends on the heart, on ourselves. And if we ask how we are to know where our hearts are, the answer is just as simple—everything which hinders us from loving God above all things and acts as a barrier between ourselves and our obedience to Jesus is our treasure, and the place where our heart is.

—From *The Cost of Discipleship* by Dietrich Bonhoeffer

✦ Holy obedience does not just fall upon our heads. There are things we can do that will draw us into this sacred sanctuary.

. . . The first step I want to give you is not something to do at all. It is something to refrain from doing. Very simply, we should not try to be less egocentric. The attempt would be self-defeating. The more we work at being unconcerned about ourselves, the more conscious of ourselves we become. And so what are we to do? Nothing. Let the matter drop. It is one of those things in life that will never yield to a frontal attack. Concentration upon the problem redoubles its strength. This matter will be cared for in due time, but only if we first forget it and turn our attention to other things.

The second step is rather like the first in that it is less a plan for action and more a call to focus our field of vision. We are to discipline ourselves to "seek first the Kingdom of God." This focus must take precedence over absolutely everything. We must never allow anything, whether deed or desire, to have that place of central importance. The redistribution of the world's wealth cannot be central, the desire for simplicity itself cannot be central. The moment any of these becomes the focus of our concern, it has become idolatry. Only one thing is to be central: the Kingdom of God. And, in fact, when the Kingdom of God is genuinely placed first, the equitable distribution of wealth, ecological concerns, the poor, simplicity, and all things necessary will be given their proper attention.

—From *Freedom of Simplicity* by Richard J. Foster

✦ Life at the center lives the reality of the presence of God in the now of every moment of every act that is done. It is a life that sees the greatness of the smallest of tasks, since these, as all others, are of God's work. Life lived at the center is an expression of God's immediate presence. It is not a life of imitation; nor one of anticipation; it is instead a life of participation, participation in the truth of its own full reality. But in saying this, no one should think that life at the center seeks some special mode of existence, some level of being somehow above the mundane toil of day to day. Just the opposite— it is life at its most human. It is not a life that ignores or avoids the ordinary, but one that lives it fully, since it knows that in so doing it expresses the profoundest of the profound. It is a life that may know pain and trouble; it certainly knows routine. It lives this as it lives everything—moment to moment—and in doing so touches the eternal.

—From *A Way in the World* by Ernest Boyer, Jr.

✦ When I was a child I often had [a] toothache, and I knew that if I went to my mother she would give me something which would deaden the pain for that night and let me get to sleep. But I did not go to my mother—at least, not till the pain became very bad. And the reason I did not go was this. I did not doubt she would give me the aspirin; but I knew that she would also do something else. I knew she would take me to the dentist the next morning. I could not get what I wanted out of her without getting something more, which I did not want. I wanted immediate relief from pain: but I could not get it without having my teeth set permanently right. And I knew those dentists; I knew they started fiddling about with all sorts of other teeth which had not yet begun to ache. They would not let sleeping dogs lie; if you gave them an inch, they took an ell.

Now, if I may put it that way, Our Lord is like the dentist. If you give Him an inch, He will take an ell. Dozens of people go to Him to be cured of some particular sin which they are ashamed of (like lust or physical cowardice) or which is obviously spoiling daily life (like bad temper or drunkenness). Well, He will cure it all right: but He will not stop there. That may be all you asked; but if you once call Him in, He will give you the full treatment.

That is why He warned people to "count the cost" before becoming Christians. "Make no mistake," He says, "if you let Me, I will make you perfect. The moment you put yourself in My hands, that is what you are in for. Nothing less, or other, than that. You have free will, and if you choose, you can push Me away. But if you do not push Me away, understand that I am going to see this job through."

—From *The Joyful Christian* by C. S. Lewis

✦ The ground floor, rising up from the natural order, is subject to its law of consequence; all the vicissitudes of circumstance, health, opportunity, the ebb and flow of energy and inclination, the temperamental reaction of the souls with whom we must live. Through these, God reaches us, deals with us, trains us; and to the uttermost. That living Spirit pressing so insistently on our spirits, filling with its spaceless presence every room of the soul's house, yet comes to us in and through natural circumstance; and makes of this circumstance, however homely, the instrument of its purifying power. The touch of the eternal reaches us most often through the things of sense. We are called to endure this ceaseless divine action; not with a sullen stoicism, but with a living grateful patience. The events by which we are thus shaped and disciplined are often as much as the natural creature can bear. God comes to the soul in His working clothes and brings His tools with Him. We need fortitude if we are to accept with quietness the sharp blows and persistent sandpapering which bring our half-finished fitments up to the standard required by the city's plan. But it is this steady endurance, born of the humble sense that everything which happens matters, yet only matters because it mediates God, and offers a never to be repeated opportunity of improving our correspondence with God, which more and more makes the house fit to be a habitation of the Spirit. It is not a weekend cottage. It must be planned and organized for life, the whole of life, not for fine weather alone. Hence strong walls and dry cellars matter more than many balconies or interesting garden designs.

—From *The House of the Soul and Concerning the Inner Life*
by Evelyn Underhill

48. Compassion

INVOCATION

Loving Father, teach me to love and care for those that need you today. Those who are passed over and do not feel love unless I love them for you. May Christ's love for others be felt through me today. In your name and by your power I pray these things. Amen.

PSALM 41

DAILY SCRIPTURE

Monday	Luke 6:27–36
Tuesday	John 15:9–17
Wednesday	John 11:1–44
Thursday	Luke 15:1–10
Friday	Job 31:13–23
Saturday	Luke 10:25–37
Sunday	Luke 11:1–44

SELECTIONS FOR MEDITATION

PERSONAL MEDITATION

PRAYER

The Word tells us that often Jesus was moved with compassion for the people with whom he came into contact. Our high-tech, fast-paced society forces us to pass hundreds of people each day without ever asking ourselves, much less God, if they could use a compassionate touch. Be sure to ask him this week if you could be more compassionate.

HYMN   "Does Jesus Care?"

Does Jesus care when my heart is pained
Too deeply for mirth and song,

As burdens press and the cares distress,
And the way grows weary and long?

Does Jesus care when my way is dark
With a nameless dread and fear?
As the daylight fades into deep night shades,
Does He care enough to be near?

Does Jesus care when I've tried and failed
To resist some temptation strong;
When for my deep grief I find no relief,
Tho' my tears flow all the night long? . . .

Frank E. Graeff

BENEDICTION

Keep me from being an ineffective, ordinary Christian; challenge me to be among those who are ready to fling their lives away for Jesus Christ, to be utterly careless of what happens to me in order that he may be glorified. I pray in his name. Amen.

Ray C. Stedman in *Jesus Teaches on Prayer*

SELECTIONS FOR MEDITATION

✦ My son-in-law, Alan Jones, told me a story of a Hassidic rabbi, renowned for his piety. He was unexpectedly confronted one day by one of his devoted youthful disciples. In a burst of feeling, the young disciple exclaimed, "My master, I love you!" The ancient teacher looked up from his books and asked his fervent disciple, "Do you know what hurts me, my son?"

The young man was puzzled. Composing himself, he stuttered, "I don't understand your question, Rabbi. I am trying to tell you how much you mean to me, and you confuse me with irrelevant questions."

"My question is neither confusing nor irrelevant," rejoined the rabbi, "for if you do not know what hurts me, how can you truly love me?"

—From *Walking on Water* by Madeleine L'Engle

✦ Living the sacrament of care for others draws a person

close to the greatest of all truths. It does this better than anything else can, but it does this in ways that are seldom obvious. It is for this reason that it is a spiritual discipline.

—From *A Way in the World* by Ernest Boyer, Jr.

✦ Classical Christian discernment involves certain underlying assumptions: human life is not accidental; it is a gift from a mysterious, loving Source. The purpose of this gift is twofold: an end in itself, loving/enjoying/creating, reflecting the nature of our Source: and a directed loving/bearing/creating, aimed at unfolding that essential lovingness wherever it is closed off in a wounded, partially blind, and hostile nature.

—From *Spiritual Friend* by Tilden H. Edwards

✦ "There is one more thing I want you to do," said Ann, when the people had left the church. "There is a lady here who lost her only son of sixteen years last month. His name was Walter. She wants you to go to the cemetery with her, pray with her, and bless the grave." I found the woman sitting on a bench in the village square. As I touched her, she started to cry bitterly. It was a sad story. Last month, Walter went to Cochabamba with a truck loaded with produce and people. As usual, the younger boys were standing on the running board of the truck holding onto the door. At one point, Walter lost his balance and fell from the truck without the driver noticing. He fell beneath the wheels and was crushed by the back tires of the truck. They took him in the truck in the hope of reaching the hospital in Cochabamba in time, but he died on the way.

Ann and I drove with Walter's mother in the jeep to the small cemetery behind the hospital. There we found the little niche where Walter's body was laid. We prayed and I sprinkled the place with holy water and we cried. "He was my only son, and he was such a good boy," his mother said with tears in her eyes. Ann told me how helpful Walter had been in the parish and how everyone was shocked by his death.

I couldn't keep my eyes from the woman's face, a gentle and deep face that had known much suffering. She had given birth to eight children: seven girls and Walter. When I stood in front of the grave I had a feeling of powerlessness and a strong desire to call Walter back to life. "Why can't I give Walter back to his mother?" I asked myself. But then I realized that my ministry lay more in powerlessness than in power; I could give her only my tears.

—From *Gracias!* by Henri J. Nouwen

✦ Compassion is not quantitative. Certainly it is true that behind every human being who cries out for help there may be a million or more equally entitled to attention. But this is the poorest of all reasons for not helping the person whose cries you hear. Where, then, does one begin or stop? How to choose? How to determine which one of a million sounds surrounding you is more deserving than the rest? Do not concern yourself in such speculations. You will never know; you will never need to know. Reach out and take hold of the one who happens to be nearest. If you are never able to help or save another, at least you will have saved one. To help put meaning into a single life may not produce universal regeneration, but it happens to represent the basic form of energy in a society. It also is the test of individual responsibility.

—From *Human Options* by Norman Cousins

✦ The cash lost each year in the United States amounts to about seventy-five dollars per capita—money that has fallen out of pockets, is misplaced, and so forth. The total average income for most of the human occupants of this planet comes to about sixty-nine dollars per person. The average American thus loses more money each year than almost anyone else earns.

There is something damnably itchy about these statistics. We feel like scratching but don't quite know where to find the bite. What do we do about unwanted distinctions? Do we celebrate the discovery that we have the biggest garbage removal bill in town? Do we congratulate ourselves on the fact that the drip from our leaky faucet in one day represents more water than the average Asian family in a drought-stricken area will drink or use in a month?

Whatever one does or does not do about these jabbing statistics, one thing at least is clear. They don't lend themselves to adjustment. No philosophical formulation, be it ever so sophisticated, can possibly provide the accommodating ointment. The notion that we have to take the world as it is doesn't quite relieve the itch. What do we do? Perhaps we had better go on scratching—at least until we find the bite.

—From *Human Options* by Norman Cousins

✦ The Father tells this story: One day one of the younger brothers was caught in fornication. The elders gathered to judge him and expel him from the community. But Abba Moses did not come. The elders then sent for him, insisting he come. Finally the old man did come, carrying on his back a large basket of sand in which he had poked a hole. The sand trailed out behind him. "Should I come and sit in judgment on a brother when my own sins trail behind me?"

—From *A Place Apart* by M. Basil Pennington

✦ It is a very small matter to you whether the man gives you your right or not: it is life or death to you whether or not you give him his. Whether he pays you what you count his debt or no, you will be compelled to pay him all you owe him. If you owe him a pound and he you a million, you must pay him the pound whether he pays you the million or not; there is no business parallel here. If, owing you love, he gives you hate, you, owing him love, have yet to pay it.

—From *An Anthology of George MacDonald.*
Edited by C. S. Lewis

✦ We bought an old building and remodeled it for offices and warehouse space. The electrician who did the work was named Richard. He was such a talker that after a while somebody in the building started calling him "Motormouth." He always had a smile and a ready answer to any question, serious or joking. He was a joy to have in the building. In a year or so we were making some additional changes that would require wiring and I asked if anyone had called Richard.

Somebody said, "Didn't you hear about Richard?" "No, I

didn't." Well, about two months ago his partner went by the trailer park to go to work with him and Richard said, "I'll just meet you up at the job in about twenty minutes."

And Richard went back to the trailer. He had been arguing with his wife and went back to the bedroom and came back and touched her on the shoulder as she stood at the sink. She turned just in time to see him pull the trigger of the pistol he had pressed against his head.

Richard, "Motormouth," always joking, always laughing, always talking, always willing to be the butt of our jokes was dead. I'd asked him lots of times how he was doing, but I guess I had never asked him in such a way that made him want to tell me.

Life in a way is like those electric bump cars at the amusement park. We just run at each other and smile and bump and away we go.

How are you doing—
    bump, bump,
Hi, Motormouth—
    bump, bump,
Great, fantastic—
    bump, bump, bump,
And somebody slips out and dies because there is no one to talk to—
    bump, bump, bump.

—From *Come Share the Being* by Bob Benson

✦ Compassion is the sometimes fatal capacity for feeling what it is like to live inside somebody else's skin.

It is the knowledge that there can never really be any peace and joy for me until there is peace and joy finally for you too.

—From *Wishful Thinking* by Frederick Buechner

✦ The Saviour looks with compassion on his people, the people of God. He could not rest satisfied with the few who had heard his call and followed. He shrank from the idea of forming an exclusive little coterie with his disciples. Unlike the founders of the great religions, he had no desire to withdraw them from the vulgar crowd and initiate them into an esoteric system of religion and ethics. He had come, he had worked and suffered for the sake of all his people. . . . There were no longer any shepherds in Israel. No one led the flock to fresh waters to quench their thirst, no one protected them from the wolf. They were harassed, wounded and distraught under the dire rod of their shepherds, and lay prostrate on the ground. Such was the condition of the people when Jesus came. There were questions but no answers, distress but no relief, anguish of conscience but no deliverance, tears but no consolation, sin but no forgiveness. Where was the good shepherd they needed so badly? What good was it when the scribes herded the people into the schools, when the devotees of the law sternly condemned sinners without lifting a finger to help them? What use were all these orthodox preachers and expounders of the Word, when they were not filled by boundless pity and compassion for God's maltreated and injured people? What is the use of scribes, devotees of the law, preachers and the rest, when there are no shepherds for the flock? What they need is good shepherds, good "pastors."

Jesus is looking for help, for he cannot do the work alone. Who will come forward to help him and work with him?

—From *The Cost of Discipleship* by Dietrich Bonhoeffer

49. Lifestyle

INVOCATION

O God, in very fact, I am finding out how not to live. I am running into ways that leave me frustrated and exhausted and hurt. Help me to find the Way. For in finding the Way I shall find you. And I would find you. Amen.

E. Stanley Jones in *The Way*

PSALM 15

DAILY SCRIPTURE

Monday	Deuteronomy 5:1–32
Tuesday	Galatians 6:1–10
Wednesday	Matthew 25:1–13
Thursday	Romans 13:1–14
Friday	John 15:1–17
Saturday	Mark 12:28–34
Sunday	Luke 11:33–36

SELECTIONS FOR MEDITATION

PERSONAL MEDITATION

PRAYER

When Jesus said that he was the Way he meant more than the Way to the Father. He was also telling us about a way to think, a way to act, a way to react, a way for all of life. This week pray that you will truly be in the Way.

HYMN   "A Charge to Keep I Have"

A charge to keep I have,
A God to glorify;
A never-dying soul to save,
And fit it for the sky.

To serve the present age,
My calling to fulfill—
O may it all my pow'rs engage
To do my Master's will!

Arm me with jealous care,
As in thy sight to live;
And O, thy servant, Lord, prepare
A strict account to give.

Help me to watch and pray,
And on thyself rely,
Assured, if I my trust betray
I shall forever die. Amen.

Charles Wesley

BENEDICTION

Today, O Lord—let me put right before interest: let me put others before self: let me put things of the Spirit before the things of the body: let me put the attainment of noble ends before the enjoyment of present pleasures: let me put principle above reputation: let me put you before all else. Amen.

John Baillie in A Diary of Private Prayer

SELECTIONS FOR MEDITATION

✦ The problem of living does not arise with the question of how to take care of the rascals or with the realization of how we blunder in dealing with other people. It begins in the relation to our own selves, in the handling of our physiological and emotional functions. What is first at stake in the life of man is not the fact of sin, of the wrong and corrupt, but the natural acts, the needs. Our possessions pose no less a problem than our passions. The primary task, therefore, is not how to deal with the evil, but how to deal with the neutral, how to deal with needs.

—From Man Is Not Alone: A Philosophy of Religion
by Abraham Joshua Heschel

✦ Every human being is a cluster of needs, yet these needs are not the same in all men nor unalterable in any one man. There is a fixed minimum of needs for all men, but no fixed maximum for any man. Unlike animals, man is the playground for the unpredictable emergence and multiplication of needs and interests, some of which are indigenous to his nature, while others are induced by advertisement, fashion, envy, or come about as miscarriages of authentic needs. We usually fail to discern between authentic and artificial needs and, misjudging a whim for an aspiration, we are thrown into ugly tensions. Most obsessions are the perpetuation of such misjudgments. In fact, more people die in the epidemics of needs than in the epidemics of disease.

—From *Man Is Not Alone: A Philosophy of Religion*
by Abraham Joshua Heschel

✦ . . . Freedom from anxiety is characterized by three inner attitudes. If what we have we receive as a gift, and if what we have is to be cared for by God, and if what we have is available to others, then we will possess freedom from anxiety. "This is the inward reality of simplicity."

. . . To receive what we have as a gift from God is the first inner attitude of simplicity. We work but we know that it is not our work that gives us what we have. We live by grace even when it comes to "daily bread." . . . What we have is not the result of our labor, but of the gracious care of God. When we are tempted to think that what we own is the result of our personal efforts, it takes only a little drought or a small accident to show us once again how radically dependent we are for everything.

To know that it is God's business, and not ours, to care for what we have is the second inner attitude of simplicity. God is able to protect what we possess. We can trust Him. . . . Simplicity means the freedom to trust God for these (and all) things.

To have our goods available to others marks the third inner attitude of simplicity. Martin Luther said somewhere, "If our goods are not available to the community they are stolen goods." The reason we find these words so difficult is our fear of the future. . . . But if we truly believe that God is who Jesus said He is, then we do not need to be afraid.

—From *Celebration of Discipline* by Richard J. Foster

✦ Each one of us has the Seed of Christ within him. In each of us the amazing and the dangerous Seed of Christ is present. It is only a Seed. It is very small, like the grain of mustard seed. The Christ that is formed in us is small indeed, but he is great with eternity. But if we dare to take this awakened Seed of Christ into the midst of the world's suffering, it will grow. . . . Take a young man or young woman in whom Christ is only dimly formed, but one in whom the Seed of Christ is alive. Put him into a distressed area, into a refugee camp, into a poverty region. Let him go into the world's suffering, bearing this Seed with him, and in suffering it will grow, and Christ will be more and more fully formed within him. As the grain of mustard seed grew so large that the birds found shelter in it, so the man who bears an awakened Seed into the world's suffering will grow until he becomes a refuge for many.

—From *Quaker Spirituality* by George Fox

✦ Monika Hellwig recently described the spiritual outlook of the Hasidim: The objective of hasidic spirituality is to become aware of God and united to God everywhere and in all things with sustained passionate and joyful self-abandonment. For the Hasidim the presence of God everywhere and in all things was understood literally. Therefore, intimate union with God was to be sought not only in seclusion but in the everyday life of the community.

—From *A Place Apart* by M. Basil Pennington

✦ The spiritual life is first of all a life.
It is not merely something to be known and studied, it is to be lived. Like all life, it grows sick and dies when it is uprooted from its proper element. Grace is engrafted on our nature and the whole man is sanctified by the presence and action of the Holy Spirit. The spiritual life is not, therefore, a life entirely uprooted from man's condition and transplanted into the realm of the angels. We live as spiritual men when we live as men seeking God. If we are to become spiritual, we must remain men. And if there were not evidence of this everywhere in theology, the Mystery of the Incarnation itself

would be ample proof of it. Why did Christ become Man if not to save men by uniting them mystically with God through His own Sacred Humanity? Jesus lived the ordinary lives of the men of His time, in order to sanctify the ordinary lives of men of all time. If we want to be spiritual, then, let us first of all live our lives. Let us not fear the responsibilities and the inevitable distractions of the work appointed for us by the will of God. Let us embrace reality and thus find ourselves immersed in the life-giving will and wisdom of God which surrounds us everywhere.

———From *Thoughts in Solitude* by Thomas Merton

✦ It is not only those who are growing old, finding the shadows of life lengthening, who are in search of meaning; there is a desire in every human being to find some kind of unity and coherence, some meaning in the diverse experiences of life. All of us instinctively want to find some kind of key that will unlock the secret and meaning of good days and bad, joy and sorrow, youth and old age, sickness and health, life and death. We want some kind of framework of understanding within which we can find perspective, and be freed from the delusion of confusing that which is truly important with the monumental trivia of life. It is, I think, only the overview of faith that can provide for us this insight into life, this meaning of life. As Dag Hammarskjöld recalls in his book, *Markings,* "On the day I first really believed in God, for the first time life made sense to me and the world had meaning."

—From *A Reason to Live! A Reason to Die!* by John Powell

✦ God is always present to us. The greatest thing we can do in life is to teach ourselves to be always present to God. The small, routine tasks that fill every day spent in the care of others may seem to be a barrier to this, but they need not. They may in fact be turned into one of the finest of spiritual disciplines, a special sacrament of the routine through which what to others appears the most ordinary and mundane of tasks is revealed to be a sacred act, an act of prayer. Prayer is nothing more or less than this, being present to God. And so this is a spirituality that makes all of life into prayer, a prayer of love, a prayer of help for others, a prayer of courage. It is a prayer that spans a lifetime, a prayer of great beauty.

—From *A Way in the World* by Ernest Boyer, Jr.

✦ The Christian message provides no technical solutions: not for environment protection, distribution of raw materials, town and country planning, noise abatement, elimination of waste; nor for any kind of structural improvements. Nor do we find in the New Testament any instructions about the possibilities of bridging the gap between rich and poor, between the industrialized and the industrially underdeveloped nations. Least of all can the Christian message offer any decision models or devices for solving the enormous problems which a change of policy would create: for instance, the problem of freezing the national and international economy to zero growth, without causing a breakdown of the different branches of industry, loss of jobs, chaotic consequences for the social security of whole population groups and for the underdeveloped countries.

But the Christian message can make something clear which is apparently not envisaged at all either in the economic theory or in the practical scale of values of the modern consumer- and efficiency-oriented society, but which perhaps could have a part to play: replacement of the compulsion to consume by freedom in regard to consumption. In any case there is some point in not constructing one's happiness on the basis of consumption and prosperity alone. But in the light of Jesus Christ it also makes sense not to be always striving, not always to be trying to have everything; not to be governed by the laws of prestige and competition; not to take part in the cult of abundance; but even with children exercise the freedom to renounce consumption. This is "poverty in spirit" as inward freedom from possessions: contented unpretentiousness and confident unconcernedness as a basic attitude. All this would be opposed to all fussy, overbold presumption and that anxious solicitude which is found among both the materially rich and the materially poor.

—From *On Being a Christian* by Hans Küng

50. Awareness

My gracious heavenly Father, with gratitude I bow before You today. I rejoice in the little, ordinary things which so often are accepted by me unrecognized and which so frequently pass by unnoticed. For life itself I give You thanks. For the breath which I borrow from You, I am grateful. For the strength to pursue a course of active labor, I offer my gratitude. That the lily of the field and the sparrow of the air are under Your guiding and protecting hand, remind me.
. . . In the name of Your Son, my Saviour, I pray. Amen.

C. Ralston Smith in *Daily Prayer Companion*

PSALM 63

DAILY SCRIPTURE

Monday	John 4:4–42
Tuesday	Matthew 13:1–23
Wednesday	Mark 8:27–30
Thursday	John 9:1–41
Friday	2 Corinthians 4:7–18
Saturday	Romans 8:18–27
Sunday	Daniel 2:20–23

SELECTIONS FOR MEDITATION

PERSONAL MEDITATION

PRAYER

The Biblical record of the outpouring of God shows mighty deeds and signs. And we are prone to look for God only in the phenomenal, the grandiose. We need to become more aware of God in the ordinary and common things of life. Let us be persuaded to look for him in all things and at all times.

HYMN "Safely Through Another Week"

Safely through another week
God has brought us on our way;
Let us now a blessing seek,
Waiting in His courts today.
Day of all the week the best,
Emblem of eternal rest!
Day of all the week the best,
Emblem of eternal rest!

While we pray for pard'ning grace,
Thro' the dear Redeemer's name,
Show Thy reconciled face,
Take away our sin and shame.
From our worldly cares set free,
May we rest this day in Thee;
From our worldly cares set free,
May we rest this day in Thee.

Here we come Thy name to praise;
May we feel Thy presence near.
May Thy glory meet our eyes,
While we in Thy house appear.
Here afford us, Lord, a taste
Of our everlasting feast;
Here afford us, Lord, a taste
Of our everlasting feast.

May Thy gospel's joyful sound
Conquer sinners, comfort saints,
Make the fruits of grace abound,
Bring relief for all complaints.
Thus may all our Sabbaths prove,
Till we join the Church above;
Thus may all our Sabbaths prove,
Till we join the Church above.
John Newton

BENEDICTION

O God and Father, I repent of my sinful preoccupation with
visible things. The world has been too much with me. You
have been here and I knew it not. I have been blind to Your

presence. Open my eyes that I may behold You in and around me. For Christ's sake. Amen.

A. W. Tozer in *The Pursuit of God*

SELECTIONS FOR MEDITATION

✦ Faith will come to him who passionately yearns for ultimate meaning, who is alert to the sublime dignity of being, who is alive to the marvel of matter, to the unbelievable core within the known, evident, concrete.

In order to grasp what is so overwhelmingly obvious to the pious man, we must suspend the trivialities of thinking that stultify unique insights and decline to stifle our minds with standardized notions. The greatest obstacle to faith is the inclination to be content with half-truths and half-realities. Faith is only given to him who lives with all his mind and all his soul; who strives for understanding with all beings not only for knowledge about them; whose permanent concern is the cultivation of our uncommon sense, education in sensing the ineffable. Faith is found in solitude for faith, in a passionate care for the marvel that is everywhere.

Highest in the list of virtues, this partisan care extends not only to the moral sphere but to all realms of life: to oneself and to others, to words and to thoughts, to events and to deeds. Unawed by the prevailing narrowness of mind, it persists as an attitude toward the whole of reality: to hold small things great, to take light matters seriously, to think of daily affairs in relation to the everlasting. It is not an attitude of detachment from reality, of passive absorption or of self-annihilation, but rather the ability to witness the holy within this world's affairs, and to entertain a feeling of shame and discontent with living without faith, without responsiveness to the holy.

—From *Man Is Not Alone: A Philosophy of Religion*
by Abraham Joshua Heschel

✦ To spy out the reality hidden in appearances requires vigilance, perseverance. It takes everything I've got.

Forty years ago it came easy. Absolutely nothing got by me then. Even now a name, a color, an aroma will come back to me from those early years with extraordinary vividness. These first sensations were not the blunted surface impressions made on a dull brain. They went deep; they sank in. My neurons must have leapt, exploded, gyred, oscillated in constant reciprocation with phenomena.

For the child, newborn, is a natural spy. Only his inherent limitations impede him from consuming all the clues of the universe fitted to his perceiving capacities. Sent here with the mission of finding the meaning buried in matter, of locating the central intelligence, he goes about his business briskly, devouring every detail within his developing grasp. He is devoted to discovery, resists sleep in order to consume more data. Never again will he seek to unearth the treasure buried in the field with such single-mindedness. He has to learn the world from scratch, but the task seems nothing but a joy. Yet gradually, over time, something goes wrong.

The spy slowly begins to forget his mission. He spends so much time and effort learning the language, adopting the habits and customs, internalizing the thought patterns flawlessly, that somehow, gradually, imperceptibly, he becomes his cover. He forgets what he's about. He goes to school, grows up. He gets his job, collects his pay, buys a house, waters the lawn. He settles down and settles in. He wakes up each morning with the shape of his mission, what brought him here in the first place, grown hazier, like a dream that slides quickly away. He frowns and makes an effort to remember. But the phone rings or the baby cries, and he is distracted for the rest of the day. Perhaps he forms a resolution to remember; still he seems helpless to keep the shape, the color of his mission clear in his mind. Then one morning he wakes up and only yawns. It must be there somewhere, buried in the brain cells, but at least superficially the memory is erased. The spy goes native.

—From *And the Trees Clap Their Hands*
by Virginia Stem Owens

✦ Transparency is one of the effects of prayer from the point of view of the one who prays. It is that growing clarity which happens, almost in spite of us, the more we give ourselves to prayer. It is a kind of immediacy, an insight—a sense of being able to enter into "things," into experience, more deeply and in a way that we had not entirely anticipated. It is a grasping of existence itself, possessing it, in an unaccountably different way. Yet by this I do not mean a peak experience in the sense of being at the heights. Instead, I mean a sense that day-to-day existence, events, persons, actions, the things that are already ours seem to be more ours than before, more open, more available to us.

—From *Clinging—The Experience of Prayer*
by Emilie Griffin

✦ Until women and men come to discover the truth of God's presence in their lives, and discover it not merely as some statement they affirm or deny but as a living reality, they will never recognize the fulfillment of the "not yet," the fulfillment of God's total gift.

—From *A Way in the World* by Ernest Boyer, Jr.

✦ If we are each obedient to our visions the cities would have green spaces, birds in their trees, and architecture to quicken the awareness of the divine life throbbing in the whole of the world. And the towns? The towns would have galleries to hold the works of their artists; theaters for the performing arts would spring up in their squares; scientists and poets would confer with each other; students would gather for debate and reflection, children would want to continue in life, and church congregations everywhere would be struggling "to make serious use of the wings the creator had given." Everyone would know what it meant to be the servant of the Most High.

—From *Letters to Scattered Pilgrims*
by Elizabeth O'Connor

✦ The question is not whether the things that happen to you are chance things or God's things because, of course, they are both at once. There is no chance thing through which God cannot speak—even the walk from the house to the garage that you have walked ten thousand times before, even the moments when you cannot believe there is a God who speaks at all anywhere. He speaks, I believe, and the words he speaks are incarnate in the flesh and blood of our selves and of our own footsore and sacred journeys. We cannot live our lives constantly looking back, listening back, lest we be turned to pillars of longing and regret, but to live without listening at all is to live deaf to the fulness of the music. Sometimes we avoid listening for fear of what we may hear, sometimes for fear that we may hear nothing at all but the empty rattle of our own feet on the pavement. But be not affeared, says Caliban, nor is he the only one to say it. "Be not afraid," says another, "for lo, I am with you always, even unto the end of the world." He says he is with us on our journeys. He says he has been with us since each of our journeys began. Listen for him. Listen to the sweet and bitter airs of your present and your past for the sound of him.

—From *The Sacred Journey* by Frederick Buechner

✦ Because God is not visibly present to the eye, it is difficult to feel that a transaction with Him is real. I suppose if when we made our acts of consecration we could actually see Him present with us, we should feel it to be a very real thing, and would realize that we had given our word to Him and could not dare to take it back, no matter how much we might wish to do so. Such a transaction would have to us the binding power that a spoken promise to an earthly friend always has to a man of honor. And what we need is to see that God's presence is a certain fact always, and that every act of our soul is done right before Him, and that a word spoken in prayer is as really spoken to Him, as if our eyes could see Him and our hands could touch Him. Then we shall cease to have such vague conceptions of our relations with Him, and shall feel the binding force of every word we say in His presence.

—From *The Christian's Secret of a Happy Life*
by Hannah Whitall Smith

✦ Determine to know more than others. "If ye know these things, happy are ye if ye do them." John 13:17.

If you do not cut the moorings, God will have to break them by a storm and send you out. Launch all on God, go out on the great swelling tide of His purpose, and you will get your eyes open. If you believe in Jesus, you are not to spend all your time in the smooth waters just inside the harbor bar, full of delight, but always moored; you have to get out through the harbor bar into the great deeps of God and begin to know for yourself, begin to have spiritual discernment.

When you know you should do a thing, and do it, immediately you know more. Revise where you have become stodgy spiritually, and you will find it goes back to a point where there was something you knew you should do, but you did not do it because there seemed no immediate call to, and now you have no perception, no discernment; at a time of crisis you are spiritually distracted instead of spiritually self-possessed. It is a dangerous thing to refuse to go on knowing.

—From *My Utmost for His Highest* by Oswald Chambers

✦ It is always on the backside of the desert that we come to the mountain of God—on the backside of the desert of self, at the end of our own dreams and ambitions and plans.

Moody said that when Moses first undertook to deliver Israel he looked this way and that way (Ex. 2:12), but when he came back from Horeb he looked only one way, God's way. But before he saw God's way he had to come to the backside of the desert.

And poor Moses had made quite a come-down from the courts of Egypt to the desert of Midian. He carried in his hand only a shepherd's rod, fit symbol of his humiliation. God demanded that he cast even that to the ground (Ex. 4:3). And when he took it up again it became henceforth the "rod of God" (4:20)!

If God has brought you to the backside of the desert, if you are reduced, as it were, to a shepherd's rod, cast even that gladly at His feet and He will restore it to you the rod of God—and with it you shall work wonders in His Name so long as you "endure as seeing Him Who is invisible."

—From *Consider Him* by Vance Havner

◆ The beach is not the place to work; to read, to write, to think. I should have remembered that from other years. . . . One falls under (its) spell, relaxes, stretches out prone. One becomes, in fact, like the element on which one lies, flattened by the sea; bare, open, empty as the beach, erased by today's tides of all yesterday's scribblings.

. . . And then, some morning in the second week, the mind wakes, comes to life again. Not in a city sense—no—but beach wise. It begins to drift, to play, to turn over in gentle careless rolls like those lazy waves on the beach.

. . . But it must not be sought for or—heaven forbid!—dug for. No, no dredging of the seabottom here. That would defeat one's purpose. The sea does not reward those who are too anxious, too greedy, or too impatient. To dig for treasures shows not only impatience and greed, but lack of faith. Patience, patience, patience is what the sea teaches. Patience and faith. One should lie empty, open, choiceless as a beach—waiting for a gift from the sea.

—From *Gift from the Sea* by Anne Morrow Lindbergh

51. Celebration

INVOCATION

Father, it is so easy for me to live automatically, so that nothing touches me or moves me. Give me the fullness of living in the now. In the name of your Son, who loved children and flowers and people, I pray. Amen.

PSALM 66

DAILY SCRIPTURE

Monday	2 Chronicles 20:20–30
Tuesday	Genesis 12:1–9
Wednesday	Matthew 21:1–11
Thursday	1 Chronicles 16:1–36
Friday	Psalm 98
Saturday	Genesis 35:1–15
Sunday	Revelation 22:1–17

SELECTIONS FOR MEDITATION

PERSONAL MEDITATION

PRAYER

We spend too much of our lives in anticipation of a time that is to come: a vacation, a day off, a weekend, and we miss the joy of the present. Begin to celebrate breath and water and food and now.

HYMN   "Come Thou Fount"

Come, Thou Fount of ev'ry blessing,
Tune my heart to sing Thy grace.
Streams of mercy, never ceasing,
Call for songs of loudest praise.
Teach me some melodious sonnet,

Sung by flaming tongue above.
Praise the mount, I'm fixed upon it,
Mount of God's unchanging love. . . .

Oh, to grace how great a debtor
Daily I'm constrained to be!
Let that grace now, like a fetter,
Bind my yielded heart to Thee.
Let me know Thee in Thy fullness,
Guide me by Thy mighty hand
Till, transformed, in Thine own image
In Thy presence I shall stand.

Robert Robinson

BENEDICTION

Father, teach me to rejoice at this moment. Teach me that it does me no good to be so busy planning to earn bread for next week that I cannot enjoy what I am eating now. Do not let tomorrow rob me of the pleasure of today. Amen.

SELECTIONS FOR MEDITATION

✦ Complementary to this daily and sometimes laborious service is that experience of God, *hitlahavut,* the going out of self, the "taste and see how good God is," that engenders a joy that seems to belong to another realm. The peak moments of ecstasy will be few and brief, but the memory of them abides, and something deep within us says that all the strivings of life are worthwhile because of them. The joy of these moments continues to flow as a deep, abiding current in our lives, to be called forth through devotion and service.

—From *A Place Apart* by M. Basil Pennington

✦ Every Christian who has been baptized into Christ shares in his priesthood, the High Priest of all creation. Every Christian is called to enter into his ultimate act of love and give to the rest of creation a divinized mind and heart with which to glorify the Maker. We need to let all the beauty, all the reality of God's creation enter into our hearts and then enfold it in our love so that it may ascend to him with that love.

—From *A Place Apart* by M. Basil Pennington

✦ We are all baptized into Christ's priesthood, the priesthood of creation. Don't let artificial light and city streets keep you from noticing sunsets and sunrises, from experiencing the spring of new life and the harvest of fall. If you don't have a farm, at least have a window box or a few pots of earth.
—From *A Place Apart* by M. Basil Pennington

✦ It would be absurd to suppose that because emotion sometimes interferes with reason, that it therefore has no place in the spiritual life. Christianity is not stoicism. The Cross does not sanctify us by destroying human feeling. Detachment is not insensibility. Too many ascetics fail to become great saints precisely because their rules and ascetic practices have merely deadened their humanity instead of setting it free to develop richly, in all its capacities, under the influence of grace.
—From *Thoughts in Solitude* by Thomas Merton

✦ And finally, we die in this room. We return in the end, as it were, to the bed which received us when we first arrived. Once more we come to the frontier, this time to step across from here to there. The point of our departure for the region from which we get no news, and from which we shall never, never return, is this bed, this couch of our weakness, set here in this room among the things that have attended most closely on our person—our shirts and dresses and shoes, and our belts and earrings and cufflinks, and our emery boards and shoe brushes and fingernail scissors. There they are, on their hangers, in their drawers, or in the little boxes on the bureau where we put them on Thursday evening when we lay down. And now they will sit there on Monday and Tuesday and Wednesday, until someone clears them out, while we— vanish to where there are no Thursdays or Mondays or any other days.

. . . And, like our birth, which would be much more impressive and (we would have thought) appropriate if it had occurred with heralds and processions and great tapestries drawn aside to reveal us there on the balcony, crowned with light, majestic in our innocence—like our birth, which happens instead all in a heap of confusion and rags, so our exit: it ought to be with the high solemnity, dignity, and grace fitting to this august moment when all our accomplishments and our relationships—nay, and our very selves—are caught away altogether and utterly. There ought once more to be trumpeters and pomps. But instead, here we are, rumpled, faded, and gasping; dressed, not in the robes of this high solemnity, but in our pajamas; borne, not in a royal couch, but on this mattress: unable to say a single syllable to these people who so earnestly listen for some sure word of reassurance and farewell from us. We struggle to get in to our life here, and we struggle to get out again. We arrive in a mess and we leave in a mess.

. . . But this will not do. All men everywhere have known that this will not do. We human beings are not quite satisfied, as dogs or aardvarks are, with this helter-skelter way of arriving and departing. After the flurry we feel we must do something. Have a christening. Have a funeral. Something big has happened, and we didn't quite have the leisure to grasp it, and mark it, and come to terms with it in all that huddle of activity. Here—let us solemnize the mystery thus, with white lace and a font and a cake; or with black crepe, a pall, and a dirge. One way or another, we must deck the event with tokens that answer somehow to how we feel about it.

—From *Hallowed Be This House* by Thomas Howard

✦ . . . through four states and eight cities we bore the Holy God on our lips, his love in our voices—the Sounds of Grace, gone singing its Thanksgiving.

Only now, on the afternoon of Thanksgiving day itself, did all our moods become one mood, and we gazed forward grimly. Tense, silent, and uncertain. Songs of love had ceased. Falsetto throats had thickened. We were scheduled to sing within the Colorado women's penitentiary.

Holy, holy, holy. Who suckered us into this?

. . . It wasn't even time, yet, for the concert to begin. No introductions had been made, either by voice or music, and this was not our program. Yet the women were coming, and the practice piece drew a spattering of applause, and Cheryl was lost. By fitful habit she led the choir into another piece for practice, "Soon and very soon, we are going to meet the king." Oh, the choir swung hard and speedily against its beat, and Timmy simply hid himself in the solo, and the women laughed at our abandon, and behold: the song itself, it took us over! The nerves left us, and we too began to laugh as we sang, as though there were some huge joke afoot, and we were grateful for the freedom in our throats, and we looked, for the first time, on one another, nodding, slapping another back, singing! And the women took to clapping, some of them dancing with their faces to the floor, their shoulders hunched, and they filled the place with their constant arrival, and some-when—no one knew when—the practice turned into an honest concert, but there was no formality to it, because we were free, don't you see, free of the restraints of propriety, free of our fears, free to be truly, truly one with these women, free (Lord, what a discovery!) in prison.

Song after song, the women stood up and beat their palms together. And they wept, sometimes. Timmy can do that to you. And at one point the entire auditorium, choir and crimi-nals together, joined hands and lifted those hands and rocked and sang, "Oh, How I Love Jesus."

My God, how you do break the bars! How you fling open the doors that imprison and divide us! This is true, for mine eyes have seen it and my heart went out to it: You are so mighty in your mercy.

—From *Ragman and Other Cries of Faith*
by Walter Wangerin, Jr.

✦ Celebrate the temporary
Don't wait until tomorrow
Live today
Celebrate the simple things
Enjoy the butterfly
Embrace the snow
Run with the ocean
Delight in the trees

Or a single lonely flower

Go barefoot in the wet grass

Don't wait
Until all the problems are solved
Or all the bills are paid

You will wait forever
Eternity will come and go
And you
Will still be waiting

Live in the now
With all its problems and its agonies
With its joy
And its pain

Celebrate your pain
Your despair
Your anger
It means you're alive
Look closer
Breathe deeper
Stand taller
Stop grieving the past

There is joy and beauty
Today

It is temporary
Here now and gone
So celebrate it
While you can
Celebrate the temporary
—From *Celebrate the Temporary* by Clyde Reid

✦ Good families prize their rituals. Nothing welds a family
more than these. Rituals are vital especially for clans without
histories, because they evoke a past, imply a future, and hint
at continuity. No line in the Seder service at Passover reas-

sures more than the last: "Next year in Jerusalem!" A clan becomes more of a clan each time it gathers to observe a fixed ritual (Christmas, birthdays, Thanksgiving, and so on), grieve at a funeral (anyone may come to most funerals; those who do declare their tribalness), and devises a new rite of its own.

... "Rituals," a California friend of mine said, "aren't just externals and holidays. They are performances of our lives. They are a kind of shorthand. They can't be decreed. My mother used to try to decree them. She'd make such a fuss over what we talked about at dinner, aiming at Topics of Common Interest, topics that celebrated our cohesion as a family. These performances were always hollow, because the phenomenology of the moment got sacrificed for the idea of the moment." Real rituals are discovered in retrospect. They emerge around constitutive moments, moments that only happen once, around whose memory meanings cluster. You don't choose moments. They choose themselves. A lucky clan includes a born mythologizer. . . .

—From *Families* by Jane Howard

52. Gratitude

INVOCATION

Rise, O Lord, into Your proper place of honor, above my ambitions, above my likes and dislikes, above my family, my health and even my life itself. Let me decrease that You may increase, let me sink that You may rise above. Ride forth upon me as You did ride into Jerusalem mounted upon the humble little beast, a colt, the foal of an ass, and let me hear the little children cry to You, "Hosanna in the highest."

A. W. Tozer in *The Pursuit of God*

PSALM 47

DAILY SCRIPTURE

Monday	Luke 1:68–75
Tuesday	Acts 2:42–47
Wednesday	1 Chronicles 16:8–36
Thursday	Philippians 4:4–7
Friday	1 Timothy 1:12–17
Saturday	Colossians 3:15–17
Sunday	1 Thessalonians 5:16–18

SELECTIONS FOR MEDITATION

PERSONAL MEDITATION

PRAYER

We are admonished to thank God for all things. St. James even says to be thankful for the trials and temptations. A grateful spirit is not readily found, but must be cultivated. Remember that every good thing comes from the Father.

HYMN   "Come, Ye Thankful People Come"

> Come, ye thankful people come;
> Raise the song of harvest home.
> All is safely gathered in
> Ere the winter storms begin.
> God, our Maker, doth provide
> For our wants to be supplied.
> Come to God's own temple, come;
> Raise the song of harvest home.
>
> All the world is God's own field,
> Fruit unto His praise to yield;
> Wheat and tares together sown,
> Unto joy or sorrows grown;
> First the blade, and then the ear,
> Then the full corn shall appear.
> Lord of harvest, grant that we
> Wholesome grain and pure may be.
>
> For the Lord our God shall come,
> And shall take His harvest home;
> From His field shall in that day
> All offenses purge away;
> Give His angels charge at last
> In the fire the tares to cast,
> But the fruitful ears to store
> In His garner evermore.
>
> Even so, Lord, quickly come
> To Thy final harvest home;
> Gather Thou Thy people in,
> Free from sorrow, free from sin;
> There forever purified,
> In Thy presence to abide.
> Come, with all thine angels come;
> Raise the glorious harvest home.
>
> > Henry Alford

BENEDICTION

Dear God and Father, I see it clearly now that only as You did come to me could I find You and know You. Now I know You and find You in available form—find You in the God-man. And what a find! Our hearts sing with gratitude. Amen.

> E. Stanley Jones in *The Word Became Flesh*

SELECTIONS FOR MEDITATION

✦ For if you go poking about the world, intent on keeping the candle of consciousness blazing, you must be ready to give thanks at all times. Discrimination is not allowed. The flame cannot gutter and fail when a cold wind whistles throughout the house.

Thanksgiving, thanksgiving. All must be thanksgiving.

It took thirty-eight thousand Levites to give thanks to God in David's day; every morning and every evening the shifts changed. Four thousand were needed just to carry the hacked carcasses of cattle, and another four thousand were needed to sing about it. The place reeked of blood, was soaked in blood. The priests stood around gnawing and chewing and giving thanks. They did not cross-stitch their gratitude on samplers to frame and hang on the wall. They wrote their thanks in blood on the doorposts every day.

Thanksgiving is not a task to be undertaken lightly. It is not for dilettantes or aesthetes. One does not dabble in praise for one's own amusement, nor train the intellect and develop perceptual skills to add to his repertoire. We're not talking about the world as a free course in art appreciation. No. Thanksgiving is not a result of perception; thanksgiving is the access to perception.

—From *And the Trees Clap Their Hands*
by Virginia Stem Owens

✦ It is a mark of religious insensitiveness that instead of grateful recognition of unworthiness to receive the gifts of God, there is so often acceptance without gratitude or contrition but with complaint when things go wrong. Though there is no single evidence by which to discern a Christian, there is an index by which one may test his own experience. Confronted by pain and annoyance does one say, "Why does this have to happen to me?" Or encompassed by God's bounties does one say, "Who am I that I should be thus blest?" The former reaction is the mark of self-pity and self-righteousness, the latter of Christian humility.

—From *Prayer and the Common Life* by Georgia Harkness

✦ All sin is a punishment for the primal sin of not knowing God. That is to say all sin is a punishment for ingratitude. For as St. Paul says (Romans 1:21) the Gentiles, who "knew" God did not know Him because they were not grateful for the knowledge of Him. They did not know Him because their knowledge did not gladden them with His love. For if we do not love Him we show that we do not know Him. He is love. *Deus caritas est.*

Our knowledge of God is perfected by gratitude: we are thankful and rejoice in the experience of the truth that He is love.

The Eucharist—the Sacrifice of praise and thanksgiving—is a burning hearth of the knowledge of God for in the Sacrifice Jesus, giving thanks to the Father, offers and immolates Himself entirely for His Father's glory and to save us from our sins. If we do not "know" Him in His sacrifice, how can it avail for us? "The knowledge of God is more than holocausts."

We do not know Him unless we are grateful, and praise the Father with Him.

—From *Thoughts in Solitude* by Thomas Merton

✦ There is no neutrality between gratitude and ingratitude. Those who are not grateful soon begin to complain of everything. Those who do not love, hate. In the spiritual life there is no such thing as an indifference to love or hate. That is why tepidity (which seems to be indifferent) is so detestable. It is hate disguised as love.

Tepidity, in which the soul is neither "hot or cold"—neither frankly loves nor frankly hates—is a state in which one rejects God and rejects the will of God while maintaining an exterior pretense of loving Him in order to keep out of trouble and save one's supposed self-respect. It is the condition that is soon arrived at by those who are habitually ungrateful for the graces of God. A man who truly responds to the goodness of God, and acknowledges all that he has received, cannot possibly be a half-hearted Christian. True gratitude and hypocrisy cannot exist together. They are totally incompatible. Gratitude of itself makes us sincere—or if it does not, then it is not true gratitude.

Gratitude, though, is more than a mental exercise, more than a formula of words. We cannot be satisfied to make a mental note of things which God has done for us and then perfunctorily thank Him for favors received.

To be grateful is to recognize the Love of God in everything He has given us—and He has given us everything. Every breath we draw is a gift of His love, every moment of existence is a gift of grace, for it brings with it immense graces from Him. Gratitude therefore takes nothing for granted, is never unresponsive, is constantly awakening to new wonder and to praise of the goodness of God. For the grateful man knows that God is good, not by hearsay but by experience. And that is what makes all the difference.

—From Thoughts in Solitude by Thomas Merton

✦ Thanksgiving was another element of which Christ's prayers were full. It was often praise and gratitude that drove him to his knees. Never did there creep into his prayers that note of aggrieved, protesting querulousness which sometimes marks our own. Always it was the amazing goodness of God his Father that filled and flooded his soul. And it was not only life's sunshine splendors that brought the cry of thanksgiving to his lips; the darkness found his gratitude unquenched. He took the broken bread, symbol of his broken body, and gave God thanks (Luke 22:19). He took the cup, seeing his own blood in it, and gave God thanks (Luke 22:17). He went out from the upper room to the sweat and agony of Gethsemane, singing a hymn and giving God thanks (Mark 14:26). In the darkness as in the light praise was the dominant note of Jesus' prayers, and not the Cross itself could silence it.

—From The Life and Teaching of Jesus Christ
by James Stewart

✦ Perhaps the importance of this day is that I completed the whole Bible. Just before Eucharist, I read the final Amen. It has been a significant experience, for which the final Book of Revelation is a soaring crescendo—only Handel has come close to a fitting response. It is not to be analyzed and "understood," but choreographed and read poetically to music. The vision of a final consummation of creation, hinted as possibility when first the spirit brooded over the primal waters; history became the plane of creativity, as God so shaped the work of his hands that the characters themselves came alive, resisting the playwright, inducing God no longer to be the sabbatical enjoyer but the tragic incarnate craftsperson, as together the dream is lost and found and reconstituted. There will be that point when all may look back from the peak and for the first time know that they would not have had it otherwise. Then and only then can there be a *Te Deum* by sound rather than fragile hope.

— From *The Province Beyond the River* by W. Paul Jones

✦ . . . I recently heard a very profound and moving sermon on prayer by my friend, Paul Garlington. At one point, he was speaking about the matter of "agreeing" with one another about a particular promise, and then notifying the Father that for him to do any less than exactly what we asked would somehow leave him breaking his own word. I don't think this preacher was decrying our getting fellow believers to pray with us for an answer. I also don't think he was remotely suggesting God would break his promises to us. He was instead pointing out a deep way of approaching our heavenly Father in trust and obedience.

To illustrate what he meant, he asked the congregation if we remembered what it was that Jesus prayed when he stood before the five thousand hungry people with five loaves and two fish in his hands. In his own style, for Garlington is dramatic as he is profound, he reminded us that Jesus did not wrinkle his brow and pray in a voice laden with earnestness and fervor, "Father, we need a miracle! And we are believing You for it just now." Instead Jesus had the people seat themselves on the hillside, and then he bowed his head and simply prayed, "Thank You."

Garlington went on to ask if we remembered the prayer of Jesus when he stood at the tomb of Lazarus. Again, to make the utter simplicity of the words of Jesus more powerful, he told us some of the things Jesus did not pray. He did not ask for a few true believers to join hands and "agree" with him that this was what they wanted the Father to do. Instead, Jesus, standing in front of the tomb from which the stone had just been rolled away and out of which the stench of death was streaming, looked up to his Father and said, "Thanks. I thank You that You hear me. And I thank You that You always hear me and even now I am only saying this so those who stand here with me will know You hear me."

Jesus did not seem to need anyone to agree with him in prayer. He and the Father already had an "agreement." The agreement was the Father's will, leaving Jesus remarkably free to lift his heart and voice in thanksgiving and praise: "Thanks, if You can make this food to go around. Thanks, if we all have to go home hungry. Thanks, if You raise Lazarus from the dead. Thanks, if we all leave this burial place with our hearts heavy with grief from the loss of our friend and brother. Thanks for Your will. Thanks for Your purpose. Thanks."

—From *He Speaks Softly* by Bob Benson

◆ If I had only . . .
forgotten future greatness
and looked at the green things and the buildings
and reached out to those around me
and smelled the air
and ignored the forms and the self-styled obligations
and heard the rain on the roof
and put my arms around my wife
   . . . and it's not too late.

—From *Notes to Myself* by Hugh Prather

◆ The boy that I am writing about here . . . left me when he was only eleven years olde . . . The birth of this son in mid-winter of 1892 was one of the supreme events of my life. He was named Lowell after my beloved poet. I took him from the arms of the doctor—which would not be allowed now in a modern hospital—and felt an unutterable emotion of joy and wonder. . . .

I never got away from this divine miracle. There was light on this child's face which I did not put there. There were marks of heavenly origin too plain to miss. Poets admit that the child trails "clouds of glory from God who is our home," but they soil it all by predicting that the glory will quickly "fade into the light of common day." It was not so with this child. A child looking at a beautiful object was told that it would soon be gone. "Never mind," he said, "there'll be something else beautiful tomorrow." The "light" kept growing plainer and more real through the eleven years he lived here on earth with me. It never became "common day."

—From *The Luminous Trail* by Rufus M. Jones

Author Index

Book Index

Hymn Index

Scripture Index

A Sample Lectionary

1. Genesis 12
2. Genesis 22:1–18
3. Exodus 2
4. Exodus 3
5. Exodus 16
6. Exodus 19
7. Numbers 13
8. Numbers 14
9. Deuteronomy 26:1–11
10. Joshua 24
11. I Kings 17:1–16
12. Nehemiah 9:9–38
13. Psalm 33
14. Psalm 46
15. Psalm 121
16. Psalm 122
17. Psalm 127
18. Psalm 137
19. Isaiah 6:1–13
20. Isaiah 10;15, 11:11
21. Isaiah 35
22. Isaiah 42:18–43:4
23. Isaiah 43:10–22
24. Isaiah 52:13–53:12
25. Isaiah 55
26. Isaiah 62
27. Jeremiah 29:1–14
28. Jeremiah 31:31–40
29. Daniel 2:20–23
30. Ezekiel 34
31. Amos 9:8–15
32. Micah 4:1–8
33. Micah 6:1–8

Matthew 25
Luke 4
Luke 6:46–49
Luke 9:51–6-
Luke 10:1–24
Luke 11:1–13
John 15
John 16:16–33
John 17
Acts 4
Acts 5
Acts 6
Acts 7
Romans 8
Romans 12
1 Corinthians 12
1 Corinthians 13
Ephesians 1
Ephesians 2
Ephesians 3
Ephesians 4
Ephesians 5
Ephesians 6
Philippians 2:1–18
Galatians 5:13–25
Colossians 2:6–15
1 John 1–2:11
1 John 3
1 Peter 1:13–2:10
1 Peter 4
Revelation 21
Revelation 22

Acknowledgments

The publisher gratefully acknowledges permission to reproduce the following copyrighted material:

Christopher Fitz Simmons Allison, *Guilt, Anger and God.* Copyright 1972 by author. Used by permission of Seabury Press, New York. All rights reserved.

Anonymous, *Orthodox Spirituality.* Copyright 1978. Used by permission of St. Vladimir's Seminary Press, Crestwood, N.Y.

John Baillie, *A Diary of Private Prayer.* Copyright 1949 by Charles Scribner's Sons; copyright renewed 1977 by Jan Fowler Baillie. Used by permission of Charles Scribner's Sons, New York.

William Barclay, *The Beatitudes and the Lord's Prayer for Everyman.* Copyright 1963 by author. Used by permission of Harper and Row Publishers, New York. *The Lord's Supper.* Copyright 1967 by author. Used by permission of Westminster Press, Philadelphia.

Bob Benson, *Come Share the Being.* Copyright 1974. Used by permission of author. *In Quest of the Shared Life.* Copyright 1981. Used by permission of author. *Something's Going on Here.* Copyright 1977. Used by permission of author. *He Speaks Softly: Learning to Hear God's Voice.* Copyright 1985. Used by permission of Word Books, Publisher, Waco.

Douglas Beyer, *Parables for Christian Living.* Copyright 1985. Used by permission of Judson Press, Valley Forge, Pa.

Raymond B. Blakney, *Meister Eckhart.* Copyright 1941. Used by permission of Harper and Row Publishers, New York.

Anthony Bloom, *Beginning to Pray.* Copyright 1970. Used by permission of Paulist Press, Ramsey, N.J.

Dietrich Bonhoeffer, *The Cost of Discipleship.* Copyright 1959 by SCM Press. Used by permission of Macmillan Publishing Co., New York. *Life Together.* Copyright 1954. Used by permission of Harper and Row Publishers, New York.

E. M. Bounds, *The Necessity of Prayer.* Copyright 1976. Used by permission of Baker Book House, Grand Rapids.

Ernest Boyer, *A Way in the World.* Copyright 1984. Used by permission of Harper and Row Publishers, New York.

Leslie Brandt, *Jesus/Now.* Copyright 1978. *Psalms/Now.* Copyright 1973. Both used by permission of Concordia Publishing House, St. Louis.

Al Bryant, *The John Wesley Reader.* Copyright 1983. Used by permission of Word Books, Publisher, Waco.

Martin Buber, *Meetings.* Copyright 1973. Used by permission of Open Court Publishers, La Salle, Ill.

Frederick Buechner, *A Room Called Remember.* Copyright 1984. *Now and Then.* Copyright 1983. *The Sacred Journey.* Copyright 1982. *Wishful Thinking.* Copyright 1973. All by author. Used by permission of Harper and Row Publishers, New York.

R. W. Burtner and R. E. Childs, eds., *A Compend of Wesley's Theology.* Copyright 1954. Used by permission of Abingdon Press, Nashville.

Leo Buscaglia, *Living, Loving, and Learning.* Copyright 1982. Used by permission of the author.

George Arthur Buttrick, ed., *The Interpeter's Bible, Vol. 7.* Copyright 1951 by Pierce and Smith. Used by permission of Abingdon Press, Nashville.

Don Helder Camara, *A Thousand Reasons for Living.* Copyright 1981. Used by permission of Fortress Press, Philadelphia.

Will Campbell, *God on Earth.* Copyright 1983. Used by permission of Crossroads, Los Angeles.

Mother Teresa, *A Gift for God.* Copyright 1975. Used by permission of Harper and Row Publishers, New York.

Howard Thurman, *Deep Is the Hunger.* Copyright 1951 by author. Used by permission of Harper and Row Publishers. *The Growing Edge.* Copyright 1956 by author. Used by permission of Harper and Row Publishers, New York. *The Inward Journey.* Copyright 1961. Used by permission of Friends United Press, Richmond, Ind.

Paul Tournier, quotations in *Reflections from The Adventure of Living.* Copyright 1965. *The Meaning of Persons.* Copyright 1957. *The Person Reborn.* Copyright 1966 by author. Used by permission of Harper and Row Publishers, New York.

A. W. Tozer, *The Knowledge of the Holy.* Copyright 1961 by author. Used by permission of Harper and Row Publishers, New York. *The Pursuit of God.* Copyright 1948. Used by permission of Christian Publications, Camp Hill, Pa. *The Root of the Righteous.* Copyright 1955. Used by permission of Christian Publications, Camp Hill, Pa.

Evelyn Underhill, *The Spiritual Life.* Copyright 1937, 1938, 1955 by Hodder and Stoughton. Used by permission of Morehouse-Barlow Co. *The House of the Soul and Concerning the Inner Live.* Copyright 1929 and 1926 by author. Used by permission of Winston/Seabury Press, Minneapolis. All rights reserved. *ABBA.* Copyright 1981 by Mowbray and Co., Providence. Copyright 1982 by Morehouse-Barlow Co., Wilton, Conn.

James Arthur Walther and William F. Orr, *First Corinthians.* Copyright 1976. Used by permission of Doubleday and Company, New York.

Walter Wangerin, Jr., *Ragman and Other Cries of Faith.* Copyright 1984 by author. Used by permission of Harper and Row Publishers, New York.

Benedicta Ward, *The Desert Christian.* Copyright 1975. Used by permission of Mowbray Co., Providence.

Kallistos Ware, *The Orthodox Way.* Copyright 1980. Used by permission of St. Vladimir's Seminary Press, Crestwood, N.Y.

Philip S. Watsons, *The Message of the Wesleys: A Reader of Instruction and Devotion.* Copyright 1964 by author. Used by permission of Macmillan Publishing Co., New York.

Reuben Welch, *Let's Listen to Jesus,* formerly titled *We Really do Need to Listen.* Copyright 1976 by Impact Books, Kirkwood, Mo. Copyright 1982 by Zondervan Publishing House. Used by permission of Zondervan Publishing, Grand Rapids.

John Wesley, *The Works of John Wesley,* Vol. 6. Sermon 48, "On Self-Denial." Copyright 1978. Used by permission of Beacon Hill Press, Kansas City, Mo.

E. B. White, *Essays of E. B. White.* Copyright 1977 by author. Used by permission of Harper and Row Publishers, New York.

John White, *Daring to Draw Near.* Copyright 1977. Used by permission of the InterVarsity Press. *The Fight.* Copyright 1976. Used by permission of InterVarsity Press, Downers Grove, Ill.

H. Orton Wiley, *Epistle to the Hebrews.* Copyright 1959. Used by permission of Beacon Hill Press, Kansas City, Mo.

Elie Wiesel, *Legends of Our Time.* Copyright 1968 by author. Used by permission.

Stephen F. Winward, *Fruit of the Spirit.* Copyright 1981. Used by permission of Wm. B. Eerdmans Publishing Co., Grand Rapids.